Philosophy of Relig...

Fundamentals of Philosophy

Series Editor: A. P. Martinich, University of Texas at Austin

Each volume in the Fundamentals of Philosophy series covers a key area of study in philosophy. Written with verve and clarity by leading philosophers, these authoritative volumes look to reveal the fundamental issues and core problems that drive interest in the field.

Philosophy of Religion

An Historical Introduction

Linda Trinkaus Zagzebski

Blackwell
Publishing

BLACKWELL PUBLISHING
350 Main Street, Malden, MA 02148-5020, USA
9600 Garsington Road, Oxford OX4 2DQ, UK
550 Swanston Street, Carlton, Victoria 3053, Australia

First published 2007 by Blackwell Publishing Ltd

2   2008

Library of Congress Cataloging-in-Publication Data

Zagzebski, Linda Trinkaus, 1946–
    The philosophy of religion : an historical introduction / Linda Trinkaus Zagzebski.
      p. cm. — (Fundamentals of philosophy)
    Includes bibliographical references and index.
    ISBN 978-1-4051-1873-6 (hardcover : alk. paper)
    ISBN 978-1-4051-1872-9 (pbk. : alk. paper)
    1. Religion—Philosophy. 2. Philosophy and religion.   I. Title.

    BL51.Z33 2007
    210—dc22
                                                    2006025791

A catalogue record for this title is available from the British Library.

Set in 10.5/13pt Photina
by Graphicraft Limited, Hong Kong
Printed and bound in Singapore
by Fabulous Printers Pte Ltd

The publisher's policy is to use permanent paper from mills that operate a sustainable
forestry policy, and which has been manufactured from pulp processed using
acid-free and elementary chlorine-free practices. Furthermore, the publisher
ensures that the text paper and cover board used have met acceptable
environmental accreditation standards.

For further information on
Blackwell Publishing, visit our website:
www.blackwellpublishing.com

Dedicated to my mother,

Doris Trinkaus

Contents

Preface

In my experience, students find the philosophy of religion one of the most interesting fields of philosophy, and since it overlaps all of the main areas of philosophy and was addressed by most of the major philosophers in the history of Western thought, it can be used as a way to introduce students to the study of philosophy. Philosophers of religion ask questions in many fields, including metaphysics, epistemology, value theory, the philosophy of human nature, the philosophy of science, and the philosophy of language. The philosophical treatment of most of the major issues in philosophy of religion began with the ancient Greeks and continued uninterrupted until some time in the twentieth century, after which it suffered a period of neglect and then enjoyed a renaissance beginning in the late fifties or sixties in England and the seventies in the US. Sometimes it is tempting to treat the field as beginning during that renaissance, but I believe that students have a much better sense of both the range of the field and the enduring importance of its questions if they can study the field historically.

I have made my text historical, but not chronological. I follow the conventional approach of dividing chapters by topic, but I have included many more ancient, medieval, and modern sources on each topic than is usual in philosophy of religion texts. I mention recent work sufficiently to give students a sense of what is being written on the topics today, but I do not attempt to survey the literature. I include my own position on some issues in a way that is designed to engage readers in a similar attempt to begin answering the questions for themselves. There are arguments in the text that are fairly sophisticated, but I do not include a careful analysis of each argument since philosophy teachers are good at doing that themselves. My purpose is to give the student sufficient background to begin thinking and writing on each issue in a philosophically and historically informed way, and to present the material in a way that makes it easier for the instructor to take over where I leave off.

I have attempted to broaden some of the standard issues. For example, the chapter on the problem of evil includes the issue of the origin of value. The chapter on immortality begins with the question of whether death is bad. The chapter on the divine nature is also on personhood and revelation. The chapter on morality and religion includes much more than Divine Command theory. The chapter on religious diversity addresses the question of why this is an issue that only became important in the modern period.

My teaching background for writing this text is a three-course sequence in the history of philosophy of religion for upper-level undergraduates at the University of Oklahoma: Ancient and Medieval Religious Philosophy, Modern Philosophy of Religion, and Contemporary Issues in Philosophy of Religion. I also teach a survey of the contemporary state of philosophy of religion for upper-level undergraduates and graduate students, as well as frequent graduate seminars.

I am grateful to the Philosophy Department at the University of Oklahoma for granting me a teaching reduction for research during spring semester 2004, and I am greatly indebted to my outstanding research assistant, Timothy Miller, whose thorough and painstaking work added immeasurably to the book. At earlier stages of research I benefitted from the assistance of Joshua Stuchlik, Sarah Price, and Kyle Johnson. I have been very fortunate to have so many supportive and stimulating students, colleagues, and friends in philosophy, and I am grateful to many authors I have never met but whose work has enriched me.

Linda Zagzebski
May 17, 2006

Chapter 1

The Philosophical
Approach to Religion

1.1 The Relation between
Religion and Philosophy

Religion has existed for as long as there have been human beings on
the earth. Philosophy was a later development, and philosophy of religion appeared later still. There would be no philosophy of religion if
philosophy were not distinct from religion and if philosophy did not
assume the role of critic of all major human practices, including the
practice of religion. These conditions never existed in the East, where
philosophies and religions are not separated as they are in the Western
world, and even in the West, philosophers did not aggressively assume
the role of religious critic until the last two or three hundred years. This
chapter will give an overview of the origin of religion and philosophy
and the historical conditions that led to the development of the field
now known as philosophy of religion. Fortunately, philosophy's role
of critic of human practices includes itself, and philosophy sometimes
scrutinizes its own methods and boundaries. In this book we will mainly
explore the questions raised within philosophy of religion, but we will
occasionally look at the contours of philosophy and its methods since
some responses to philosophical arguments about religion are criticisms
of the method employed.

1.1.1 The origin of religion

Religion is probably universal in the way morality, art, and music are
universal, and like these other practices, it is doubtful that it can be
defined with any precision. Fortunately, that does not matter. All of us

know a lot about morality, and many of us know a lot about art, but few people attempt to define either one, probably because they have the good sense to know they will fail. The need for definition arises only in special situations anyway. For example, when the US Supreme Court ruled that something is pornographic only if it is devoid of artistic merit, the ruling could not be applied without a way to determine what has artistic merit and what does not.[1] But most of the time we can study art, enjoy art, and even produce art without the ability to draw a sharp line between art and non-art. We are in the same position with respect to religion. We do not have to spend a lot of time attempting to define religion in a way that permits us to answer a series of questions that sets the boundaries of religion – e.g., What distinguishes a cult from a religion? Is Marxism a religion? If my next-door neighbor, Harriet, invents Harrietism, a practice that has only one adherent, can her practice qualify as a religion? We are all familiar with some of the non-controversial examples of religions, and we need to worry about the difficult cases only in situations that rarely arise in the philosophical study of religion. So a rough account of religion should suffice.

I would begin by saying that religion is a complex human practice involving distinctive emotions, acts, and beliefs. It is doubtful that there is any belief common to all religions, but all religions express and foster a sense of the sacred. I am convinced that the sacred is indefinable for the same reason that the lovable, the admirable, the awesome, the frightening, and the offensive are indefinable. In each case we can identify some of its descriptive features, but we do not really understand it unless we have had the characteristic emotion that goes with it. I think that to understand the lovable one must have felt love; to understand the frightening one must have felt fear; to understand the rude one must have felt offended; to understand the pitiful one must have felt pity; to understand the sacred one must have felt reverence. Reverence is an emotion directed towards the sacred. There can be sacred spaces, sacred times, and sacred objects. A sacred space is usually a special place set aside for religious worship and ritual, such as a temple or church, but there can be sacred places in nature. For example, the Navajo (Diné) believe that their ancestral land within the Four Sacred

---

1   *Miller v. California*, United States Supreme Court, 413 US 15, 24 (1973).

Mountains is a vast sacred place, and some never leave it.[2] Sacred times are typically the days and times set aside for religious ritual or prayer. Through ritual, religions use sacred objects and places to contact that part of reality that most human beings do not encounter in the ordinary course of their lives – a deeper or higher part.

In my theory of emotion,[3] emotions have two inseparable aspects: an aspect of feeling and an aspect of seeing. Emotions are feelings directed towards something seen in a way characteristic of the emotion, but it is doubtful that a distinctive way of seeing requires a belief. When we feel fear we see something *as* dangerous, but we need not actually believe that the thing we fear is dangerous. I can fear heights without believing there is danger that I will fall. Similarly, when we feel love we see someone as lovable, but it is possible to love without believing that the loved one has qualities that make him or her lovable. When we feel reverence we see or experience something as sacred, but a person can feel reverence without believing that the object of reverence is sacred. Perhaps she is too young or too naive to conceptualize the sacred and is unable to form beliefs about it, or she may be skeptical that the sacred is a real property of anything and so she is wary of the significance of her own emotion, but that need not prevent her from having the emotion. Beliefs typically appear when a person becomes reflectively aware of his or her emotion and trusts it, so beliefs are consequent to the emotion. If so, the emotion of reverence is a more basic feature of religion than any belief. This may turn out to be important because philosophers usually focus attention almost exclusively on beliefs.

---

2   The four mountains are (1) Mont Blanc, or as the Navajo call it, Tsisnaasjini, the sacred mountain of the east in San Luis Valley, Colorado; (2) Mount Taylor (Tsoodil), the sacred mountain of the south, north of Laguna, New Mexico; (3) San Francisco Peaks (Doko'oosliid), the sacred mountain of the west, near Flagstaff, Arizona; and (4) Mount Hesperus (Dibé Nitsaa), the sacred mountain of the north, in the La Plata Mountains, Colorado. The area within the four mountains is in the area known as the Four Corners, where New Mexico, Arizona, Colorado, and Utah come together. The Navajo believe the Creator gave the land to their ancestors, First Man and First Woman. The four mountains form the compass points of a huge, cosmic hogan. Only those who live inside the area within the mountains can build hogans, the centers of religious worship, and only within the sacred area can they perform ceremonies such as special forms of the Blessing Way, or create medicine bundles.

3   See Zagzebski (2003; 2004).

3

Another religious emotion is awe. Awe is directed towards something unfathomable that is at once frightening and thrilling. The awesome transcends the ordinary categories of good and bad. Clearly, primitive peoples faced a huge, unmanageable, and often threatening world, but paradoxically, as humans have progressed in understanding the natural world and managing some of its more perilous aspects, this has been accompanied by the discovery that the universe is even more massive and less controllable than early humans thought. Awe does not disappear as we gain more understanding of the natural world, but now it is less likely to be aroused by thunder, and more likely to be aroused by photographs of the earth from space or the development of the human fetus.

Like other emotions, awe need not be accompanied by any particular belief. The well-known atheist biologist Richard Dawkins (1997) says he finds scientific discoveries awe-inspiring:

> It's exactly this feeling of spine-shivering, breath-catching awe – almost worship – this flooding of the chest with ecstatic wonder, that modern science can provide. And it does so beyond the wildest dreams of saints and mystics. The fact that the supernatural has no place in our explanations, in our understanding of so much about the universe and life, doesn't diminish the awe. Quite the contrary. The merest glance through a microscope at the brain of an ant or through a telescope at a long-ago galaxy of a billion worlds is enough to render poky and parochial the very psalms of praise. (p. 27)

I have no idea if Dawkins has the same emotion as the religious person whose emotion he does not hesitate to denigrate, but if he does, he has one of the basic components of religion – a particular kind of emotional experience.

In an important book on religion, *The Idea of the Holy*, the early twentieth-century German philosopher Rudolf Otto proposed the term "the numinous" for a category of emotion whose object he calls "mysterium tremendum." Otto analyzes a number of components of the numinous, including a feeling of dread, the sense of being over-powered, an element of urgency, an element of fascination, and a sense of the wholly other. Otto (1958) says, "There is no religion in which it [the numinous] does not live as the real innermost core, and without it no religion would be worthy of the name" (p. 6). If Otto is right, my use of the word "awe" may be too feeble, and I invite interested readers to undertake a study of religious emotion, a much neglected topic for philosophical examination.[4] But for the purpose of introduction, I will leave it to the reader's experience to identify the distinctive emotions related to reverence and awe that lie at the root of religion.

In addition to reverence and awe, there are distinctively religious forms of such emotions as faith, hope, love, guilt, peace, and joy. Many religions encourage, develop, and direct these emotions in certain ways. I think, then, that to fully understand any particular religion, it is not enough to understand its history and doctrines; one must also have had the emotions it cultivates. A significant way these emotions are expressed is in works of art. Occasionally I have had the experience of wanting to possess a certain artwork primarily because it expressed an unnamed emotion better than anything else I had ever seen, and I doubt that my experience is unusual. That probably means that there are emotions that are more suited to expression in art than in words, and many of them probably have no names. The fact that there is so much variety in the art and music of the world's religions may indicate that religions differ in the emotions they express and foster as well as in the doctrines they teach.[5] But there are no doubt also commonalities, given that the art, music, and literature of one religion are often understandable to people raised in another, even if not completely so. A common experience when traveling in a country with a radically unfamiliar culture is to feel delight at discovering what one has in common with the people one meets there, accompanied by the sense that there is a barrier beyond which one can never go. In a similar way, we may feel that we can appreciate an emotion while simultaneously recognizing it as alien, an emotion we could never have save in imagination.

Religious emotions lead to religious acts. For early humans ritual in a sacred place alleviated fear and satisfied the desire to be part of a larger world. By performing sacrifices to the gods, they believed that the gods gave them benefits, including the most basic benefit of survival,

4   Two important exceptions are Wainwright (1995) and Wynn (2005).
5   There are religions that have not produced visual art. The English art historian Kenneth Clark (1969) says, "It's a curious fact that the all-male religions have produced no religious imagery – in most cases have positively forbidden it. The great religious art of the world is deeply involved with the female principle" (p. 177).

a practice that led Freud to describe religious sacrifice as bribery.[6] An important Christian teaching is that blood sacrifice is no longer needed, but sacrifice continues to play an important role in some of the world's major religions, including the bloodless sacrifice of the Catholic Mass. The idea of sacrifice is also connected with the giving of gifts to a ruler, a theme that was developed in the legend of the Magi. In one version that can be traced back to Tertullian in the second century, the Magi are kings, suggesting that even earthly kings must do homage to a higher ruler.

A type of religious act that is virtually universal is rituals for the dead. We know there were burial rituals at least as far back as 100,000 years ago among the Neanderthal, prior to the rise of *homo sapiens.*[7] Probably such rituals indicate a concern for the afterlife, although we can only guess what the Neanderthals believed about the world entered by the dead.[8] The idea that a god or gods can see and hear us led to the practice of personal and communal prayer. In addition to religious emotions, then, there are characteristic religious acts – worship, sacrifice, burial rituals, and prayer.

Human beings are almost continuously and painfully aware of human finitude. Suffering and death are universal, and no doubt everyone believes human life is not as it ought to be. Curiously, many cultures have independently arrived at an explanation for this predicament

---

6   In *The Future of an Illusion*, Freud (1961) says that by personifying the forces of nature, humans render themselves less defenseless. "We can apply the same methods against these violent supermen outside that we employ in our own society; we can try to adjure them, to appease them, to bribe them, and, by so influencing them, we may rob them of a part of their power" (pp. 20–1).

7   A recent discovery in Spain may have turned up evidence for the oldest known burial. A stone axe was found in a pit among the fossilized bones of 27 humanoids of the species *Homo heidelbergensis*, which dominated Europe 600,000–200,000 years ago and is thought to have given rise to both the Neanderthals and modern humans. Spanish researchers suggest that the axe might have been put there deliberately as part of a burial ritual, although other scholars think it more likely that the remains were accidentally washed into the pit. See Rincon (2003).

8   Some researchers dispute the significance of the Neanderthal burial sites, claiming that a requirement for belief in an afterlife is abstract thinking, which appeared around 50,000 years ago in modern humans (Rincon 2003). But at a minimum, burial rites associated with belief in an afterlife have been practiced as long as the human species has existed. However, burial rites are not sufficient for belief in an afterlife, as we see from the example of the Navajo.

through a myth of a fall from a previously ideal state. Most Westerners know the stories of the fallen angels and the fall of Adam and Eve in Genesis, but numerous cultures around the world have such myths. For example, the Sre of Indochina believe that man once lived immortally in a paradise with the god Ong Ndu, eternally young and with no need for work. But the primordial man and woman disobeyed the god by jumping in a well, and as a result humans now have to endure suffering, old age, and death. The Yombe tribe of Africa say that the god Nzondo drove human beings from their paradise home and scattered them over the earth while setting off an unceasing chain of disasters (Ries 1987, p. 257). In the ancient Babylonian myth *Enuma elish* the rebellion and fall of the world takes place before humans are created (as in the story of the fallen angels). After the mother goddess Tiamat creates other gods, they conspire against her and murder her, and then make human beings for the purpose of having them work to serve the gods (p. 259). In one version of the ancient Egyptian fall myth,[9] the sun god, Re, rules over the earth at a time when humans and divine beings live together. When Re is old, humans plot against him, taking advantage of his weakness and senility. Re stops the rebellion by sending his eye, in the form of the goddess Hathor, to kill the rebellious humans. When Hathor returns after killing the humans in the desert, Re tells her not to kill the rest of mankind. However, she so enjoyed killing them that Re is forced to protect the rest of mankind from her by getting her drunk on strong beer dyed red to look like human blood. After this, the goddess Nut transforms herself into a cow and the weary Re climbs onto her back. When men see Re on her back they repent for their rebellion and kill the remaining humans who plotted against him. Nut becomes the sky so that the majesty of Re will be seen by human beings, who are henceforth separated from the gods.

These myths are easy to dismiss as pre-philosophical, but there is even a story of a fall in Plato. In the Platonic dialogue *Phaedrus*, the human soul is allegorically portrayed as a charioteer with a pair of winged horses that strives for perfection, but inevitably loses its wings and falls to the ground. Plato then offers the hope of rising again, saying that after 3,000 years the soul might regrow its wings if it is "the

9   This summary is based on "The Book of the Heavenly Cow," in Simpson (2003), pp. 289–98.

soul of a man who practices philosophy without guile" or the soul of a lover who "is not devoid of philosophy" (*Phaedrus* 249). In the *Timaeus* Plato says there are as many souls as there are stars, and each soul is originally allotted to a star. The souls fall to earth and become embodied, resulting in the experience of passions, but if they are able to master their emotions and love justice, they are sent back to their native star (*Timaeus* 41d–42d).

There are a number of recurrent themes in these myths: rebellion, a fall to a lower state, punishment and separation of humans from the divine, and, in some versions, hope for rising again. It is interesting to speculate about the widespread use of these motifs. Virtually all religions offer an explanation for the pitiable state of the human condition and offer human beings a way to cope with it. A myth of a fall is one way to do that. Coping with the human condition might be aided by the promise that suffering will eventually be overcome or transformed in some way, and that humans can become divine. The remedy for the problem usually includes moral behavior as prescribed by the particular religion, and most religions teach that the ultimate goal of moral living is unattainable without the practice of that religion, a point to which we will return in Chapter 6. In summary, many religions not only offer sacred places for the performance of ritual acts, they also structure human life, teach the nature of a good life, explain the pitiful lot of human beings, and show them the right attitude about suffering and death and what morality requires.

Philosophers care about whether the teachings of any religion are true because many religions offer answers to questions philosophers ask: What is the origin of the material world? What is the nature of the human person? Is there a God? Where did good and evil come from? Is there an afterlife? I assume it is obvious that truth is important, but from the perspective of many religions, the importance of belief in its teachings is not limited to the fact that it is important to accept the truth. Belief is important because the ultimate good the religion promises – salvation or something comparable – is impossible without the right beliefs. For Christianity, conversion from non-belief to belief is critical. For religions that do not emphasize personal belief, it is not. Conversion was not important in the ancient Greek and Roman religions because theirs was a religion for their own people and it was not intended to transform their life or to give them a world view. The Jewish religion did have a world view, and the prophets repeatedly called

8

the Israelites to reform their lives, but this was a type of conversion intended for the Jewish people; it was not for the gentiles (although there were some gentile converts). Arthur Nock argues that conversion as a key component of religion made its appearance in the Western world with Christianity.[10] Christianity not only had a world view, it taught that the suffering and death of Jesus Christ had saved the world, a message that needed to be spread to all human beings. If salvation requires faith, and faith includes particular beliefs, beliefs must be changed for people to be saved. The idea that belief is necessary for salvation has a complex history in Christianity, and the Christian churches do not all teach that salvation requires a particular cognitive attitude towards specific doctrines. Nonetheless, both ordinary believers and non-believers wonder what they should believe about religion, whether or not they think their salvation depends upon believing the right thing. Anyone who cares about the truth wonders what the truth is about important matters, and the more important the truth that is at stake, the more insistent the wonder. Philosophers also want to know what to believe, usually in much greater detail and with much stronger standards for the justification of belief. So the question "What should I believe?" is *the* question at the intersection of philosophy and religion. Philosophy addresses the issue of what it is rational to believe. In comparison, religion understands belief as part of something else that one should do that is more important than the belief itself. Religion is a practice, not an academic field.

1.1.2   The origin of philosophy

Philosophers in the West insist on very rigorous standards for the evaluation of the truth of a belief, and the reason can be traced to ancient Greece, where philosophy originated in the sixth century BC. Because of the Greeks, philosophy took a very different path in the Western world than in the East. The German philosopher Karl Jaspers has called attention to an interesting feature of the period of human history centering on the fifth century BC, but extending two or three hundred years in each direction. Many of the most important thinkers in the history of the world lived at that time, but few of them knew of the existence of

10   Nock (1998) ch. 1 and pp. 134–5.

the others. In China there were Confucius and Lao Tze, the founder of Taoism; in India there were the writers of the Upanishads, Mahavira, the founder of Jainism, and the Buddha; in Persia there was Zoroaster; in Palestine, the Hebrew prophets; and in Greece, there was a series of important philosophers including Pythagoras, Socrates, Plato, Aristotle, and the Stoics. This period has been called the Axial Age because it was a time in which human consciousness was immensely enlarged and the basic categories for understanding the world were developed, categories that continue to be used by a large portion of the peoples of the world.[11]

I do not know why so many powerful thinkers lived at close to the same time or whether there is any significance to that fact, but I want to call attention to one curious feature of the list given by Jaspers. The great minds of the Axial Age were religious thinkers in every country except one: Greece. In Greece they were all philosophers, not founders of religions. The Greek religion had modest pretensions. Unlike the religions of India, Persia, China, and Israel, the ancient Greek religion did not attempt to answer ultimate questions about the origin of the universe and human fate. The Greek gods faced a pre-existent universe themselves and had no control over final human destiny. The Greek religion provided rituals and traditions that enabled humans to gain benefits from the gods and to have continuity with the past and future, but belief was not important. At least, there was no question of the Greek religion transforming a person's consciousness or giving him meaning and purpose in his life, or answering his questions about the nature of the universe. Instead, the Greeks looked to philosophy to answer questions about the origin of the universe and how it is put together, whether there is any world besides the world of our experience, whether we can control our destiny, and what makes something good or evil. Answers to these questions were proposed by the great Greek philosophers, beginning with Thales. These philosophies therefore had something in common with the great religions of the East. Nonetheless, they were not religions. With very few exceptions, they did not create sacred spaces and rituals to contact a higher world. They attempted to understand the world and to reach a higher world, if there

---

11   See Jaspers (1949). Many other religious historians have commented on the Axial Age. See also Hick (2004).

is one, through the mind.[12] So in Greek culture the functions of religion that we now consider central were divided between philosophy and religion. Religion gave the individuals of a community a sacred place where they performed rituals to propitiate the gods and to connect them to their cultural forebears, but philosophy asked and attempted to answer questions about the ultimate nature of the universe. The same point applies to ancient Roman religion. The effect of this split continues in the division between philosophy and religion in the West. Eastern religion and philosophy has no such split.

All the pre-Socratic philosophers were struck by the difference between appearance and reality and the great difficulty in distinguishing them. They subjected traditional beliefs to critical scrutiny and developed highly original views about the basic constituents of the universe. What sets Greek philosophy apart from religion, then, is the method. Some religions and some philosophies ask the same questions, and they might even propose some of the same answers, e.g., the answer to the question "Where did the universe come from?", but Greek philosophers firmly believed in the ability of the independent human mind to figure out the truth. Western philosophy still uses the methods inherited from the Greeks, and Western philosophy is still separate from religion.

Christianity arose within Judaism but was brought to the gentiles very early by St Paul, who spoke Greek and was a Roman citizen. Christianity had features of both Greek religion and Greek philosophy. It gave answers to ultimate questions and it was a practice to which its adherents made an exclusive commitment. Christianity was therefore a competitor to both the religions and the philosophies of the Roman empire. It overcame Roman and Hellenistic religion rather easily; it was more difficult to overcome the philosophies of the time. Ancient philosophies offered a comprehensive outlook on the world that was intended to provide the best foundation for human life. Stoicism, Epicureanism, and Pyrrhonian skepticism were all philosophies one could live by and to which one could be converted. To confront these philosophies, Christian philosophers adopted the categories of thought of Greek philosophy and engaged in argument with non-Christian philosophers. Within a few centuries most of the main Western philosophers

---

12   The Pythagoreans stressed ritual and may be an exception.

were Christian. As Christians their history included the Bible, the founding of the Church, and the tradition of spiritual reflection on the Christian life, but as philosophers their history was Greek.

Since the eastern Roman empire was Greek-speaking, the centers of philosophy were in the Eastern centers of learning. The complete works of Plato were available to Byzantine philosophers, and Plato was translated into Arabic beginning in the ninth century in Baghdad, mainly by Nestorian Christians living there, but while Neo-Platonism was known in the Latin West, the only Platonic dialogue that was translated before the twelfth century was the first third of the *Timaeus*, in which Plato speaks of the material world as formed out of pre-existing matter by God (the Demiurge) with the eternal Forms as patterns. The works of Aristotle were unknown in the West for hundreds of years while they were translated and critically examined by Arabic philosophers. Until the twelfth century, the only works of Aristotle available in the West were two works of logic, *Categories* and *De Interpretatione*, and even these works were not translated into Latin until the sixth century. Aristotle's works were reintroduced to Western Europe from Moorish Spain in the twelfth century, and the great Christian philosophers of the thirteenth century, including St Thomas Aquinas, studied Aristotle through the works of Arabic writers. The medieval Islamic philosophers are therefore part of the history of Western philosophy, an ironic fact when we consider the place of Islamic thought in the contemporary world. Today the West does not recognize Islam as part of its own heritage, and Islam considers the West an adversary. Nonetheless, much of Greek philosophy came to the West via Islamic philosophers and Jewish philosophers such as Maimonides who wrote in Arabic, and both Christian and Muslim philosophy began with the Greeks.

Islamic philosophy was an important link between ancient Greek philosophy and the philosophy of the Western high Middle Ages, but just as medieval philosophy in the West reached its zenith, Islamic philosophy began a decline. The reason is unclear. William Craig (1980, p. 8) says that Islamic philosophy never recovered from the blow it received from Al-Ghazali's work, *The Incoherence of the Philosophers* (1997 [1095]). This book included an important argument for theism that we will discuss in Chapter 2 (the *kalam* cosmological argument), but it concentrates on attacking philosophy, which to the Muslims meant Aristotelian-influenced thought. Subsequently, the Muslim philosophers (*falsafa*) would produce only one more great philosopher, Averroes (Ibn Rushd). Another factor in the decline has been suggested by the distinguished Middle Eastern historian Bernard Lewis, who points to the cultural changes that ended the translations into Arabic of works from the outside. The medieval translators rendered into Arabic what was thought to be useful at the time – works on medicine, astronomy, physics, mathematics, and philosophy – but the period in which philosophy was regarded as useful ended, and as the medieval period waned, there were no more translations or commentaries on works produced by non-Muslims.[13] I am not convinced that this is sufficient to account for the decline of Islamic philosophy, since philosophy can flourish without input from the outside; nor am I convinced that a work by one important Muslim philosopher can explain it either, so I will leave the question unanswered.

1.1.3 The origin of philosophy of religion

So far I have argued that philosophy of religion only makes sense if philosophy and religion are separated. They are not separated in the East, but they are separated in the West because of the Greeks. So philosophy of religion is part of philosophy, not religion, and this leads to the question of how philosophy of religion became distinguished from other branches of philosophy. When you look at the topics discussed in this book – Is there a God? What is the origin of the universe? What happens after death? Why does evil exist? What is the relation between God and morality? – all of the major philosophers up to the nineteenth century discussed some of these topics and some discussed all of them. They did not recognize a field called philosophy of religion and did not think of themselves as writing in any such field; they were just doing philosophy. Certainly, Plato did not take himself to be doing philosophy of religion in the *Phaedo*, where we get the first extended set of arguments in Western philosophy for life after death. Aristotle did not think he was doing philosophy of religion in his argument for a First Mover or in his argument that the universe did not have a beginning. Medieval philosophers did not distinguish philosophy of religion from other branches of philosophy either. The distinction they thought important was something else – the difference between revealed theology, on the

---

13   Lewis (2002), pp. 139–40.

one hand, and what they called natural theology, which was philosophy. They were not concerned with distinguishing philosophy of religion from other branches of philosophy, but to distinguish philosophy from theology. The difference is that theology presupposes divine revelation, particularly, in the Bible; philosophy does not.

So when and why was philosophy of religion invented? James Collins (1967) argues in his book *The Emergence of Philosophy of Religion* that it was in the eighteenth and nineteenth centuries. He says that in David Hume, Immanuel Kant, and G. W. F. Hegel we find a "study of religion . . . free from functional dependence upon any theology, sensitive to the full power of the skeptical challenge in its religious implications, and thoroughly philosophical in nature" (p. 353). Similarly, Merold Westphal (1997) argues in his paper "The Emergence of Modern Philosophy of Religion" that "we owe to [Hegel] more than to anyone else the notion that there is a subdivision of philosophy called the philosophy of religion" (p. 111), and Hegel's (1821) *Lectures on the Philosophy of Religion* was one of the earliest works to use the term "philosophy of religion" for its subject matter.[14] Westphal points out that in the eyes of many philosophers Hume and Kant destroyed the traditional proofs for the existence of God, which we will discuss in Chapter 2. After that, scholars began to focus less on God and the truth of religious beliefs, and more on the psychology and sociology of religious belief and practices. Some followed what has come to be called a "hermeneutics of suspicion" that looked for ulterior motives for religion. Notably Kant did not subscribe to the hermeneutics of suspicion, but Hume is generally credited with beginning it, and it continued through the works of Marx, Nietzsche, and Freud, whose writings made a significant impact on the twentieth century (Westphal 1997, p. 116). We will return to the origin of philosophy of religion in Chapter 2 and will discuss Freud in Chapter 6.

---

14   Hegel was not the first however, since the Cambridge Platonist Ralph Cudworth had used the term "philosophy of religion" in the seventeenth century. Charles Taliaferro (2005) argues that Cudworth and Henry More set up the arguments and terminology that shaped the agenda for subsequent English-language philosophy of religion. According to Taliaferro, the important but neglected Cambridge Platonists are crucial in understanding the shift from medieval to modern thinking about religion.

Many of the celebrated philosophers of the first fifty or sixty years of the twentieth century were atheists – Bertrand Russell, the Logical Positivists, John Dewey, Martin Heidegger (for much of his life), Jean-Paul Sartre, and W. V. Quine – and there was very little philosophy of religion written in English during that period. The exceptions were works by committed Christians such as the Catholic philosophers who participated in the neo-Thomist revival of that period. But by the late fifties and sixties, some well-known philosophers took up the task of bringing back into the philosophical mainstream the traditional philosophical topics that are examined in this book. An important impetus for the new vigor that philosophy of religion enjoyed in the last third of the twentieth century was the collection *New Essays in Philosophical Theology*, first published in 1955.[15] This was followed by a movement among Calvinist philosophers that came to be known as Reformed Epistemology, an approach that presented a philosophically rigorous defense of the rationality of religious belief without evidence.[16] In the last few decades there has been an enormous amount of work in philosophy of religion in the English-speaking world, employing a variety of methods, and inspired by many different traditions in the history of Western philosophy. Philosophy of religion tends to track developments in other branches of philosophy. Changes in epistemology (theory of knowledge) are reflected in changes in religious epistemology. New arguments and positions on such metaphysical issues as free will, the mind/body problem, and the nature of time are reflected in arguments about divine foreknowledge and human free will, life after death, and the question of whether God is timeless. To a lesser extent, changes in approaches to ethics have been reflected in changes in approaches to religious ethics. Some of these developments will be topics for later chapters. What is generally unrecognized, I think, is that at least once in the history of Western philosophy the influence went in the other direction. One of the most important concepts in Western philosophy has its roots in Christian theology. That is the concept of a person, to be discussed in Chapter 4.

15 MacIntyre and Flew (1964).
16 The first major publication on Reformed Epistemology was a collection of essays titled *Faith and Rationality* (Plantinga and Wolterstorff 1983). This book initiated a movement that now has a large literature.

1.2 The Idea of God

1.2.1 Monotheism

There are religions that are non-theistic, such as Theravāda Buddhism, but the idea of God is central to the Abrahamic faiths of Judaism, Christianity, and Islam, as well as to some of the religions of the East, such as monotheistic Hinduism and Sikhism. The conception of God prevalent in Christianity today has both Greek and Hebrew roots. For the Jews God is a person who has relationships with human beings, and the Jewish people eventually came to believe that there is only one god. In Greek philosophy there developed the idea of an absolutely perfect being with intelligence and some personal characteristics, but no relationship with humans.[17] By the second cent AD the two ideas were combined in the Christian conception of God.

Monotheism developed during the Axial period, although it probably originated earlier. Our earliest record of monotheistic teaching seems to be that of the Egyptian Pharaoh Akhenaten, who ruled in the fourteenth century BC. Akhenaten taught the worship of one god, Aten, a universal, omnipresent spirit who created and ruled the world. But Akhenaten's religion was suppressed by his successor, Tutenkamen, and it does not seem to have been influential in subsequent Egyptian religion. Elsewhere, the Jewish religion gradually moved from monolatry, the worship of one god, to monotheism, the belief in the existence of one god. Notice that monolatry and monotheism are not the same thing. The covenant with the God of Israel ruled out the worship of other gods, but not necessarily their existence. But by the eighth century BC the prophet Amos declared that both the Israelites and neighboring kingdoms would be judged by Jehovah for their evil acts, thereby implying that God was the ruler of other peoples besides the Israelites and that the Israelite neighbors could not justify their behavior by claiming that it was endorsed by their local gods. Amos may not have been explicitly monotheistic, but he was moving in that direction. One important consequence of monotheism, then, is that it was associated with the development of the idea of a universal moral code.

---

17 But Paul Gavrilyuk (2004) argues that by the first century BC divine involvement in the world was a hotly disputed topic among pagan philosophers.

As already noted, the religions of ancient Greece and Rome were polytheistic, but the vast majority of philosophers in antiquity believed in one god who governs the universe. Thales of Miletus (sixth century BC), almost always credited with being the first Greek philosopher, wrote that "all things are full of gods,"[18] but his younger contemporary Anaximander wrote of something he called the "Infinite." Aristotle describes Anaximander's view as follows:

> But there cannot be a principle of the infinite, for that would be a limit of it. Further, as it is a principle, it is both uncreatable and indestructible. For there must be a point at which what has come to be reaches its end, and also a termination of all passing away. That is why, as we say, there is no principle of *this*, but it is this which is held to be the principle of other things, and to encompass all and to steer all, as those assert who do not recognize, alongside the infinite, other causes, such as Mind or Friendship. Further they identify it with the Divine, for it is deathless and imperishable as Anaximander says, with the majority of the physicists. (*Physics* 203b6–15)

One of the pre-Socratic philosophers who most influenced Plato was Parmenides, who lived in the fifth century BC in Elea, a Greek colony in southwestern Italy. Parmenides believed that Being is one. It is perfect, simple, indivisible, immovable, and eternal, existing beyond time without any temporal parts. It is nothing like a person, since it does not even direct the course of events as Anaximander's Boundless does, but in addition to influencing Plato, and probably through the works of Plato, the Parmenidean conception of Being is remarkably similar to the God of Aquinas and other medieval philosophers, except that they combined it with the conception of a personal deity coming from the Jewish and Christian Scriptures. We will investigate this conception of God in Chapter 4.

The God of one of Socrates' followers, Antisthenes (445–365 BC) designs and regulates everything in the universe, but Antisthenes says God "resembles nothing with which human beings are acquainted. His reality transcends human knowledge and language, for which reason we can neither know him nor talk about him" (Navia 2001, p. 47). In Aristotle (384–322 BC) there is an Unmoved Mover, which he

---

18   See Aristotle (1984), *On the Soul*, 411a8–10.

describes as Thought thinking on itself, a blissful, eternal being that draws everything else in the universe towards itself like a giant metaphysical magnet (*Metaphysics* XII, 1072b21). Many of the Platonists, the Peripatetics (followers of Aristotle), and the Stoics of later antiquity believed in a god who is unique in that he is a first principle of the universe, providentially governs reality, and enjoys eternal bliss. Michael Frede argues that although the view that there are lesser "divine" beings was widespread among the Greeks, most of the Greek philosophers were monotheistic, and in later antiquity, by the time Christianity was spreading in the Hellenistic world, the dominant position among educated Greeks was monotheism.[19] What was difficult for educated people in the early centuries of the Christian era to accept was not monotheism, but the distinctive doctrines of the Incarnation and the Resurrection.[20]

Monotheism has great philosophical importance because a single god is very different in kind from one god among many. Obviously, one god has more power than one of many gods, and I have already noted the ethical significance of one god, but in addition, one god has the potential to play a significant metaphysical role in explaining the existence of the universe. Monotheism can be mythological, but it is potentially the basis for a unitary metaphysical system. The appearance of monotheism also created the potential for a new kind of conflict between belief systems that did not occur within polytheism. Compare a passage in I Kings 20, in which the Israelites fight the Arameans and defeat them.

19   See Frede (1999). Other papers in this volume address the same issue.

20   Arthur Nock (1998) argues that the pagan would find some things familiar in Christianity and other things unfamiliar and unpalatable. What was familiar was a sacrament of rebirth (p. 209), the idea that a god could have a son (p. 232), the idea that the son of a god could die and a god could have a passion and resurrection (p. 234), and the idea of a single god, the supreme cause and source of good (p. 235). Nonetheless, there was objection to the doctrine of Incarnation (p. 236), since it was thought that, whereas a mortal being could become immortal, humanity was a liability. No god would become human unless it happened in the very distant and mythical past (pp. 236–7). Christian teaching on the last things was also seen as strange (p. 242). The Resurrection was particularly unpalatable in a culture influenced by Platonism. There was something like a resurrection in Zoroastrianism (p. 243), but in Mithraism, a descendent of Zoroastrianism, the idea of resurrection disappeared (pp. 245–6). Platonism and Orphism taught that there is a divine element in the human being that makes the soul naturally immortal. This is at odds with the doctrine of Resurrection and it made redemption unnecessary.

The Arameans say of the Israelites, "Their gods are gods of the hills, and so they are stronger than we; but let us fight against them in the plain, and we shall be stronger than they" (RSV). Notice that the Arameans do not doubt the existence of the Hebrew gods; they simply think they have a different jurisdiction than their own gods. There is no question of one side being converted to the other side or of one side believing in the true gods and the other side not. They simply worship the gods of their place, rather like the way we root for the team of our home town or university. But when someone believes in one god who is the god of all peoples, there is a conflict not only between their belief and the beliefs of other religions, there is also a conflict with the beliefs of those who do not believe in any religion at all, but whose beliefs about the origin of the universe are purely naturalistic. Monotheism therefore conflicts not only with polytheism, but with non-theistic metaphysical systems. This makes monotheism very important philosophically. It is doubtful that philosophy of religion would exist were it not for the monotheistic religions.

1.2.2   The *imitatio dei*

Religions in many parts of the world teach that human beings do or should imitate a god or gods. In the Hebrew Bible God makes human beings in his own image, and in the Gospel of John, Jesus says, "Is it not written in your law [Psalm 82:6], 'I have said, You are gods'?" (John 10:34). Many other religions exhort humans to become as gods, some teaching that this can be literally accomplished after many reincarnations, although that is not a view prevalent in the West.[21] In Athens, by the fifth century BC it was widely believed that the human being is latently immortal and divine. Some thought that this divinity can be manifest only if a person purifies himself by performing certain rites. But in Plato and the Stoics human beings become like God by becoming virtuous. There are examples of this view throughout the Platonic dialogues. In the *Republic* Plato says that to be virtuous is to be like God, who takes good care of those who are like him (*Republic* X, 613a–b), and in the *Theaetetus* he says, "In God there is no sort of wrong whatsoever; he is supremely just, and the thing most like him is the

---

21   See Passmore (2000), first two chapters, for a history of the idea of imitating God or a perfect being.

man who has become as just as it lies in human nature to be" (*Theaetetus* 176c).[22]

This Platonic idea recurs in the philosophy of the Stoics, who made virtue as likeness to God central to their ethics.[23] In the first century, the Roman Stoic Seneca writes:

> Need you refuse to believe that there's something divine in one who is a part of God? All the world that contains us is one, and is God: we are his colleagues and his members. Our spirit is able: it arrives there, if its blemishes don't hold it down. As our body stands erect, its eyes fixed on the sky, so our spirit, free to expand as far as it will, is formed by nature to desire equality with godhead.[24]

In Christianity the *imitatio dei* has an interesting history because it is in tension with the idea of God as a perfect being. It is impossible to imitate an absolutely perfect, simple, self-sufficient, disembodied, immutable being, even though traditionally such a being is considered the most deserving of worship. In Christian theology this tension is resolved in the doctrine of the Incarnation, in which God becomes man and Jesus Christ is fully God and fully human.[25] For the Christian religion, then, the *imitatio dei* is the *imitatio christi*. As in the Stoic and Platonic tradition of imitation mentioned above, the idea of imitation of Christ stresses the ethical, while the high metaphysical view of God is important in Christian mysticism. The monastic literature weaves both strands into practices that can be incorporated into the daily life of the man or woman with an unusually strong desire to imitate the divine. Near the beginning of the Prologue to the Rule of St Benedict, the preeminent rule for monastic orders for almost 1,500 years, Benedict says, "Let us open our eyes to the light that can change us into the likeness of God."[26] This theme appears in many of the Church Fathers, particularly in the East, and continues in the contemporary spiritual literature.[27]

---

22 See Russell (2004) for a discussion of virtue as divine imitation in Plato and the Stoics.
23 See Long (2004), ch. 6, especially pp. 144–6.
24 *Seneca's Letters to Lucilius*, 92.30. See Seneca (1932) [c. 60–70].
25 This doctrine was defined at the Council of Chalcedon, AD 451.
26 See Marett-Crosby (2003), p. 11.
27 For a very well-written recent devotional reflection on this theme, see Casey (2004).

In summary, the idea of God that dominates Western philosophy is of a being who is both a metaphysical and moral exemplar. God is supreme both in being and in goodness. This view has important implications for metaphysics, philosophy of human nature, and ethics. In other chapters of this book we will explore the idea of God, defenses of it, and criticisms of it. God as metaphysical source of everything else in existence will be the topic of Chapters 2, 3, and 4. God as source of morality will be the topic of Chapter 6. The most serious problem with the view that God is supremely good is the problem of evil, the topic of Chapter 7.

1.3 Religion and Philosophy: the View from the Other Side

Religion and philosophy have not always had a harmonious coexistence, a problem that will become apparent from time to time in this book, and will be the topic of Chapter 10. The second-century Christian theologian Tertullian is famous for his frustrated exclamation, "What indeed has Athens to do with Jerusalem?"[28] The fact that this remark has been repeated so many times during the course of Christian history suggests that it hits a nerve with religious believers, particularly Christians who think that Christianity should emphasize its biblical basis more than its philosophical heritage. Most philosophers agree that the practice of religion does not require philosophical investigation. The latter is for a special sort of person. Not everyone likes philosophy or has the talent and the time to pursue it. But some people think philosophy can actually be harmful, and this complaint does not come only from those who think that philosophy is detrimental to faith. Look at the words of the English poet John Keats:

> Do not all charms fly
> At the mere touch of cold philosophy?
> There was an awful rainbow once in heaven:
> We know her woof, her texture; she is given
> In the dull catalogue of common things.
> Philosophy will clip an angel's wings.
> (*Lamia*, pt II, 229–34, in Keats (1978) p. 472)

28   See ch. 7 of his *Prescription Against Heretics*: Tertullian (1870a [199]), p. 9. There is a similar passage in his *Apology*, 46: Tertullian (1869 [197]).

Many of us who love philosophy are sure that philosophy does not clip an angel's wings. Recall that in the *Phaedrus* Plato says philosophy helps the soul to regrow its wings after it falls to the ground. Philosophy also corrects such excesses of religion as superstition and fanaticism, and philosophy sharpens the minds of those who study it, whether or not they have any religious beliefs. It is also an exciting pursuit. Philosophers agree on very little, but all are convinced that philosophy is hard. The questions it investigates are among the most difficult human beings have ever asked, and it is difficult to tell when we have reached the right answer, or even an answer that remotely approaches the truth. Philosophy requires the discipline to constantly battle wishful thinking and other emotions that lead us away from the truth, and often the arguments philosophers propose are initially convincing, yet closer investigation reveals them to be unsound. It takes intense and rigorous thinking to tell when an argument should be accepted.

This means that in order to have knowledge we need reasons that must be carefully scrutinized, and the reasons differ in important ways from those that are emotionally satisfying. Some philosophers conclude that emotions are irrelevant, but that is a mistake. Even the passion for truth is an emotion, and the passion to avoid falsehood is a different emotion, as we will see in the last chapter. My position is that many emotion-dispositions that are components of intellectual virtues have an important role in evaluating any kind of belief. These virtues include open-mindedness, intellectual fairness, intellectual humility, and sympathetic understanding of those with a contrary position. Some intellectual virtues aim at helping us to get the truth or to avoid falsehood, but some aim at other intellectual goods such as understanding and wisdom. Philosophers sometimes undervalue understanding and wisdom and overvalue certainty, but almost all philosophers agree that the value of getting the truth is non-negotiable. This makes it problematic to ever choose against truth. In Dostoyevsky's novel *The Devils* Shatov says to Stavrogin, "Didn't you tell me that if it were mathematically proved to you that truth was outside Christ, you would rather remain with Christ than with truth?" (Dostoevsky 1871, p. 255). With the possible exception of Kierkegaard, I seriously doubt that any philosopher we will discuss in this book would answer yes. Compare what Socrates says on the day he dies: "Give but little thought to Socrates but much more to the truth. If you think that what

I say is true, agree with me; if not, oppose it with every argument" (*Phaedo*, 91b).

What is the starting point for philosophy of religion? Changes in views about where philosophy begins have revolutionized philosophy more than once in its history. Prior to the seventeenth century, philosophy usually began with metaphysics – a comprehensive description of reality, including human beings, the rest of nature, and the supernatural realm. After Descartes, however, many philosophers adopted the method of starting with our individual consciousness. The purpose was to go as far as we can with what we can embrace with our own experience and powers. This method has continued to be influential, in spite of the fact that some philosophers have replaced it with other starting points – sometimes language, sometimes science. It is very difficult to tell whether or not to accept the philosophical arguments given in this book without some sense of the ultimate starting point for philosophical investigation. One assumption almost all philosophers make is that philosophical arguments *can* be assessed. Philosophy is very democratic in its presupposition that any intelligent, interested person is in a position to evaluate philosophical arguments for their soundness. A time-honored view among many of the world's religions, however, is that some truths are accessible only to the wise or to those who have prepared themselves to understand what a particular religion teaches. This makes it questionable whether those outside a given religious tradition have the capacity to either accept or reject its teachings, since one can neither accept nor reject what one cannot comprehend. You might expect this to be a point of view expressed only by religious persons who feel misunderstood, but that is not the case. As we will see in Chapter 3, the great twentieth-century philosopher Ludwig Wittgenstein stated it clearly, and he was expressing his own lack of understanding of something he nonetheless deeply respected.

I have chosen to begin with the traditional starting point of philosophy of religion: the question of whether there is a God, a single being of incomparable greatness whose existence is worthy of special attention from human beings. We will approach this question from several different directions. As I argued above, monotheism has tremendous philosophical as well as religious importance. If there is no God, some chapters of this book still make sense, but some do not. In any case, this book is for those who wonder and for those who are perplexed.

Further reading

There are many useful anthologies and reference works in philosophy of religion, but readers should be aware that they usually do not include many medieval sources and even fewer ancient sources. The *Blackwell Guide to Philosophy of Religion*, edited by William E. Mann (Malden, Mass.: Blackwell Publishing, 2005), and the *Oxford Handbook of Philosophy of Religion*, edited by William Wainwright (New York: Oxford University Press, 2005) are excellent collections of recent essays on major topics in philosophy of religion. The Blackwell *Contemporary Debates in Philosophy of Religion*, edited by Michael Peterson and Raymond VanArragon (Malden, Mass.: Blackwell Publishing, 2004), features essays on opposing sides of major issues in philosophy of religion. Students who wish to investigate the historical background of modern philosophy of religion should consult James Collins, *The Emergence of Philosophy of Religion* (New Haven: Yale University Press, 1967). John Haldane's short book *An Intelligent Person's Guide to Religion* (London: Duckworth, 2003) is a highly readable defense of religious faith in the modern world.

Chapter 2

The Classical Arguments for the Existence of God

2.1 What Question Does a Theistic Argument Answer?

Inquiry is the process of finding out the answer to a question, so inquiry into the existence of x can be expressed by asking the question "Does x exist?" Normally we do not inquire whether something exists unless we do not already believe that it exists. To find out, we may look for it ourselves, if we can, or we may rely upon the testimony of others, or we may infer its existence from other things whose existence we accept. Sometimes we discover the existence of something without looking for it, but we can't ask whether something exists without the idea of the thing we are seeking. Nobody would ask whether the Fountain of Youth exists unless he had heard of the Fountain of Youth. Nobody would ask whether the moons of Saturn exist unless he had heard of Saturn and moons. People have been known to roam the world searching for happiness. Presumably they couldn't do that without some idea of what they were hoping to find. There are people who ask whether God exists in the same way others ask whether happiness exists. They have at least a vague idea of what they are looking for, and a limited number of ways to go about finding it.

The classical arguments for the existence of God can be confusing because they have not always been offered in response to an inquiry whether God exists. The theistic arguments have a number of different functions and have been offered as responses to a variety of questions, sometimes posed to oneself and sometimes posed to someone else. Unless we know what question the argument is attempting to answer and who is asking it, it is impossible to tell whether any of the arguments succeed and whether the arguments fail when they fail to convince the questioner.

One type of questioner is the agnostic inquirer. She does not believe one way or the other in the existence of God, and is looking for an answer to the question "Does God exist?" in the same way Ponce de Leon was looking for an answer to the question "Does the Fountain of Youth exist?" She might turn both to theists and to atheists to help her get an answer, considering both positions live options. Another type of questioner is the atheist attacker. She already believes there is no God and challenges the theist to defend his belief. But it may not be clear what she expects him to do. Perhaps she just wants him to show her that, if she were in his place, she might very well believe what he believes. But she might expect something stronger – to convince her that theism is rational, given the conditions she is in herself. If she is predisposed to atheism, that may be hard to do. But why does that matter? Whether or not it matters is an important issue in contemporary religious epistemology. It is not obvious that the rational justification of any of our beliefs depends upon what other people think. But surely, at least *some* other persons are in a position to evaluate our beliefs, and if we are intellectually humble and open-minded, we must take their evaluation seriously. An advantage of close dialogue among open-minded theists, agnostics, and atheists is that any criticisms one has of another will be more serious challenges than the attacks of someone who has already ruled out the other's position in advance. Answering an aggressive and unsympathetic opponent almost never teaches us anything we didn't already know.

Let us look at the first kind of questioner, the agnostic inquirer. In a celebrated piece of dialogue between the nineteenth-century Indian sage Ramakrishna and a spiritual inquirer who subsequently became his disciple, the inquirer asks,"Do you believe in God, sir?"

"Yes," the Master replies.

"Can you prove it, sir?"

"Yes."

"How?"

"Because I see Him just as I see you here, only very much more intensely."[1]

---

1 Quoted in Sterling (1993), p. 88.

Ramakrishna's inquirer must have been one of the first kind, since he became Ramakrishna's disciple, but clearly this bit of dialogue would not convince the typical modern inquirer. One reason it would not is that the scientific method enjoys a very high status in our culture, and that method requires that answers to questions about the existence of some entity be based on observations that are repeatable by anybody else. Science is very egalitarian. You do not have to be a special person with a special kind of wisdom or insight to make discoveries. This is the virtue of science, and it may also be its vice, because we certainly do not know that all truths are accessible to everyone. As I mentioned at the end of Chapter 1, many religions since antiquity have taught that a person must prepare himself to receive certain kinds of truth or even to understand them. The preparation may take discipline and the guidance of a person farther along the spiritual path. Trust in such a person may be necessary to succeed at the inquiry. I imagine that Ramakrishna's inquirer was not primarily convinced by the words Ramakrishna uttered, but by trust that he was a person worth following. If the aim is to be in Ramakrishna's position some day with respect to someone else, one cannot do it by simply believing him and repeating his words to others. Personal experience cannot be transferred that way. Belief based on such experience cannot be transferred that way either.

The classical arguments for the existence of God do not presuppose any special experience and rely on principles it is presumed any intelligent person can know. One kind of argument concludes that God exists on the grounds that God's existence is the best explanation for some phenomena everyone can observe: the orderliness of the universe. Another kind of argument concludes that God exists on the grounds that if God does not exist, there is no adequate answer to a sensible question: Where did the universe come from? A third kind of argument claims something much more subtle: There is something about a certain concept that requires the existence of a divine being. The first is the Teleological or Design Argument. The second is the Cosmological Argument. The third is the Ontological Argument.

What type of questioner is the one to whom these arguments are directed? It is doubtful that any of them has often succeeded in convincing an agnostic, and it is even less likely that any of them has changed the mind of an atheist. As John Henry Newman said, "It is as absurd to argue men, as to torture them, into believing,"[2] although there are some noteworthy exceptions.[3] But until the seventeenth century, or thereabouts, the arguments were used primarily to show theists that their *own* belief could be rationally justified. So if you lived in the thirteenth century and had become a Dominican novice, Aquinas had five ways to prove to yourself that what you believed was defensible using reason alone, without referring to divine revelation. Given the shortage of atheists or agnostics among Aquinas' acquaintances, it is unlikely that he addressed either of the two kinds of inquirer I've mentioned. On the contrary, Aquinas was more concerned to respond to philosophers such as St John Damascene, who maintained that knowledge of God's existence is innate.[4] Knowledge of God needs to be brought out by a process of reasoning from experience, Aquinas thought. Notice that this is not a response to either an atheist or an agnostic, but rather to someone who thinks God's existence is so obvious that there is no need for argument at all.

Some time during the early modern period in the West, the Teleological, Cosmological, and Ontological Arguments acquired the use of responding to the second kind of questioner mentioned above, the atheist challenger. The historical background of this shift is interesting. The work of Descartes not only revolutionized philosophy, it had an extensive and profound effect on religion. Descartes intended his skeptical method to have a constructive purpose: to strip our beliefs down to a foundation in certainty, and to reconstruct the edifice of our beliefs on a firm foundation. I think it is fair to say that the negative side of Descartes' philosophy had more influence on subsequent philosophy than the positive side. As applied to religion, it led to the position that entire religions rest upon the success of one of the theistic arguments, and it led to the invention of the field of philosophy of religion. How did this happen?

Michael Buckley, S.J. argues in his book on the rise of modern atheism that Catholic theologians turned to philosophers and scientists

---

2 See Newman (1997), p. 63. An eminent religious leader in England, Newman (1801–90) was an Anglican priest who later converted to Catholicism and achieved the office of cardinal in 1879.

3   The well-known atheist Antony Flew has recently said that he now accepts some form of the Design Argument. See Flew and Habermas (2004).

4   Copleston (1962), pp. 55–6.

in the early seventeenth century to answer non-existent attacks from atheists, endorsing the view that only philosophical and scientific arguments can be the basis for religious belief.[5] When the new forms of the Teleological and Cosmological Arguments they developed were attacked, atheism did break out, beginning with a small group surrounding the Baron Paul d'Holbach (1723–89), but ironically, their arguments came out of the polemics of orthodox Catholics.

If Buckley is right, the modern attempt to secure religion on a philosophical or scientific foundation was bound to fail, and atheism among intellectuals arose from the perceived failure of theistic arguments. But earlier forms of these same arguments had been used for many centuries without serious problems for religion. The problem arose when the arguments were used to answer a different kind of question, a challenge from the skeptic rather than a bolster to a pre-existing belief. But what really led to a crisis was the picture of the structure of religious belief that also was inherited from Descartes, the structure now called foundationalism. The idea was that a system of religious beliefs has a structure like an inverted triangle with belief in God at the bottom. All other religious beliefs rest upon belief in the existence of God. There is no point in even looking at the rationality of religious beliefs without first examining the rationality of belief in God, since if belief in God cannot be independently justified, no other religious belief is justified. This foundationalist picture has been the subject of serious criticism for at least a century, but it does have an intuitive appeal and still has many supporters.

A second reason that made the theistic arguments supremely important in justifying religion has already been noted. It was the assumption that these arguments must be constructed and evaluated in such a way that they make no reference to religious experience or insight, or anything inaccessible to the skeptical inquirer. Obviously, Ramakrishna's answer to his disciple given above would be ruled out. Buckley (2004) finds the bracketing of religious experience and the interpersonal dimensions of religious consciousness particularly objectionable, and says that it is unsurprising that atheism was the result (p. xvi).

A third reason that the theistic arguments became pre-eminent in justifying religion is that another kind of foundationalism was

5   See Buckley (1987; 2004).

presupposed as well. Not only was it assumed that theistic belief is the foundation for all other religious beliefs, it was also assumed that beliefs are the foundation of religion. Religion is a practice in which beliefs come first, and the rest of the practice, including religious emotions, acts, and rituals derive their justification from the independent justification of religious beliefs. In Chapter 1 I suggested that it is a mistake to understand emotions as deriving from or resting upon beliefs. For that reason it is a mistake to understand religious emotions as deriving from religious beliefs. If emotions are ways of grasping external reality without resting upon prior beliefs, the ways in which emotions indicate the existence of religious reality should not be ignored. Furthermore, religious practice may not be justified through features of individual components of the practice – beliefs, emotions, acts, etc. Rather, the practice may have features that justify it as a whole. For example, some practices may lead to or be partially constitutive of a life of human flourishing, whereas others are not. I think this possibility deserves more attention.

One can criticize all of the assumptions that portrayed religions as standing or falling with the theistic arguments, but there are many philosophers who believe that at least one of these arguments has a form that can withstand even the most rigorous criticism from the second kind of questioner mentioned above. In the next three sections we will examine these arguments. In each case I will survey the history of the argument very briefly and will formulate some of the strongest versions of the argument I know of. Interested readers will want to consult the extensive contemporary and historical literature on the classical arguments.

2.2   The Teleological Argument

The Teleological Argument gets its name from the Greek word *telos*, which means end or purpose. In philosophy, the idea that nature is purposive comes from Plato and Aristotle. Aristotle thought that all things move towards the Final Cause (the Unmoved Mover mentioned in Chapter 1) as towards a cosmic magnet. There are versions of the Teleological Argument that follow Aristotle by focusing on the evident directionality of change in the natural world, whereas others focus on the orderliness and implicit design of nature. The Teleological

Argument is therefore sometimes called the Design Argument. The conclusion of the argument may be that there is an intelligent designer who originated the universe, or it may include the idea that a designer continuously directs the processes of nature providentially.

The ancient Stoic philosophers argued for a divine providential designer of the universe. Cicero, the famous Roman orator and statesman (first century BC), was not a Stoic, but often wrote in sympathy with Stoic doctrine. An especially elegant statement of the Design Argument appears in his writings:

> Who would not deny the name of human being to a man who, on seeing the regular motions of the heavens and the fixed order of the stars and the accurate interconnexion and interrelation of all things, can deny that these things possess any rational design, and can maintain that phenomena, the wisdom of whose ordering transcends the capacity of our wisdom to understand it, take place by chance? When we see something moved by machinery, like an orrery or clock or many other such things, we do not doubt that these contrivances are the work of reason; when therefore we behold the whole compass of the heavens moving with revolutions of marvelous velocity and executing with perfect regularity the annual changes of the season with absolute safety and security for all things, how can we doubt that all this is effected not merely by reason, but by a reason that is transcendent and divine?[6]

Cicero uses analogy to argue for divine governance, not simply for an originating intelligent cause. The conclusion that the evident order of the universe reveals governance is also the central idea of Aquinas' Fifth Way:

> The fifth way is taken from the governance of the world. We see that things which lack intelligence, such as natural bodies, act for an end, and this is evident from their acting always, or nearly always, in the same way, so as to obtain the best result. Hence it is plain that not fortuitously, but designedly, do they achieve their end. Now whatever lacks intelligence cannot move towards an end, unless it be directed by some being endowed with knowledge and intelligence, as the arrow is shot to its mark by the archer. Therefore some intelligent being exists

---

6   See *De Natura Deorum* bk II, 97 in Cicero (1979).

by whom all natural things are directed to their end; and this being we call God.[7]

Governance is not something we can observe in nature, nor is purpose. I assume that we do not actually *see* governance, nor do we see purpose. It is more plausible that we see design, but even that is normally thought to be inferred from something else.[8] In the argument of Aquinas, what we see is orderliness leading to the best result. Cicero says something similar: "Thus every line of reasoning goes to prove that all things in this world of ours are marvelously governed by divine intelligence and wisdom for the safety and preservation of all."[9] So both Cicero and Aquinas seem to think that we observe in nature or infer from what we observe, not merely order, but an orderly movement towards a good end.

In the early modern period the idea of governance and the idea that the processes of nature lead to the best end were dropped in favor of arguments going from the observed order of nature to the conclusion that nature was created by an intelligent designer. Probably the most well known of these arguments was given by William Paley (1743–1805), whose analogy with a watch has been repeated many times.[10] Paley asks the reader to imagine you are walking across a heath and come across a watch lying on the ground. If you picked it up and examined it, your observation of the intricate complexity of the parts and their operation to produce the movement of the hands around the dial would indicate to you that the watch had been designed for a purpose, and presumably you would make the same inference even if you had never seen a watch and did not know what watches are for.

Paley's argument can be formulated as follows:

Paley's simple analogical argument
(1) We observe in artifacts such as a watch order and regularity of parts.

7   Aquinas (1981 [1273]) pt I, q. 2, art. 3.
8   Proponents and critics of the Design Argument share the assumption that design is inferred, not directly perceived. For a recent defense of the view that design is perceived directly see Ratzsch (2003).
9   *De Natura Deorum* bk II, 132 in Cicero (1979).
10   See Paley (1802).

(2) We know that a watch could not have these features without a designer, a conscious being who creates it intentionally.
(3) Nature itself exhibits order and regularity of parts.
(4) Therefore, nature must have a designer, a conscious being who created nature intentionally.

Objections to this kind of argument were given by David Hume (1711–76) in one of the most influential works of early modern philosophy, *Dialogues Concerning Natural Religion*.[11] Before giving objections, Hume presents a more elaborate analogical argument in the mouth of Cleanthes, one of the participants in the dialogue:

Hume's analogical argument[12]
(1) Nature is a great machine, composed of lesser machines, all of which exhibit order.
(2) Machines caused to exist by human minds exhibit order.
(3) Nature resembles machines caused to exist by human minds.
(4) If effects resemble each other, the causes do as well.
(5) So the cause of nature resembles human minds.
(6) Greater effects require greater causes.
(7) Nature is a much greater machine than the machines produced by human minds.
(8) So the cause of nature resembles but is much greater than human minds.

Hume offers several objections to the analogy between the universe and artifacts in the mouth of Philo, the skeptic of the dialogue. One objection is that human thought is never the ultimate cause of human artifacts. A human designer gets ideas from nature and other people and the process is far from predictable. Another objection is that the universe is too singular a phenomenon to be analogous to any of its parts. Since we have no experience of other universes, we are in no position to draw any conclusions about the similarity of causes of the universe to causes of components of the universe.

11   See Hume (1779).
12   The synopsis I am presenting here can be found in part II when Cleanthes first speaks.

An historically more important problem encountered by the Design Argument was the theory of evolution. Although Paley and other early modern philosophers had parted with the ancients by limiting their conclusion to the thesis that the universe had an intelligent originating designer rather than an ongoing governing being, they were aligned with the ancient Stoics in focusing on apparent purpose in biological nature, particularly in animals and in organs of the human body, such as the eye. Darwin's evolutionary theory explained the order and change in biological nature in terms of the adaptation of organisms to their environments, which made it seem unnecessary to posit a God to explain the kind of order that fascinated Paley. Darwin's theory also undermined Paley's analogy between a watch and natural organisms, since watches do not contain any internal principles of adaptation. Biological nature is different from artifacts.

Why does the theory of evolution seem to make the hypothesis of an intelligent designer unnecessary? Richard Dawkins (mentioned in Chapter 1), describes how order comes out of chance by using the model of disorder plus a sieve.[13] Pebbles in the ocean are tossed about randomly, but the action of the waves on the pebbles is different for larger pebbles than for smaller pebbles, and if you walk along the beach, you see that the larger pebbles are farther from the shoreline than the smaller pebbles. Order comes from disorder plus a mechanism that sorts without any intelligent plan. Genetic mutations are chance events, which nature permits because, when cells duplicate, they do not always do so perfectly. So evolution requires a degree of chance that results in variability of traits among the animals of a certain population. Presumably that would be analogous to a variety of pebbles. The mechanism of natural selection is the sieve, analogous to the action of the waves that results in sorting of the pebbles. Animals with certain traits are more likely to live long enough to reproduce themselves and thus to pass on to the next generation the traits they have. Small chance mutations when passed through the same mechanism over and over again result in the development of new complex species, just as the tossing of pebbles by the waves over and over again results in an orderly arrangement of the pebbles on the beach.

13   Dawkins (1996), pp. 43–4.

There are a number of well-known responses to evolutionary theory among theists. One response is to accept the theory, but to view the entire evolutionary process as another instance of nature operating to achieve an end. Richard Swinburne (1979) suggests that the theory of evolution shows the natural universe to be "a machine-making machine" (p. 135). Keith Ward argues that God could just as well have used the mechanism of natural selection rather than direct creation of species if he wanted to create a world of diverse species, including intelligent humans who can appreciate their creator. In fact, Ward thinks that Darwinism is more probable on the hypothesis of theism than on the hypothesis of atheistic naturalism. It is improbable on the theory of evolution that the human species would evolve unless the evolutionary process were directed, argues Ward. The causal activity of God is a better explanation.[14] Returning to Dawkins' analogy with the pebbles on the beach, we could express Ward's position this way: The fact that there is a mechanism in nature that produces order by a sorting mechanism operating on disorder is itself in need of an explanation. The way in which the random tossing of the pebbles by the waves results in an orderly arrangement of the pebbles on the sand does not need to be explained. What needs explanation is the entire system of waves, pebbles, and sorting. Similarly, says Ward, what needs explaining is the whole system of evolutionary processes. That system is more probable on the hypothesis of design than on the hypothesis of naturalism.

Ward's response to Darwinism is indicative of a trend among contemporary supporters of the Design Argument who use modern theories of probability. The question they address is not the origin of the human species, but the prior question of the origin of the biological universe or the entire physical universe. Recent versions of the argument look to physics rather than to biology for the evidence of purpose and design, and rather than to propose analogies between human artifacts like watches and the universe as a whole, they are probabilistic arguments or arguments to the best explanation. The question they pose is this: Given the data of the universe as we know it, is it more likely that the particular universe we have would have occurred by chance or by design?

14   Ward (1996), pp. 76–8.

A number of philosophers and physicists have argued that the universe at its beginning had to be "fine-tuned" to an extraordinary degree to result in a universe with such interesting properties as the possession of intelligent beings like ourselves. The probability that the initial conditions of the universe would have been such that it was possible for a universe to evolve that supported conscious life is extraordinarily low. This leads to a different form of the Design Argument:

A contemporary argument from probability
(1) The universe has a large number of life-facilitating coincidences between causally unrelated aspects of the physical universe. For example, the ratio of the density between an open universe that goes on expanding for ever and a closed universe that collapses upon itself is extremely narrow, and the density of the universe is in that range. In addition, if any of the fundamental physical constants (strong and weak nuclear forces, electromagnetic force, electron charge) had differed even minutely from what they in fact are, the universe would not have supported life. Intelligent life could only have evolved in an extremely narrow range of possible universes.
(2) The probability that this could have occurred by chance is infinitesimally low.
(3) Therefore, it is much more probable that our universe was intelligently designed than that it occurred by chance.[15]

There are a number of objections that have been offered to this form of the Design Argument. One is that intelligent life of a very different kind than what we know of might have evolved out of a completely different kind of universe with different physical constants. Another is that perhaps an infinite number of universes coexist with ours or have existed sequentially in an infinite amount of time prior to now. This is the "Multiverse" hypothesis.

It is very difficult to know how we could evaluate the probability of either of these hypotheses, but this response is a two-edged sword

---

15   These "fine tuning" arguments are discussed in Corwin (1983), Craig and Sinnott-Armstrong (2004), and in many of the essays included in Manson (2003).

because it means that it is also difficult to know how we can evaluate the probability of the hypothesis of theism, given that we do not know the probability of its competitor hypotheses. Nonetheless, many people are impressed with the intuitive low probability of a universe that has the precise conditions necessary for the evolution of consciousness. Consciousness that includes self-consciousness has a singular place in the universe that sets it apart from everything else and demands an explanation. The Design Argument therefore leads into the areas of philosophy that address the nature of consciousness and attempt to unravel its mystery.

2.3   The Cosmological Argument

The Cosmological Argument aims at demonstrating that there must be an external cause of the universe with a nature superior to anything in the universe. There are two basic forms of the argument. One assumes the impossibility of an infinite series of temporal moments extending back into the past. Everything in the physical universe has a cause prior to itself in time. Since the series cannot go back to infinity, there must be a First Cause. The second form of the argument does not assume that time cannot extend infinitely into the past, and in fact it need not make any assumption about the size or shape of time. The key premise of the second argument is that the universe is a dependent entity, the sort of thing that cannot exist without something external to it upon which it depends for its existence. The first form of the argument aims to demonstrate the existence of a First Cause in the sense of first that means an initiator or first in a series, whereas the second form aims to demonstrate the existence of a First Cause in the sense of first that means highest or ultimate. There are both ancient and modern versions of both forms of the Cosmological Argument.

2.3.1   Did the universe and time have a beginning?

Richard Sorabji says that the Greeks separated the idea of a creation from the idea of a beginning, and they separated the question of whether the orderly physical universe had a beginning from the issue of whether matter and time had a beginning. With few exceptions, he says, the idea that time had a beginning was denied by everyone in

European antiquity outside the Judeo-Christian tradition.[16] There was dispute over Plato's *Timaeus*, since it was sometimes interpreted as maintaining that time had a beginning and sometimes not.[17] However, the dominant view was the Aristotelian one that time had no beginning and will have no end. And since Aristotle defined time as the measure of motion, this meant that the motion of matter had no beginning and will have no end. Nonetheless, Sorabji says, all sides agreed that the physical universe with its present orderly arrangement had a beginning. So the Greeks distinguished three questions about the beginning: (1) Did the orderly cosmos have a beginning? (2) Did matter have a beginning? (3) Did time have a beginning? The answer to (1) was assumed to be affirmative. The dispute was over (2) and (3), not (1). To make matters more complicated, they distinguished all of the questions about a beginning from the parallel questions about causation or creation. In particular, question (2) was distinguished from (4) Was matter created?

A clarification is also needed for the orthodox Judeo-Christian view on the beginning of time and the universe. The standard reading of the opening of Genesis is that the material universe had a beginning, but it is unclear whether it is formless matter that begins, or only the ordered universe whose creation is described so vividly in Genesis I. It is doubtful that Genesis gives an affirmative answer to questions (2) and (3). Of course, the author of the beginning of Genesis was not aware of what would become the dominant Greek position on the origin of time and matter, so he should not be expected to take a clear stand on that issue. And if Genesis does not state that God created matter and time, neither does it say that matter pre-existed for ever. It is not clear, then, whether Genesis conflicts with the dominant Greek view. However, it was generally interpreted as affirming a first moment of time and a temporal origin of the universe. This is important historically because the topic of the origin of time and the universe was perhaps the first case in which

---

16   See Sorabji (1983), p. 193.

17   In the *Timaeus* Plato implies that time came into being upon the creation (37c–38), but he also says that God (the Demiurge) created order out of disordered matter (30a). The latter seems to presuppose time prior to the creative activity of God. One interpretation suggested by Sorabji (1983) is that God created ordered time, but disordered time existed previously along with disordered matter (pp. 272–5). Personally, I cannot make any sense out of the idea of disordered time.

there was the perception of a direct clash between Greek and Hebrew positions on a critical metaphysical issue.[18]

Among the Christian fathers, Clement of Alexandria (second century) declared that matter is timeless in one of his works, and Origen attacks the idea of the eternity of matter as a view held by others, so there must have been disagreement on the question. It seems to me that the Prologue to the Gospel of John (approximately AD 90) suggests a creation out of nothing, albeit through the divine *Logos*, but in any case, the doctrine became universal among Christian philosophers by the end of the second century.[19] It was defended by Augustine (fourth–fifth centuries), who says that God created time along with motion, but it is interesting that Augustine suggests that time might have begun with the creation of the angels, not the creation of the physical universe. The angels are created beings even though they exist in all time.[20]

By the thirteenth century there was uncertainty again among Christian philosophers after the rediscovery of Aristotle's works. Recall that the works of Aristotle were known to the Arab philosophers for many centuries after they had been lost in the West, and their introduction into the Latin West reinvigorated the position that the world had no beginning and will have no end. Al-Ghazali (eleventh–twelfth centuries) had recorded arguments of "the theologians" for a beginning of the universe, and arguments by "the philosophers," who took the Aristotelian view against it. In reply, Averroes maintained that neither set of arguments was conclusive. His Jewish contemporary Maimonides had the same position. Maimonides maintained that since neither side can be proven, we are free to accept a beginning of the universe on the authority of Scripture. In the following century Aquinas was influenced by this position and concluded that it is revelation, not reason, that shows the universe had a beginning. According to Aquinas, the finitude

18 There is a second "creation account" in Genesis 2:4–25, but this does not actually concern the origin of the world.
19 This is the interpretation of David Winston (1971) who argues that the *ex nihilo* doctrine arose at the end of the second century in controversy with the Gnostics. He cites Theophilus of Antioch as the first to give a clear statement of the doctrine.
20 See Augustine (1950 [427]) XII, ch. 15. Augustine says that there would be time with the creation of the angels if there was motion among the angels, presumably meaning mental motion, since he assumes the angels have no bodies.

of time and the universe is an issue that reason cannot decide one way or the other. In fact, he thought this position actually has a theological advantage, since if both positions are possible, it shows that God had a choice. He could have created a universe that exists in infinitely extended time, but chose instead to create a universe with a beginning.[21]

In the twentieth century it was widely accepted that the issue of whether the universe had a beginning had been settled empirically. The expansion of the universe was predicted in 1922 by the Russian mathematician Alexander Friedman and was verified by Hubble in 1929. A time-reversed extrapolation from the rate of expansion of the universe led to the conclusion that the universe had a beginning a finite amount of time in the past. That figure has varied somewhat over the decades, but it is generally put at around 15 billion years ago. This event, commonly called the Big Bang, brought back into vogue the form of the Cosmological Argument that relies on the idea that there must have been a first moment of time, and some philosophers and physicists believe that Big Bang cosmology gives empirical support to this argument.

Others disagree. An assumption that has almost always been taken for granted in philosophical reflections on time, both ancient and modern, is that time is linear. For example, the intuition that time goes back infinitely into the past is supported by the idea that for any finite number of moments n that have elapsed before now, it always makes sense to ask, "What happened n +1 moments ago?" On the other side, some argued that if an infinite number of moments of time have already elapsed before now, we would never have gotten to now, for if there has been an infinite number of moments before now, there would have been an infinite number of moments of time before *any* moment in the past. But then how did we get from then to now? This was one of the arguments of Philoponus, a Christian philosopher of the early sixth century who attacked the infinity of the past as nonsensical.[22] Notice that the intuitions on both sides of the issue assume the linearity of time. But all of these arguments are avoided if time is non-linear.

21   See Aquinas (1981 [1273]) pt I, q. 46.
22   Sorabji (1983), pp. 214ff.

Stephen Hawking postulates that time is finite but unbounded in his well-known book *A Brief History of Time*, using a spherical model of time rather than a linear one. On the surface of a sphere there is no boundary, yet the size of the surface is finite. No matter where you start, you can go "backwards" or "forwards", but you never run up against an edge. On this model it makes no more sense to ask what happened "before" the Big Bang than to ask what is happening on the earth's surface a hundred miles above the North Pole.[23]

The possibility that time is not linear, or differs in some other dramatic way from the way we ordinarily think of it, leads to the issue of how the nature of time affects the Cosmological Argument we are about to consider. What exactly is at stake? What is most obviously at stake is that a Cosmological Argument that depends upon the linearity of time and finitude of the past may be an argument for a different kind of First Cause than an argument that is compatible with the infinity of past time or a non-linear model of time. In the next section we will look at several different Cosmological Arguments. One requires that there was a finite amount of time in the past and that time is linear. The others do not.

2.3.2 Cosmological Arguments

In Plato's late dialogue *Laws* he briefly presents a Cosmological Argument for the existence of a self-moved Mover (or Movers) as part of a discussion about the laws pertaining to religion. Plato argues that that which is moved by another cannot be the primary element in change. Only a self-moved Mover can be. He also maintains that if everything was first at rest, only a self-moved Mover could begin the process of change (*Laws* 893–6). Plato's argument is loose and it is probably not intended to be an argument for a single self-moved Mover. It can be interpreted to imply that there was a first moment of time, although that is doubtful also. But an argument explicitly relying on the assumption that there was a first moment of time is the Kalām Cosmological Argument developed by medieval Arabic thinkers such as al-Kindi (ninth century) and al-Ghazali (eleventh century). They were called the *kalām*, or "the theologians," as opposed to the

---

23   Hawking (1988) ch. 8, esp. pp. 135–49.

falsafa, or "the philosophers" who followed Aristotle. In its general form the argument is very simple:

The Argument from the Kalām
(1) Whatever begins to exist is caused to exist by something else.
(2) The universe began to exist.
(3) Therefore, the universe was caused to exist by something else.[24]

The major advocate of this argument among contemporary philosophers is William Lane Craig.[25] The defense of the argument is basically the defense of premise (2), which we have already considered. Rarely has anyone attacked premise (1) unless it is on the grounds that there is a self-caused cause, as we just saw in Plato's *Laws*. But few would be so bold as to suggest that something can come from nothing. An exception is the physicist Alan Guth, whose recent inflationary theory[26] includes the proposal that the universe could have evolved from an initial seed that came from nothing.[27]

The second kind of Cosmological Argument does not assume that time had a beginning. In fact, those arguments influenced by Aristotle often assumed the contrary. In the *Physics* Aristotle argues that motion

24   I am following the form of the argument in Plantinga (1998).
25   See Craig (1979). This argument has generated a great deal of literature, both defending and criticizing it. The debate in Craig and Sinnott-Armstrong (2004) covers this argument, along with several other theistic arguments.
26   A summary of Guth's theory is provided by Lemley (2002). Guth's inflationary theory is the theory that between 10^{-37} and 10^{-34} seconds after the Big Bang the universe expanded exponentially. Guth maintains that according to this theory, the universe did not have to be especially fine-tuned at the start to end up with a universe precisely divided between closed and open. For a more detailed account see Guth (1997).
27   This part of Guth's theory comes from the work of Edward Tryon (1973), who proposed in *Nature* that the universe could be a vacuum fluctuation, which is close to the proposal that it came from nothing. In principle, anything could materialize as a vacuum fluctuation, but the probabilities get smaller as the thing's mass and complexity increase (Guth 1997, p. 272). Most scientists ignored Tryon's theory because vacuum fluctuations are usually subatomic in size; they considered Tryon's suggestion that the entire universe is a vacuum fluctuation simply too unlikely. Although Guth (1997) does not necessarily endorse all the details of Tryon's theory, he does think that his inflationary theory makes the general approach promising. He claims that "the inflationary theory can explain how the universe might have evolved from an initial seed as small as Tryon's vacuum fluctuations" (p. 14).

has no beginning and no end. The cessation of a motion requires a destructive agent, and the destructive agent would have to be destroyed after the thing it destroys has been destroyed, and then the thing that destroys *it* would subsequently have to be destroyed, so there is no end to the sequence (*Physics* 252a). In *Metaphysics* XII Aristotle uses this point to conclude that there must be an indestructible substance. Substances are the primary existents, so if all substances are destructible, everything is destructible. But since it is impossible that all movement be destroyed, it is impossible that everything is destructible. There must be an indestructible substance, the Unmoved Mover, mentioned in Chapter 1. Aristotle does not refer to the UM as a creator, but ingenious Muslim philosophers assimilated the Aristotelian view of the UM to the idea of a Creator of the universe. The idea that there can be a cause outside of time that creates infinitely long time is admittedly hard to grasp, but probably no harder to grasp than the idea of a cause outside of time creating finitely long time. The only reason the latter seems easier to imagine is that we may give in to the temptation to think that a timeless God somehow pre-exists time in order to create it, but of course that makes no sense. If you can imagine that a timeless being can create time by creating a temporal world, the length of time should not matter.

The Muslim philosopher Avicenna (980–1037), a Persian by birth, employed the Aristotelian argument for an Unmoved Mover to argue that everything contingent comes from the creative will of God, thus bringing the Aristotelian conception of God in line with Muslim belief. Avicenna defines a *contingent* being as a being whose existence requires a cause. A *necessary* being, in contrast, is a being whose existence does not require a cause. Here is one way Avicenna argues for the existence of a necessary being:

Avicenna's Argument[28]

(1) Every being is either contingent or necessary.
(2) If a being is necessary, then a necessary being exists.
(3) If a being is contingent, then a necessary being exists for
    (a) a contingent being requires a cause for its existence (whether or not the cause precedes it in time).

28 I am adapting the form of this argument from Craig (1980), pp. 89–96.

(b) if this cause is also contingent, then there is a series of contingent beings.

(c) there cannot be an infinite series of causes of the existence of any being.

(d) the ultimate cause of any contingent being must be a being that does not itself need a cause.

(4) Therefore, a necessary being exists.[29]

In twelfth-century Muslim Spain, Averroes (Ibn Rushd) produced a form of Avicenna's argument that he considered valid,[30] and when his works were translated into Latin and became known in Paris, they caused a sensation. The influence of forms of this argument on Aquinas is apparent in the latter's Second Way, which is very similar to it. When people first read the Second Way's claim that there cannot be an infinite sequence of causes, they often assume it implies that there must have been a first moment of time, but Aquinas intended the argument to be compatible with the Aristotelian view that the world had no beginning. To make sense of the argument, we must follow the Greeks in separating the idea of being caused from having a beginning, as we see in Avicenna's version.

Whatever one thinks of the implications of the Second Way about a beginning, Aquinas' Third Way quite clearly does not presuppose that there was a first moment of time. On the contrary, it seems to me that the argument is more plausible under the assumption that there was infinite time in the past. This argument is also an argument from contingency, but notice that Aquinas begins with a different notion of contingency than the one used by Avicenna. Aquinas adapted the argument from one given by Maimonides:

Aquinas' Third Way[31]

(1) We see in the world things which have the possibility either to be or not to be. That is to say, their existence is contingent, not necessary.

---

29 Notice that the conclusion on line (5) is not the same as the implied conclusion of line (2). The necessary being of line (5) is one that is not only necessary, but is that upon which contingent beings depend for their existence. There is no implication that the necessary being of line (2) has any connection with contingent beings.

30 See Craig (1980), pp. 106ff.

31 Aquinas, *Summa Theologica* I, q. 2, art. 3.

(2) It is not possible that all things are contingent, for

(a) if a thing is contingent, then there is some time at which it does not exist.

(b) if all things were contingent, then at some time in the past all things did not exist; there was nothing in existence.

(c) nothing can come into existence from nothing.

(d) so if all things were contingent, nothing would exist even now.

(e) but some things do exist.

(f) hence, not all things that exist are contingent; a necessary being exists.

(3) A necessary being either owes its necessity to something else or it does not owe its necessity to something other than itself.

(4) There cannot be an infinite chain of beings upon which a necessary being owes its necessity.

(5) Therefore, there is a necessary being that owes its necessity to nothing other than itself.

There is a problem with the move from (2a) to (2b). (2b) says that if everything that has ever been in existence is contingent, then there was some time in the past when nothing existed. But why the past? First, Aquinas apparently thinks that a contingent thing cannot exist for an infinite amount of time. But even if this is true, there is no reason to think that a contingent thing would have failed to exist at some time in the past unless an infinite amount of time has already gone by. But even if there is an infinite amount of time in the past, why say that *everything* would have gone out of existence by now if all things were contingent? Why couldn't a new contingent thing come into existence as each one goes out of existence? To answer that, Aquinas could use the idea that even a series of contingent beings is contingent, or he could rely on the idea that no contingent thing can cause an infinite sequence of contingent things (the argument of the Second Way), or he could use the idea that the basic constituents of every contingent thing are contingent pieces of matter, so the basic building blocks of the universe are contingent, and if the building blocks go out of existence, so does everything they build.

So I think that assuming:

(i) a contingent thing only exists for a finite amount of time, and

(ii) there has been an infinite amount of time in the past,

it would follow that if all things in the universe, including their basic constituents, are contingent, there would have been a time in the past at which nothing existed. And if nothing existed at some time in the past, nothing would exist even now. But obviously something does exist now. Therefore, it cannot be the case that everything in existence is contingent.

I find the Third Way the most interesting of the Five Ways, but it clearly relies on disputable assumptions about time and the relationship between contingency and temporality. A version without these assumptions would be preferable. Such an argument appeared in the seventeenth century, and the final version of the Cosmological Argument for our review is one that developed at that time.

The modern versions of the Cosmological Argument make no mention of the structure of time. Instead, they use an important principle of early modern metaphysics, the Principle of Sufficient Reason (PSR), which has a number of variations, but can be briefly stated as follows: Every contingent fact requires an explanation for its truth. (Presumably necessary facts are self-explanatory.) Gottfried Leibniz[32] and Samuel Clarke both accepted this principle and used it in arguing for the existence of God. Here is a rendition of Clarke's argument:

Clarke's Argument from the Principle of Sufficient Reason[33]
A necessary being = a being that cannot not exist. A contingent being = a being that can not exist.
(1) Every existent thing must be either contingent or necessary.
(2) Assume that everything in existence is contingent.
(3) The fact that the world of contingent things exists is contingent.
(4) The fact that the world of contingent things exists needs explanation (by PSR).
(5) The fact that there is a world of contingent things cannot be explained by something outside it since, by hypothesis, nothing else exists, but its existence could not be explained by anything inside it since the existence of a whole cannot be explained by the existence of a part.

---

32   See his *The Monadology*, section 32ff in Leibniz (1989).
33   See Clarke (1998 [1705]).

(6) So if everything in existence is contingent, the existence of the world of contingent things has no explanation.

(7) Therefore, there must exist a necessary being whose existence explains the existence of the world of contingent things.

This argument involves the idea that the collection of all contingent things is itself a contingent thing – a thing depending upon something else that explains its existence. Therefore, there must be something in existence in addition to all the contingent things. But Hume objected in the mouth of Cleanthes that a collection of contingent beings is not itself a contingent being in want of an explanation. Says Hume:

> in tracing an eternal succession of objects it seems absurd to inquire for a general cause or first author. How can anything that exists from eternity have a cause, since that relation implies a priority in time and a beginning of existence? . . . But the *whole*, you say, wants a cause. I answer that the uniting of these parts into a whole, like the uniting of several distinct countries into one kingdom, or several distinct members into one body, is performed merely by an arbitrary act of the mind, and has no influence on the nature of things. Did I show you the particular causes of each individual in a collection of twenty particles of matter, I should think it very unreasonable should you afterwards ask me what was the cause of the whole twenty. This is sufficiently explained in explaining the cause of the parts.[34]

For some kinds of collections Hume's objection seems sound. For example, suppose you want to know why your philosophy class has assembled in a certain room at a certain time. It is surely enough to know why each member of the class decided to come to class that day. Once you have that information, your question is answered. It is not necessary to find out something else – why the class itself is there. That is because *the class* is really nothing over and above a collection of individuals. On the other hand, suppose you want to know why your dogwood tree died. Your question is about an organism whose parts are not independent of each other and whose death is an event that cannot be reduced to a collection of events occurring in its parts. Is the

---

34   See part IX of the *Dialogues Concerning Natural Religion*, pp. 59–60 in Hume (1948 [1779]).

universe more like an organism or more like a philosophy class? Or is it in a third category of collection? I will leave it to the reader to consider possible answers to that question.

2.4   The Ontological Argument

Unlike the Teleological and Cosmological Arguments, the Ontological Argument is not the sort of argument that ordinary people think of on their own, and when they first hear of it, most people think there has got to be something wrong with it. But it is remarkably difficult to say exactly what that is. It turns out that the argument is not guilty of any simple mistake of logic. Bertrand Russell (1967) says in his autobiography that one day when he was out walking to buy some tobacco, he suddenly threw his hat in the air and exclaimed, "Great God in boots! – the ontological argument is sound!" (p. 84). He later changed his mind, but the argument has continued to fascinate philosophers. One of the most fascinating aspects of it is that it is the only major theistic argument that is purely *a priori* – that is, it has no premise acquired from experience, and while that means that it cannot gain support from science, it also means that it cannot be refuted empirically.

2.4.1   Anselm's arguments

Historians agree that the first person to think of this argument was St Anselm of Canterbury in the eleventh century.[35] Descartes and Leibniz proposed versions in the seventeenth century, and several more philosophers proposed versions during the twentieth century, when there was a burst of interest in the argument, using the techniques of modern modal logic. Many other famous philosophers have rejected it, including Aquinas and Immanuel Kant.

---

35   Earlier in the eleventh century the Arab philosopher Avicenna (Ibn Sīnā) distinguished necessary from possible beings as follows: "The necessary being is that which, if assumed to be non-existent, involves a contradiction. The possible being is that which may be assumed to be non-existent without involving a contradiction" (quoted in Craig (1980), p. 87). Craig observes the similarity to the ontological argument, but notes that Avicenna does not draw the conclusion that therefore there must be a necessary being, as Anselm does.

Anselm was a monk who became abbot of the Benedictine monastery of Bec in Normandy, and then was elected Archbishop of Canterbury in 1093. While at Bec he wrote his greatest philosophical works, including the *Monologion* and *Proslogion*. The latter is written as an address of the soul to God and was modeled on Augustine's *Confessions*. There are two versions of the Ontological Argument in the *Proslogion*, one in Chapter 2 and one in Chapter 3. Both arguments have created a lot of controversy, and it was not always recognized that there are two distinct arguments. Nowadays it is usually agreed that the argument in *Proslogion* 3 is the better of the two. Another source of controversy is the issue of the purpose of the arguments. In *Proslogion* 1 Anselm says he does not understand in order to believe, but believes in order to understand, and the work is addressed to God, so it is unlikely that Anselm intended the argument to answer either agnostic inquirers or atheist attackers. On the other hand, many subsequent philosophers have judged the argument at least as good as the Cosmological and Design Arguments, and it follows the rule of using nothing inaccessible to the skeptical inquirer.

Anselm's Argument in Proslogion *2*

In *Proslogion* 2 Anselm (1965 [1078]) argues that the idea of perfection entails existence. Let G = that than which nothing greater can be conceived. Anselm argues in the form of a *reductio ad absurdum* that the "fool who says in his heart there is no God" is committed to a contradiction as follows:

(1) We can conceive of G, which is to say, G exists at least in our understanding.

(2) Suppose that G does not exist in reality.

(3) We can conceive of G existing in reality.

(4) It is greater to exist in reality than to exist merely in the understanding.

(5) So we can conceive of G (i.e. that than which nothing greater can be conceived) being greater than it is.

But (5) is a contradiction.

(6) Therefore, the supposition (2) is false. G exists in reality.

The opposition to this argument generally focuses on premise (4). This premise appears to maintain that existence is a great-making property. Kant disputed this on the grounds that existence is not a property at all, but even if it is, surely existence is not a great-making property of everything.[36] For instance, we would not want to say that an existent terrorist is better than a non-existent one. The sense in which it is better for G to exist than not to exist must apply only to certain kinds of beings. Brian Leftow suggests that nothing that does not exist ought to be worshiped.[37] If worthiness of worship is included in G, then G would be greater if it exists in reality, not merely in the understanding, and it would be greater partly *because* it exists in reality.

Anselm's contemporary, the monk Gaunilo, argued in a famous piece called "On Behalf of the Fool" that an argument exactly parallel to Anselm's could be given to prove the existence of the greatest conceivable island.[38] But we all know that no such island exists. Therefore, Anselm's argument must be unsound. The fact that Gaunilo chose an island for his example is, of course, arbitrary. He could have made up the concept of the greatest conceivable human being, the greatest conceivable book, the greatest conceivable flower, and so on. The point is that we know in advance that no such object exists. Therefore, there must be something wrong with arguing from the concept of such a thing to its existence. Likewise, there must be something wrong with arguing from the concept of the greatest conceivable being to its existence.[39]

The contemporary philosopher Alvin Plantinga (1974a) has replied on behalf of Anselm that things like islands have no maxima. We cannot even conceive of the greatest conceivable island, whereas we can conceive of the greatest conceivable being. Such a being would have properties of perfect goodness, omnipotence, omniscience, etc. One could reply that there are no maxima to these properties either, but it is clear that Anselm thought that the fact that existence is entailed by G is a special case. The concept of that than which nothing greater

---

36 See Kant (1781), A592/B620–A602/B630.

37 Leftow (2005), p. 86.

38 Gaunilo's "On Behalf of the Fool" is included in Anselm (1965 [1078]).

39 Notice that there is a difference between *that than which nothing greater can be conceived*, which is the concept Anselm uses in *Proslogion* 2, and *the greatest conceivable being*. The latter implies that nothing conceivable equals it in greatness, whereas the former implies only that nothing surpasses it. The usual points of controversy over the argument do not turn on this difference, so I have ignored it in the text. The different versions of the argument can easily be modified to reflect the difference in wording, if desired.

can be conceived entails existence in a way in which, he thinks, nothing else does.

Much more could be said about whether Gaunilo's analogy still works, but in any case, the analogy cannot be used to refute Anselm's argument in *Proslogion* 3. This argument can be worded either in terms of the conceivable or in terms of the possible. Anselm seems to equate the two, but it is the latter that lends itself to variations using modern modal logic, so I will present the argument in that form:

Anselm's Argument in Proslogion 3

(1) It is possible that there exists something whose non-existence is impossible.

(2) A being whose non-existence is impossible is greater than a being whose non-existence is possible. (A necessary being is greater than a contingent being.)

(3) Suppose that the greatest possible being does not exist.

(4) The non-existence of the greatest possible being is possible (from 3).

(5) The greatest possible being is not the greatest possible being (2, 4). But (5) is a contradiction.

(6) Therefore, the greatest possible being exists.

Notice that Gaunilo's island analogy does not apply to this argument because nobody would propose the parallel first premise: It is possible that there exists an island whose non-existence is impossible. However, a modification of Kant's objection to (2) would still apply in that any reasons for thinking that existence is not a property would presumably also be reasons for thinking that necessary existence is not a property. A form of the argument that does not use premise (2) is therefore preferable, and in the twentieth century several such arguments have been proposed. I will present the simplest one.

In the following ontological argument there is only one premise.

Contemporary modal ontological argument

(1) It is possible that there is a being whose non-existence is impossible.

(2) Therefore, there is a being whose non-existence is impossible.

This argument is valid in standard systems of modal logic. The idea is that a being whose non-existence is impossible is either necessary or impossible. If such a being is possible, its existence is necessary. If its existence is necessary, then it actually exists. To put the argument another way, there are four alternatives to be considered:

(a) God exists necessarily.

(b) God exists contingently.

(c) God does not exist and his non-existence is contingent.

(d) God does not exist and his non-existence is necessary (his existence is impossible).

What the Ontological Argument succeeds in doing is to show that options (b) and (c) are ruled out. So either (a) or (d) is true. If the possibility of God's existence is granted, option (a) follows. The issue, however, is whether God's existence is really possible. It might seem obvious that God's existence is possible because it is conceivable, but the sense of possible in the above argument cannot be the same as the conceivable. It is unclear, then, whether it is possible that there is a being whose non-existence is impossible.

Ontological arguments are fun for people with a certain kind of mind, and students who enjoy these arguments will find many variations of them in the contemporary literature. This is one of the areas of philosophy of religion in which advances track developments in other areas of philosophy, in this case, the logic and metaphysics of modality.

2.5   Conclusion: Connecting the Arguments

In the *Critique of Pure Reason*, Kant argued that the three classical arguments are the only three possible theoretical arguments for God's existence and they all reduce to the Ontological Argument. Here's why. The Teleological Argument is an analogy which only works if the universe is similar to a human artifact. But if the universe is similar to a human artifact, the argument proves only that the universe has a maker that is analogous to a human artificer. But humans don't create anything. We can rearrange matter into a different form, but we don't create the matter itself. Therefore, the Teleological Argument can prove at most that there is an *architect* of the universe, not a creator.

To prove that the architect of the universe is also a creator, we need a proof of the contingency of the universe, that it depends upon a necessary being that created it. But that is the Cosmological Argument. Now the Cosmological Argument is supposed to be based on experience, but it really is not. The only part of it that uses experience is the first premise, which says that contingent things exist. The argument then proceeds *a priori* to a necessarily existent being upon whom the contingent universe depends for its existence. But how do we know that such a being is the *highest being, a perfect being*? We need an argument that necessary existence is a perfection, and that is the Ontological Argument. So, Kant argues, the only real argument for the existence of God is the Ontological Argument, and as we saw above, Kant thinks the Ontological Argument fails.[40] Kant's own argument is one in which the existence of God is a postulate of practical reason, a demand of morality. We will look at Kant's Moral Argument in Chapter 6.

I am not convinced that Kant is right that the Teleological and Cosmological Arguments depend upon the Ontological Argument, but he surely is right that if we suppose that all three arguments lead to the same conclusion – that God exists, then we need linking arguments to show that the designer of the Teleological Argument = the necessary being of the Cosmological Argument = the perfect being of the Ontological Argument. Of course, some readers may not think it is important that we have linking arguments, since they may not think it is important that all three arguments succeed. It may be enough if only one succeeds. But in assessing the arguments for theism, Richard Swinburne argues that even though none is conclusive, together they form a cumulative case for theism. Each argument raises the probability that God exists, and together they can raise the probability substantially.[41] Notice that Swinburne's approach only works if the arguments show the probable existence of the same being, so Swinburne's position needs linking arguments that demonstrate that the above identities probably hold. We will return to such linking arguments in Chapter 4.

Linking arguments are needed for another reason. One objection to the classical arguments is that they do not demonstrate the existence of a being with the properties of the God of any monotheistic religion, so they lack religious usefulness. Of course, an argument can be useful without proving everything you want, but it does mean that there need

---

40   See Kant ([1965] 1781) A630/B658.
41   He develops this argument in Swinburne (1979), which was revised in Swinburne (2004). The argument is also presented in a simplified form for a more popular audience in Swinburne (2002).

to be arguments linking any argument one may accept for theism and the conclusions that religious believers hold central to religious practice. Chapter 4 will include some of these arguments as well.

The arguments we have investigated in this chapter are by far the most famous of the arguments for the existence of God. Philosophers never tire of them even though the great interest in the arguments arises from highly dubious assumptions about their importance. As I mentioned at the beginning of this chapter, there are at least three historical explanations for the importance they have assumed in justifying religious belief. First, there are two legacies of Descartes: the threat of radical skepticism and a foundationalist picture of the structure of rational belief. When applied to religious belief, foundationalism is the view that all the beliefs of theistic religions rest upon the belief in God. If belief in God is not justified, neither is any other religious belief. In a skeptical age, the standards for the justification of theistic belief tend to be very high. Another legacy of modern philosophy is intellectual egalitarianism. Whatever is used to justify a belief in something of the order of importance of theism must be accessible to any normal person. No reference to special insight, wisdom, or experience may be used in justifying theistic belief. The reason for this is not just egalitarianism, but the fact that the arguments for theism in the modern era arose from the perception that they had to convince religious skeptics. If you are going to try to convince a skeptic, clearly you cannot appeal to anything inaccessible to the skeptic.

Finally, there is another assumption that I find important – the idea that beliefs are more basic in the structure of religious practice than are emotions and acts. I am willing to accept that beliefs are more basic than acts, but not that they are more basic than emotions. It would take more than an introductory book to investigate the nature and importance of religious emotion, but I will mention it occasionally in this book to tempt readers to think about whether emotions can be paths to truth, particularly truths that can only be expressed inadequately or in a distorted fashion by ordinary propositions whose cognitive content we can all comprehend.

Further reading

For an outstanding debate between a theist and an atheist, students will want to consult J. J. C. Smart and John J. Haldane, *Atheism and Theism*,

2nd edn (Malden, Mass.: Blackwell Publishing, 2003). There is also a very large literature on each of the classical arguments for the existence of God. For the Teleological Argument, see the collection of essays, *God and Design: The Teleological Argument and Modern Science*, edited by Neil Manson (New York: Routledge, 2003). For the Cosmological Argument, see William L. Rowe, *The Cosmological Argument* (New York: Fordham University Press, 1998), and William Lane Craig, *The Cosmological Argument from Plato to Leibniz* (New York: Barnes and Noble Books, 1980). Graham Oppy, *Ontological Arguments and Belief in God* (New York: Cambridge University Press, 1995) is an excellent book on that style of argument. Stephen T. Davis's book *God, Reason, and Theistic Proofs* (Edinburgh: Edinburgh University Press, 1997) includes a good discussion of the point of the theistic arguments.

Chapter 3

Pragmatic and Fideist Approaches to Religious Belief

3.1   Introduction

In Chapter 2 we considered three different kinds of questioner to whom a theistic argument might be offered: (1) the agnostic inquirer, (2) the atheist attacker, and (3) the believer searching for understanding. The traditional arguments in their best-known forms were mostly developed by philosophers in the third category. For many hundreds of years these arguments had been used to show intellectual theists that belief in God could be supported by reason in a way that illuminated the nature of God and the relationship between God and the created world. But by the seventeenth century Catholic theologians began to use them to answer questioners in the second category (before these people even existed, according to Buckley (2004, pp. 30–1)). Both sides accepted certain assumptions that derive at least indirectly from Descartes: (1) the justification for the practice of religion rests upon the justification of religious beliefs, (2) the justification of religious beliefs rests upon the justification of theism, (3) the justification of theism requires demonstration by argument whose premises are accessible to any normal, intelligent person, including the religious skeptic. This was an era dominated by the awareness of the difficulty of giving a plausible response to the threat of global skepticism, another Cartesian legacy, and it is unsurprising that by the eighteenth century the classical arguments for theism were perceived to be failures and the practice of religion rejected by many intellectuals. This chapter is part of the story of the response to the perceived failure of the classical arguments.

Some theists took the conservative approach of continuing to accept the three assumptions mentioned above, while trying to bolster the classical arguments by producing ingenious and more rigorous forms of such arguments. Others took the position that the problem was in the assumptions themselves. There followed an era in which the rules were questioned, an era from which we have still not emerged. Those questioning the rules were not necessarily motivated by religious concerns. Some philosophers thought the assumptions stultified philosophy in general, not just religious philosophy. Some thought they were just plain false.

Notice that the difficulty in answering the skeptical challenge can be treated as an advantage for theism. If the threat of skepticism is global, and belief in God is no worse off than belief in the existence of trees, of a past, and of other minds, then skepticism about theism is not very threatening. The idea here is that the farther skepticism spreads, the less people feel its bite. Religious skepticism need not be taken too seriously if it is the same kind of skepticism that allegedly threatens basic commonsense beliefs that most of us would never give up. Parity arguments of this kind were developed during the last third of the twentieth century.[1]

The focus of this chapter will be three responses that involve rejecting one or more of the assumptions I've mentioned. One response was to argue that religious practice is an activity whose justification need not derive from the epistemic justification of religious beliefs. The justification of religion may be pragmatic. One of the earliest and most famous defenders of this position was Pascal. Another response was to attack the idea that religious belief is produced or even aided by objective reasoning. This was the position of Kierkegaard. Another was to argue that religious concepts and beliefs get their meaning from within a practice. Someone outside the practice can neither affirm nor deny the claims made within a religious practice. This was the view of Wittgenstein. Wittgenstein was not a theist, so his approach was not intended to be a defense of theism or an inducement to become a theist, but it was an approach that some theists found congenial. The approaches of Pascal and Kierkegaard, in contrast, are probably the first approaches we have encountered in this book clearly intended for the first kind of questioner, the agnostic inquirer.

1 See Plantinga (1967).

3.2   Pascal

3.2.1   Pascalian fideism

One of the most important proponents of the anti-rationalist approach to religion lived and worked before it was widely believed that the rationalist attack on religion had succeeded. Blaise Pascal, a brilliant seventeenth-century mathematician and philosopher, wrestled with one of the most critical issues of his age – how knowledge is possible; but contrary to the dominant view of his time, he concluded that reason is not the only path to knowledge. Pascal's statement, "The heart has its reasons, which reason does not know" (1941 [1670], p. 95) has been repeated many times, not just because the words are so well chosen, but because the passion and insight of his own writing seems to verify his point.[2] If Pascal is right about the reasons of the heart, the assumption that theism is unjustified unless the existence of God can be demonstrated is false.

In the *Pensées* Pascal raises skeptical questions like Descartes, but he argues that what skepticism shows us is not that knowledge is impossible, but that knowledge cannot rest solely upon reason, which is never immune to attack by argument. As a devoted Christian, Pascal explains this problem by the doctrine of the Fall. A long tradition of theological commentary on the Fall explains the weakening of the human will and reason as the result of Original Sin, and Pascal argues that our passional nature was weakened as well. Sometimes disbelief in God is not a problem of feebleness of intellect, but of insensibility to the things of the heart. This marks an interesting departure from the medieval view of emotions, which generally classified them as part of our "lower" nature. Pascal does not deny that passion can lead to falsehood, but he claims that it can also lead to truth.

Pascal was a fideist. Fideism comes from the Latin word for faith, *fides*. So fideism is faith-ism. It can be characterized as the view that faith is higher than reason, does not need the support of reason, and should not seek it. According to moderate fideism, faith is directed

---

2   Some philosophers can be understood just as well by reading a commentator's summary, and some philosophers probably can be understood even better that way, but to appreciate Pascal, one has to read him in his own words, even if in translation.

towards a higher order of reality than reason, but it is not opposed to reason. Pascal was a moderate fideist. He maintained that religious belief needs grounds that are not philosophical, although, as we will see next, his wager is intended to be rational. In contrast, radical fideism claims that faith is not only higher than reason, it is opposed to it. Kierkegaard was a radical fideist Christian. He maintained that Christianity is a paradox and the person with Christian faith looks absurd from a rational viewpoint. The history of radical fideism goes back to the early centuries of the Christian era, in which the second-century theologian Tertullian was notorious for his claim that he believed not in spite of the absurdity of Christianity but because of it.[3]

Above I mentioned that skepticism can be perceived as an ally of theism when it is used to generate parity arguments between religious belief and the commonsense beliefs that the skeptic attacks. Some fideists in the modern period thought of skepticism as an ally in a different way. If the skeptic exposes the impairment of human reason, faith can fill the gap the skeptic has revealed. The doctrine of the Fall explains the source of the impairment, and the doctrine of grace explains what gets us out of it. Of course, the skeptic can reply that in revealing our intellectual incapacities, he has shown us something that is nobody's fault; it is just the human condition. It is no different than having physical incapacities.

There are other gaps attributed to the Fall that are harder to explain, however. There is the gap between our perception of what is morally demanded of us and our ability to live up to it. John Hare (1996) has called this "the moral gap." The Christian doctrines of faith and grace are intended to explain what fills both gaps. These features of faith are important in understanding Pascal because Pascal's wager has often been construed as a bloodless bet, the kind of thing done by somebody who has no idea what faith is all about. That accusation hardly applies to Pascal.

3.2.2 The wager

Pascal's wager is famous, not because it is about faith, but because it is not. The wager does not deny the rule that an argument for theism

---

3 See Tertullian (1870b [205]), ch. V.

should not appeal to anything inaccessible to the skeptic, nor does it deny the assumption that belief is at the heart of religious practice. What it denies is that religious belief must be *epistemically* justified in order to be justified. That is, it denies that a religious belief can be justifiably held only if it can be shown that it is likely to be true, given premises that are also likely to be true. In the wager, Pascal argues that a religious belief can be justifiably held if it can be shown to be beneficial to the believer. Arguments that aim at showing that believing a certain proposition is good for a person are called pragmatic arguments. Pragmatic arguments are benefit-directed rather than truth-directed.

There are two kinds of pragmatic argument. In the first kind it is argued that a belief benefits a person whether or not it is true. These are truth-independent pragmatic arguments. Many psychological studies indicate that the majority of people have excessively positive beliefs about themselves; for example, the vast majority assess their own driving skills as better than average. Clearly not all of these self-assessments can be true. However, some psychologists believe that having such beliefs about oneself can be beneficial even though they are inaccurate because people who assess themselves more accurately are more likely to have lower self-esteem and be depressed.[4] These studies could be used to provide a truth-independent argument justifying the belief that one is a better-than-average driver (or a better-than-average student, better-looking than the average, etc.).

The second kind of pragmatic argument is one in which it is argued that a belief benefits a person provided it is true. These are truth-dependent pragmatic arguments. Most people wouldn't start a business unless they believe they will be successful. They get a benefit if the belief is true and only if it is true, yet there may be little epistemic justification for thinking it is true. Pascal's wager is an argument of that kind. It is a truth-dependent pragmatic argument.

Pascal gives the wager more than once, and it is not exactly the same each time.[5] In one of his arguments he proposes a situation in which reason cannot decide between theism and atheism. Neither can be proven, and the implication is that the prior probability that there is

---

4   See Taylor and Brown (1988; 1994) for discussion of these studies.
5   For his own statement of the argument, see Pascal (1941 [1670]), pp. 79–84.

a God is roughly equal to the prior probability that there is not. The person we are considering is "on the fence," and cannot make up his mind using the standard ways of figuring out whether something is true. In this situation, Pascal says, one should compare the outcomes of the options of believing and not believing. The choice is forced, he says, because not betting on God's existence has the same outcome as betting against God's existence. Analogously, not deciding to start a business has the same outcome as deciding not to start the business. Either way, you don't do anything.

The decision procedure one should use requires some assumptions about the price of belief and non-belief, and the gains promised by God for believing in him. Pascal assumes that if there is a God, the gain for belief is eternal heaven, an infinite gain. Notably he does not assume that the price for non-belief is eternal hell. The mathematics of the model works even if there is no eternal hell for non-believers. The wager also needs a way to assign values to belief and to non-belief if there isn't a God. This also can be done in various ways, but the mathematics of the model allows for wide variations in the assignment of the latter values, provided that they are finite. Believing in God if there isn't one may involve a small loss. It takes time to go to church, money and effort to follow the Beatitudes, and so on. However, there is probably also some finite gain in that the believer has peace of mind and the ability to face suffering, although obviously there is considerable individual variability in these outcomes. The outcome of disbelieving in God if there isn't one is neutral, assuming that if there is no God, neither is there an afterlife. The disbeliever neither gains nor loses if there is no God since presumably he wouldn't find out that he was right. (Notice also that we need a standard of neither negative nor positive value against which we measure the other outcomes.) If the disbeliever is wrong and there is an afterlife, there would probably be some finite loss, since he would find out he was wrong after death. But this is something I am assuming, not Pascal. The reader can adjust the values as he or she sees fit. With the assumptions I have made, the wager looks like this:

Pascal's wager

Bet God exists		Bet God does not exist	
Right	Wrong	Right	Wrong
Infinite gain	finite loss + finite gain	neutral	some finite loss

On this model it is clearly better to bet that there is a God, since you stand to gain infinitely and lose little or nothing if you are wrong. In contrast, if you bet there is no God, the best outcome you can have is neither good nor bad. (And, of course, if there is a hell, you may be in big trouble.) As I've said, I have adjusted the values the way that makes the most sense to me, but Pascal makes it clear that it doesn't matter what the values are as long as the outcome of betting on God when God exists is infinitely greater than any of the other outcomes.

What's more, the wager works even if the prior probability that there is a God is much lower than the prior probability that there is no God. Suppose there is only a 10 percent chance that there is a God. Even then, the wager tells you to bet on it, and in one of his descriptions of the wager, Pascal does not assume that the prior probability that there is a God equals the probability there is no God.

Pascal does not assume that mere belief in God is sufficient for the infinite reward, but he says that once a person bets on God, that will lead her to practice religion (the Catholic religion, in his view), and eventually she will get herself into the kind of faith that is rewarded by God. To get herself in that position, he says, she should go to Mass, pray, and undertake the other practices of religious people.

Pascal's wager is clever because of the infinite gain the believer reportedly gets by betting on theism. But variations of the wager have been proposed that do not rely on that aspect. Lord Byron (1979) wrote, "Indisputably the firm believers in the Gospel have a great advantage over all others – for this simple reason – that if true – they will have their reward hereafter, and if there be no hereafter – they can be but with the infidel in his eternal sleep – having had the assistance of an exalted hope – through life – without subsequent disappointment" (p. 76).[6] Byron's idea seems to be that the believer comes out at least as well as the non-believer whether or not there is a God and whether or not the anticipated reward is infinite.

Pascal's wager has a number of well-known objections, some of them coming from theists and some from non-theists. Let us consider three of them.

1. *The many gods objection*. Pascal assumes the wager is over belief in the Christian God. It is a God who promises eternal life for belief in him.

6   The passage is from a letter to John Sheppard dated December 8, 1821.

But this means that the wager is between the existence of a God of a certain kind and no God. That is not a forced wager because there are other possibilities. To put the point another way, there are many wagers: Christian God or no Christian God, Muslim God or no Muslim God, Hindu God or no Hindu God, etc. And this is a problem because for some of these you could make the same kind of wager, yet you really can only bet on one, assuming that betting on one commits you to betting against the others. But which one should you bet on?

One answer to this objection is that Pascal is thinking of live options, something you could really believe. Presumably he thinks that the God of only one religion would be a possibility for you. Pascal's era was not one in which there were churches, temples, mosques, and synagogues within easy driving distance of the average person making the wager. So it means that Pascal's wager is not intended for everybody. It is for people who: (1) think both Christianity and atheism are intellectually unproven but also unrefuted, so from a rational viewpoint both are live options; (2) have a roughly Christian view of God as a being who rewards his worshipers with heaven; and (3) are in the emotional position of struggle, trying to choose. Presumably that would apply to many people, and many other people would be in the analogous position of betting on the God of a different religion. Clearly, though, the situation is much more complex for a person for whom more than one religion that promises an infinite payoff is a live option.

2. *The wager presupposes a low view of God and religious faith.* A second objection is that God does not want believers who believe on the basis of a wager motivated by self-interest. This is not what religious faith is all about. This objection is often expressed by religious people who find the wager repugnant. The reply to this objection is that Pascal is formulating an appeal to a certain kind of person, one who is perched precariously between belief and unbelief. Given that he thought of the wager as the precursor to real faith, not faith itself, the person who makes the wager would sincerely try to believe in God. She would not remain indefinitely in the state of the gambler who is motivated only by potential gain. There is no guarantee that she will eventually acquire real faith, but she won't unless she tries, just as the entrepreneur has no guarantee of success in business, but he knows for sure that he won't succeed if he doesn't make the attempt. If the theistic bettor succeeds, her original motive will eventually be replaced by the attitude of religious faith. Notice that this means that the box in the diagram

for betting on God if there is one should indicate that there is a certain finite probability of getting an infinite gain, since not every bettor on God will get the payoff. But a finite probability of getting an infinite payoff is still an infinite payoff.

3. *We can't believe by making a choice.* There are many things you can't just decide to believe. Suppose somebody tries to bribe you into believing there will be an earthquake in Antarctica on April 19, 2020. Could you do it? You can't just believe because it is in your interest to do so. No matter how much money you are offered, it is probably impossible to make yourself believe certain things if the evidence does not support it. If the choice is not forced, your reason tells you to withhold judgment. And it is hard to see how you could muster the motive to believe, given that earthquakes in Antarctica probably do not connect to anything you already care about at all.

But there are several disanalogies between the Antarctica example and Pascal's wager. As we have seen, Pascal does not think you can start believing in an instant. Second, Pascal thinks the choice is forced, and it is about something you already care about. If you take the time to cultivate the belief by acting as if you believe, you may eventually end up really believing. Here is an analogy given by James Cargile (1982) defending Pascal's view that you could get yourself to believe in God given (a) the right motivation, (b) no firm belief to begin with, and (c) a bit of time. Suppose a billionaire jazz lover declares that in two years he will toss a coin. If it comes up heads he will give a million dollars to every devoted jazz fan. If it comes up tails he won't do anything. Every Sunday for the next two years a one-hour jazz concert is scheduled. If you attend these concerts religiously, listen to jazz at every other opportunity, and avoid listening to any other kind of music, it is quite likely that you will become a lover of jazz. Of course, it's not likely to work if you hated jazz from the beginning, but if you start out neutral, there is a good chance it will work. In any case, Pascal is addressing someone who is neutral about the existence of God.

But here is another analogy that is more problematic. It highlights both the issue of whether you can make yourself feel something, and whether it is morally reprehensible to do so even if you can. Suppose a wealthy man falls in love with a poor woman and wants to marry her, but she feels nothing for him, neither positive nor negative. If she can get herself to love him, she will get a lot of money. One problem is that she has to try to love the man, and while the chances that she will succeed vary with the case, there is rarely a very high probability that it will. But that is not an unsurmountable problem, since even a low probability of success may be enough to make the effort to love him worthwhile. The real problem is that the motive is suspect. No one objects when a woman tries to love a man in order to have a happy relationship with someone she does not want to hurt, but the situation is problematic when she is motivated by the prospect of a reward external to the relationship itself. Nonetheless, human motives are complex, and we often consider it acceptable, even commendable, when people consider the external rewards of a marriage to some extent. Parents routinely advise their children to pick a mate with a good income, and nobody considers that deplorable. But it would be a foolhardy parent who would advise her child to choose a mate with the best income and *then* try to love the person. Is Pascal's wager analogous to the foolhardy parent? If so, can it be altered to avoid the problematic features of the marriage analogy?

3.3   Kierkegaard

3.3.1   The stages on life's way

Søren Kierkegaard was an early nineteenth-century Danish writer of philosophy, theology, devotional literature, and fiction, often called the father of existentialism. He had a tortured personal life, which he both expressed and attempted to overcome in his writing. As a young man he broke off his engagement to a young woman named Regina Olson, even though he still loved her deeply. This was a decisive event in his life, and his first book, *Fear and Trembling* (1983 [1843]), a profound meditation on Abraham's sacrifice of Isaac, was written to explain to Regina why he could not marry her. As Kierkegaard interprets the story in Genesis, Abraham could only make the decision to sacrifice his son through a "leap of faith," and he thought of his own sacrifice of Regina as a comparable act.

Kierkegaard believed that Christianity is fundamentally a way of existing, and that people have forgotten what it means to be Christian because they have forgotten what it means to exist. Existentialism gets its name from the attempt to understand existence, particularly human existence, and to make existence itself, rather than the abstract ideas that fascinate most philosophers, central to the way philosophy is conducted. Kierkegaard describes human existence as an unfinished process in which the individual must take responsibility for achieving an identity as a self through free choices. He describes such a choice as a leap to highlight his idea that intellectual reflection alone can never motivate. A decision to end the process of reflection is necessary and such a decision must be generated by passion. The passions that shape a person's self constitute an individual's inwardness or subjectivity. The most significant passions such as love and faith do not merely happen; they must be cultivated and chosen.

In *Stages on Life's Way* (1988 [1845]) Kierkegaard describes the process by which the individual becomes a self as ideally moving through three stages. Since human development does not occur automatically, but by choice, the individual can become fixated on one level. So the stages confront each other as rival ways of life. The three stages are the aesthetic, the ethical, and the religious.

The *aesthetic life* is a life lived for the moment. It aims at the satisfaction of desires, and in its highest form the aesthetic person acquires the ability to enjoy life reflectively, through the arts. What the aesthetic person lacks is commitment. Commitment is necessary for the unity of the self because a true self endures through time. One cannot have a self that exists in the moment.

The *ethical life* is a life lived through universal principles, a life lived for the future and with respect for the past. It is the highest kind of life of which human beings are capable by themselves, using reason and natural moral principles. What the ethical person lacks is awareness of the transcendent realm. Persons at this stage do not realize that the true ideals of the ethical cannot be realized in this life and require an order of life beyond the human.

The *religious life* is a life lived in contact with the transcendent realm. It is a life of faith, of commitment to God. Objective reasoning, which is appropriate on the ethical level, is not appropriate on the religious level. Christianity is a paradox, since the idea of the Incarnation, of God becoming man in order to establish a relationship with humans, does not make sense. It takes a leap of faith to move from the ethical level to the religious.

The movement from one stage to the next is accompanied by anxiety. Irony and humor appear when one is at the boundary of a higher stage on life's way. So the person who has discovered his or her "eternal validity" can look back ironically at the relative values that captivate most people who live their lives aesthetically. Such a person is at the border of the ethical life. Similarly, the "existential humorist," who has seen the incongruities that necessarily pervade our ethical projects, is on the border of the religious life. Consider how often moral reasoning clashes with itself. When that happens, you can always say that somebody is making a mistake, and that is often the case, but repeated clashes show that something is distorted in reasoning itself; something important is being overlooked that cannot be fixed by making the reasoning clearer. The person who has discovered that for himself is near to discovering the transcendent realm.

Each stage of life is seen by the ones below as absurd. So the ethical life looks silly to the aesthetic person and the religious life looks absurd to the ethical person. This is why faith looks absurd from the rational point of view. The story of Abraham and Isaac reveals the irresolvable conflict between the ethical life and the religious life. When God commands Abraham to sacrifice his son, Isaac, Kierkegaard writes, Abraham's act of obedience to God requires a "teleological suspension of the ethical." That act cannot be understood in ethical terms since in those terms it is a conflict of moral duties: one to obey God, and the other not to kill. Instead, we must read the story as one in which Abraham makes a choice to "suspend" the ethical in favor of a higher religious duty. Abraham's relationship to God requires a leap of faith, underwritten by his willingness to bet his son's life that he is right.

In *Concluding Unscientific Postscript*, Kierkegaard's longest work, he presents his idea that truth is passion and passion is subjectivity. One important point to make about this is that it is very hard to describe his view, since any description tends to counteract what it is attempting to describe. The problem is not just that truth is indescribable and cannot be defined; the point is stronger than that. Kierkegaard thinks that truth is opposed to objective reasoning and conceptualizing is a way of objectifying what it is about. The act of grasping truth is opposed to the act of conceptualizing, so the very attempt to explain what truth is is self-defeating. Truth has to be communicated indirectly. If truth is passion, since you don't teach passion by explanation or argument, truth cannot be taught by argument. Many of Kierkegaard's works were written under pseudonyms, and commentators have debated whether that means he was not speaking in his own voice. But that is what you would expect him to do if he was trying to convey the truth indirectly. The author must be hidden in order for the work to be a stimulus for the reader to make certain choices, to see things in a new way, not as a set of arguments that are objectively evaluated and which the author portrays as his own.[7]

The main point here is that truth is not a property of a proposition, but an engagement of the self with a higher reality. Kierkegaard will often say truth is subjectivity or inwardness or passion, where inwardness is the set of passions that define the self. Subjectivity is the self, the kind of consciousness that makes you a self. But it is not a consciousness that is defined by an objective object. It is a relationship of self to another self, and the highest kind of engagement of self to self is the relationship of a self to God. Sometimes Kierkegaard will say Christianity is truth. Christianity is a way of existing in passion, a way of existing in a relationship with God through Faith. This is mysterious, but I think it is meant to be. Kierkegaard's words are intended to put the reader into a state that is not one of belief or of grasping *what* he is saying. In that sense it is non-cognitive. But it is not just a feeling state. It has an object that one takes to be in the real world and one commits oneself to the object.

Kierkegaard is a radical fideist. His stages on life's way make the stage of religious faith higher than the ethical stage, and the stages are to some extent opposed to each other since reason operates at the ethical level, not the religious, and the latter is characterized by paradox. Kierkegaard thinks that, if Christianity made sense rationally, faith would not be required and we would lose the ability to move to the stage of contact with the transcendent. The attempt to make Christianity rational reduces it to an ethical system. To do that we would lose what makes it so important. The point of Christianity is passionate concern.

3.3.2   Kierkegaard's arguments that faith and reason are opposed

Philosophers always try to make sense of even those philosophers who maintain that making sense is not the goal. But it *can* be helpful to try to make sense of the idea that it is not a good idea to make sense of

---

7   Kierkegaard's idea of indirect communication makes it very hard to tell if he is serious when he makes such provocative statements as "Truth is passion" or "Christianity is truth."

certain things. That is what some philosophers have done with Kierkegaard's arguments against objective reasoning in religion. Robert M. Adams (1977) has identified three such arguments, which I have summarized here.

The Incommensurability Argument[8]

(1) Christianity is an historically based religion.

(2) Rational evidence for historical events can never be more than approximate.

(3) But religious faith involves an "infinite interest."

(4) There is an incommensurability between the individual's desire for assurance and the historical evidence.

(5) This incommensurability means that faith and reason are incommensurable. There is no common measure that allows them to be joined together.

(6) The gap between evidence and faith can only be bridged by making a decision.

The Postponement Argument[9]

(1) Rational deliberation is in principle open-ended. No matter how much evidence one has, more evidence may appear later.

(2) So the scholarly debate on the historical reliability of scriptures and philosophical arguments for religious belief is ongoing.

(3) If faith has to be based upon such a process it would have to be postponed forever. You would die before it would be complete.

(4) Therefore, there must be a decisive commitment to end the process of deliberation.

(5) This is faith.

The Passion Argument[10]

(1) Passion always involves risk and faith is the highest passion.

(2) So faith by its very nature requires risk. It is the contradiction between infinite passion and objective uncertainty. Christian faith is faith in the Incarnation, a paradox.

---

8   See Kierkegaard (1992 [1846]) pt I, ch. 1, esp. pp. 23–4. Adams (1977) calls this the approximation argument.

9   See Kierkegaard (1992 [1846]) pt I, ch. 1, esp. p. 27.

10   See Kierkegaard (1992 [1846]) pt II, ch. 2, esp. pp. 203–4.

(3) The greater the uncertainty, the greater the passion, and the more intense the appropriation of truth. So there is a greater appropriation of truth in faith because it is opposed to reason.

All three of these arguments for the idea that faith is a kind of passion that goes beyond objective reasoning have parallels with passionate love. Think of the gap between the objective reasons for loving someone and the infinite interest you have in your lover when you fall in love. Reasons for and against making a commitment to that person can go on for ever, like the postponement argument. At some point you just make a decision and make a commitment. The same point applies to the passion argument. There is risk in falling in love, and some people have trouble doing it for just that reason. Faith according to Kierkegaard is like that.

Now in one way his view seems just right. All three of the arguments above seem to apply both to passionate love and to faith. In both cases there is no sufficient objective reason for the passion, and in both cases the passion requires risk. He also seems right when he says that from an objective viewpoint one would have to postpone the decision to make a commitment forever, since the evidence changes all the time and there may be more evidence tomorrow either for or against the commitment. But the situation of passionate love does not involve making a commitment to an absurdity, a paradox. Even though other people often smile at the passion you feel for someone whom they regard as basically like any other person, friends and parents are not going to say your choice is "absurd," a paradox that you recognize yourself. They might say you are making a leap into the unknown, but they will not say that you are crazy. (If they do, you probably should worry and rethink the matter.) In Kierkegaard's case, nobody, as far as I remember from reading his biography, told him that he was nuts to want to marry Regina.

It seems to me, then, that it is one thing to say that there is an infinite gap between the conclusions of objective reasoning and the leap of making certain kinds of commitments (whether or not "passion" is the right word to describe the basis for the commitment). It is another thing to say that the leap is paradoxical or absurd from the point of view of the objective reasoner. Notice that the conclusions of the incommensurability and postponement arguments as paraphrased here say nothing about paradox or absurdity. The conclusion of the passion argument does emphasize the paradox and the opposition to reason of the leap of faith, so that argument is the most extreme of the three. I do not find the third argument convincing, but the other two seem reasonable.

This raises the issue of whether there is a sense in which the radical fideist, Kierkegaard, is nonetheless quite reasonable. It is perhaps a truism that we should not believe anything without good reason. But what is a good reason? Don't Pascal and Kierkegaard give reasons for belief? Pascal's reasons are pragmatic, but they are still reasons, and his point is that it is rational to believe in God for reasons that are different in kind from the reasons provided by a standard truth-directed argument with premises and conclusion. Kierkegaard also gives reasons for making the leap of faith. His reasons have to do with his distinctive idea of what truth is and the importance of appropriating Christianity in order to reach a higher level of existence – the religious level. But that is a reason. It is an existential reason – the religious life is better than the objective, moral life, but it is still a reason. It makes sense of the belief.

So if a reason for a belief is something that makes sense of it and that makes it a good thing to do, then fideists like Pascal and Kierkegaard agree that there are reasons for religious belief. They are not simply being stupid. What's more, Adams (1977) suggests at the end of his paper on Kierkegaard's three arguments that Kierkegaard's views about religious passion suggest that the religious believer would be pragmatically justified in taking the leap of faith for reasons parallel to Pascal's wager. The person with Kierkegaardian passion could desire attaining the truth through Christianity so ardently that he would be willing to sacrifice everything else for the sake of the smallest chance of getting it. Such a person's religious belief would be based on objective reasoning after all.

3.4   Wittgenstein

3.4.1   Background

At the end of the first chapter I mentioned that philosophy has been revolutionized more than once in its history, changing the shape of the philosophical approach to religion. Wittgenstein was clearly a revolutionary, one of the most important philosophers of the twentieth century, and one of the first to focus on the philosophical study of language. Wittgenstein thought that to understand the things philosophers talk about one must clarify the language we use in expressing these things, and often we find that what we are really talking about is something quite different from what we thought. Philosophers do not all agree that Wittgenstein's attempt to subvert traditional philosophy was successful, but many philosophers think that the Wittgensteinian approach is particularly well suited to the domain of religion, whether or not it should be embraced by philosophers in other fields. Wittgenstein actually has very little to say about religion, but what he says is powerful, and perhaps more importantly, what he says about other philosophical topics exhibits a passion that may make him an example of what Kierkegaard has in mind when he speaks of the person who lives in truth.

Around 1916 Wittgenstein went to Cambridge and impressed everyone with his brilliance, including Bertrand Russell and G. E. Moore, who treated him as an equal. He was never an official student, but after he wrote his first important work, *Tractatus Logico-Philosophicus*, in 1922, they decided he had earned a PhD.[11] In the *Tractatus* Wittgenstein proposes his "picture theory" of meaning. Words are combined in a sentence to form a picture of a possible state of affairs. The structure of sentences reflects the structure of the world those sentences are about. If the way things are arranged in the world corresponds to the way the words are combined in the sentence, the sentence is true. If not, it is false. But he stresses that there are many things that cannot be said. Words can picture facts, but once we try explaining *how* words picture facts, we are going beyond what language can do because the way words picture facts is not itself a fact. Philosophy goes beyond the reach of language, and so does religion. So, for example, the words "God exists" do not picture a state of affairs that can or cannot correspond to reality. Language is incapable of expressing some of what is most important. Wittgenstein concludes, "What we cannot speak about we must pass over in silence" (1961 [1922], p. 151).

---

11 Wittgenstein joined the Austrian military and wrote the *Tractatus* during his enlisted time. Later he was taken prisoner by the Italians, but was allowed to send the manuscript of the *Tractatus* to Bertrand Russell from the prison camp. When Wittgenstein returned to Cambridge in 1929, he submitted the work as his doctoral thesis.

Wittgenstein left philosophy for several years, but came back to it in 1929. During the 1930s his philosophy of language was dramatically transformed. In this period he wrote and lectured extensively, but none of this work was published until after his death. The most important work of this later period of his life is the *Philosophical Investigations* (2001 [1953]). In this work Wittgenstein abandoned the idea that a proposition is a picture made up of names arranged in the way the things they stand for are arranged in a fact. In the earlier period he had thought that language always has the same purpose: to describe or picture the facts. In the later period he came to the conclusion that language has many purposes, that we have many "language-games" that set the rules of meaning for the sentences used within the game. The meaning of a word is its use within such a game. The use of language to express religious beliefs is very different from its use to describe facts. He continued to maintain that religious propositions do not express facts, but he dropped the view of the *Tractatus* that they should not be expressed at all because they go beyond the limits of language. Now he maintained that it is not a misuse of language to express those propositions. Words like "sin," "redemption," "grace," and "God" play an important role in a form of life. That role is something like a passionate commitment to a system of pictures.

It is a mistake to think of statements about sin or grace or redemption as *describing* anything, nor do they make predictions. Evidence neither confirms nor disconfirms them, and they are neither true nor false. In short, they are not empirical beliefs. To think of religious beliefs as like empirical beliefs would make them obviously irrational. People who are very careful to weigh the evidence for claims made on the news do not treat the evidence for their religious beliefs in the same way at all. The explanation is that in religion "controversies look quite different from any normal controversies. Reasons look entirely different from normal reasons" (Wittgenstein 1972, p. 56). They are not reasonable in the way empirical beliefs can be reasonable, but they are not unreasonable in that way either. When religious beliefs are treated as empirical beliefs they become superstitions, and Wittgenstein (1972) ridicules one Father O'Hara who thinks that religious beliefs are descriptive facts. O'Hara makes a fundamental error because he mistakes the grammar of religious beliefs for something else.

When someone utters a sentence in religious discourse, he or she can be right, but she is only right within the form of life that defines that discourse. She can also be wrong (Wittgenstein says "make a blunder"), but again, she can only make a blunder in a particular system (p. 59). For someone outside that form of life, what she says is not wrong; the outsider just doesn't say it. Wittgenstein refers to thinking of illness as a punishment: "If someone said: 'Wittgenstein, you don't take illness as punishment, so what do you believe?' – I'd say: 'I don't have any thoughts of punishment'" (p. 55). Similarly, take the belief "I believe that there will be a last judgment." If this does not describe anything and does not make a prediction, how is it being used? Wittgenstein replies, "Here believing obviously plays much more this role: suppose we said that a certain picture might play the role of constantly admonishing me, or I always think of it. Here, an enormous difference would be between those people for whom the picture is constantly in the foreground, and others who just didn't use it at all" (p. 56). The belief seems, then, to express a commitment to a certain attitude about oneself in the world. The last judgment picture is one the believer has passionately embraced, and it guides her behavior. The alternative is not the thought that her belief is false or unreasonable, but not to be committed in that way. A person who says, "Well, it's possibly true," doesn't get it.

Wittgenstein says that empirical evidence is not only unnecessary to make religious belief reasonable, it is not sufficient either. He says that even if propositions about Christ's life were established with as much certainty as facts about Napoleon's life, that would not be enough. "The indubitability wouldn't be enough to make me change my whole life" (p. 57). Compare that remark with Kierkegaard (1992 [1846]): "If all the angels united [to seek historical evidence], they would still be able to produce only an approximation, because in historical knowledge an approximation is the only certainty – but also too little on which to build an eternal happiness" (p. 30).

As we have seen, Wittgenstein defends two principal doctrines about religion: (1) a doctrine about the meaning of religious discourse, and (2) a doctrine about the epistemology of religious beliefs. The first is that the expression of religious beliefs in words is not a prediction or a description of a state of affairs, but a passionate commitment to a system of pictures by which the religious person guides her life. The second is that religious beliefs are immune to falsification and verification. Critics and apologists who mistake religious beliefs for hypotheses and marshal evidence for or against them confuse religious faith with superstition. Religious beliefs are not immune to criticism, but they need to be criticized from within a practice.

Can a religious practice be criticized as a whole? Isn't it possible that an entire practice can be skewed, perhaps rooted in superstition or corrupt values? Wittgenstein says, "It is true that we can compare a picture that is firmly rooted in us to a superstition; but it is equally true that we *always* eventually have to reach some firm ground, either a picture or something else, so that a picture which is at the root of all our thinking is to be respected and not treated as a superstition" (1980 [1977], p. 83). Stephen Mulhall (2001) says it is unclear what Wittgenstein has in mind when he speaks of a picture at the root of our thinking, but it does not follow from the fact that there is such a picture that it ought to be treated with respect:

> from the fact that certain religious pictures guide an individual's life, and lie at the root of all that she says and does, it certainly does not follow that they are worthy of respect. Why, after all, should the depth or pervasive influence of a picture make it incoherent to judge that it embodies a degrading or immature attitude to life? What is needed for me to make such a criticism is, as Wittgenstein says, some firm ground from which to evaluate the religious picture, a competing picture or something else of the kind that is fundamental to my life; but such pictures are precisely designed to provide a base from which to criticize opposing pictures that lie at the root of other people's lives. (p. 107)

In Chapter 9 we will turn to the issue of the diversity of religious practices. My position is that we need self-trust in order to judge that a practice is degrading or immature or vicious, and self-trust operates in a way that commits us to trusting some others more than ourselves and some others less so. We need to trust our emotions of admiration, contempt, and disgust, whether those emotions are directed towards another practice or towards our own. A practice can be evaluated, but the bottom line is always something in ourselves, something we trust more than that which we are evaluating.

Wittgenstein and Kierkegaard have approaches to religious belief that are not only at odds with the traditional defenses of theism, but which also present radically different interpretations of what the believer is doing when he or she is a religious believer. Philosophers almost always speak as if the object of knowledge or belief is a proposition and it makes no difference who the person is who apprehends it. The proposition that *God exists* is like an object lying around waiting for somebody to pick it up, and it can be picked up by more than one person. You either pick it up or you don't. Wittgenstein and Kierkegaard want to say that what it means to believe that God exists and loves us depends upon who the person is who believes it. The object picked up by one person differs from what is picked up by another, so the subject cannot be separated from the object. More radically, Wittgenstein implies that there is no object there at all before somebody picks it up. Kierkegaard does think that there is religious truth, which is the passionate appropriation of a religious object. So for Kierkegaard religious belief is an object plus something else that is more important than the object. For Wittgenstein there is only the something else.

Further reading

Non-traditional approaches to religious belief do not have the long history of the classical arguments, but they have become increasingly popular, and there is a large literature on religious pragmatism, fideism, and non-cognitivism in religion. The following is just a sampling of the books on the approaches discussed in this chapter. For Pascal's wager, see Jeff Jordan, *Gambling on God: Essays on Pascal's Wager* (Lanham, Md: Rowman and Littlefield, 1994) and Nicholas Rescher, *Pascal's Wager: A Study of Practical Reasoning in Philosophical Theology* (Notre Dame, Ind.: University of Notre Dame Press, 1985). There is much more to Pascal than the wager, and students will enjoy reading the *Pensées* (New York: The Modern Library, 1941). Kierkegaard is much more difficult, but some of the secondary literature is accessible. See, in particular, Stephen Evans, *Faith Beyond Reason: A Kierkegaardian Account* (Grand Rapids: W. B. Eerdmans, 1998). For Wittgensteinian philosophy of religion, see Robert L. Arrington and Mark Addis, *Wittgenstein and Philosophy of Religion* (New York: Routledge, 2001), D. Z. Phillips, *Wittgenstein and Religion* (New York: St Martin's Press, 1993), and Brian R. Clack, *An Introduction to Wittgenstein's Philosophy of Religion* (Edinburgh: Edinburgh University Press, 1999).

Chapter 4

Who or What Is God?

4.1   Introduction

The classical theistic arguments conclude that there exists a being of a certain description – the designer of the universe, the First Cause, or the greatest conceivable being. Suppose that one of these arguments is convincing. What follows from that? The different arguments we have considered are supposed to point to the existence of the same being, but, as we saw at the end of Chapter 2, we can reasonably ask whether something could be a designer without being a creator, or be a creator without being a necessary being, or be a necessary being without being perfect. It would help to have linking arguments that connect the conclusions of the various arguments together and reveal the basic attributes of the deity. As we will see, Aquinas painstakingly argued for a logical connection among the divine attributes. The First Cause must be pure being, pure goodness, infinite, incorporeal, immutable, eternal, simple, one, omnipotent, omniscient, and so on. He thought this could be discovered by reason, without personal experience of God, and without the aid of sacred scriptures by which God is revealed to humankind. But even assuming that the divine attributes can be determined by reason from one of the classical arguments, the great Abrahamic religions maintain that God is personal. Can it be determined by reason that the being with the classical attributes is a person or persons? Even if we get past that problem and answer in the affirmative, there is still the problem that we can never know a person by analyzing concepts. The most that can be expected out of an *a priori* approach to the existence and nature of God is that there is a being with the qualities that make it worthy of worship, including personhood, but we could never know the person who is God by reason alone. That is not the way we know persons.

Here is another way of looking at the problem. What is the connection between finding out *that* a certain being exists and finding out *what* the being is like? The way of Aquinas and other medieval philosophers was to begin with the former, which involved arguing for the existence of a being with a single important attribute such as necessary existence or perfection, and then to argue that that attribute entails a string of other important attributes. That is fine if it works, but there is no guarantee that the most significant attributes of such a being will be revealed by this method, and puzzles generated by the attributes will be discussed in section 4.3. The problem is even worse if we are talking about a person, since finding out who a person is is distinct from finding out what the person is like. With persons, then, we ask a further question. Which comes first: (1) finding out *that* the person exists, (2) finding out *what* the person is like, or (3) finding out *who* the person is? Normally, (3) is accomplished through communications, which we call revelations when we are speaking about God. In section 4.4 we will look at the connection between (1) and (3) as applied to God and we will consider the possibility that finding out that God exists need not be prior to finding out who God is. In section 4.2 we will look at the connection between (1) and (2). Most of this chapter presupposes an affirmative answer to the question whether God exists, although section 4.4 will return to the agnostic questioner from a different direction.

4.2   The *Via Negativa*

According to a long and important tradition in Christian religious thought, there is a big gap between (1) and (2). That is, there is a gulf between knowing that God exists and understanding God's nature. It is plain that the Cosmological and Ontological Arguments conclude that a being exists that radically transcends anything in the human realm, so we cannot expect to get a clear understanding of God from such arguments. But neither one of these arguments is the source of the tradition that human beings are woefully in the dark about what God is like, although not necessarily lacking the sense of a personal connection with God. In fact, the idea that God is incomprehensible predates the Christian era. A poignant expression of the elusiveness of the deity without doubt of God's existence can be found in the Book of Proverbs:

> Why, I am the most stupid of men,
>   and have not even human intelligence;
> Neither have I learned wisdom,
>   nor have I the knowledge of the Holy One.
> Who has gone up to heaven and come down again –
>   who has cupped the wind in his hands?
> Who has bound up the waters in a cloak –
>   who has marked out all the ends of the earth?
> What is his name, what is his son's name,
>   if you know it? (Proverbs 30:2–4)

We also see the painfulness of failing to understand God in the Book of Job, since one of the many ways in which Job suffers is in not understanding why God lets him suffer. This lack of understanding is at the root of the problem of evil and other problems discussed in this book. There is a gap between understanding and acceptance that some say is filled by faith.

In *Summa Theologica* I, q. 13, Aquinas addresses the "names" of God, but before doing that, he makes it clear that God cannot be known in his essence. We ascribe attributes to God by mentally removing properties from God. So at the beginning of q. 3, right after he has gone through his famous Five Ways, Aquinas (1981 [1273]) says, "Now, because we cannot know what God is, but rather what He is not, we have no means for considering how God is, but rather how He is not." The idea that we know God by what he is not more than by what he is is called the apophatic tradition, which owes much of its influence in medieval thought to St Gregory of Nyssa (*ca.* 335–*ca.* 395) and Dionysius the Areopagite. The latter is sometimes called the "pseudo-Dionysius" because in the Middle Ages he was thought to be the convert of St Paul who wrote to Timothy. Actually, he was a Syrian monk of the early sixth century. He influenced both Eastern mysticism and Western Christianity, partly because of the mistake about his identity. Aquinas cites him frequently.[1]

---

1 The influence of Dionysius on both the Eastern and Western mystical traditions is interesting. Probably the most fascinating mystical manual I have ever read is the fourteenth-century text *The Cloud of Unknowing* (Anonymous 1983), whose northern English author bases his method of contemplation on the idea that God is transcendent and unseeable, above a "cloud of unknowing," which cannot be penetrated by the intellect, but only by love.

According to Dionysius there are two ways in which we can know God – the way of reason and the way of mystical contemplation. Theology and philosophy use the first method, but mystical contemplation is superior, giving an intuitive knowledge of the ineffable deity. The reason mysticism is superior is that God's essence is hidden, vastly superior to anything we can comprehend. The mystic does not try to comprehend it, but can intuit it. Aquinas himself had a mystical vision near the end of his life after which he said that everything he had written about God was "so much straw" as compared to what he had seen in his vision.[2]

So according to Aquinas, the best a rational approach to the nature of God can do is to focus on what God is not. For example, since no sensible thing resembles God, we remove from our conception of God anything pertaining to the body. We say God has no body, and that is the most revealing way to explain what we mean when we say God is a spirit. We really do not have a conception of a spirit except by negating the conception of a body. The same point applies to attributes such as immutability, timelessness, and simplicity. An immutable being is one that cannot change; a timeless being is one that is not in time; a simple being is one that has no parts or distinguishable differences within its nature. But there are other properties of the deity that humans do have in some degree, and we attribute to God the perfection of such attributes rather than negate them. We do that when we say God is good, powerful, knowing, loving, and so on. Because these qualities are possessed by God in an unimaginably higher way than they are possessed by us, they can only be applied to God through analogy. So when we say that God is perfectly good, we do not mean that God is good in the way humans are good, only more so. The parallel point applies to knowledge and power. The perfection of an attribute is not merely the maximal degree of an attribute we already understand and possess to some degree ourselves. There is a difference of kind, not merely degree, between the way God is good, knowing, and powerful, and the way earthly beings are good, knowing, and powerful. So everything we can say about God is either by negating a property with which we are familiar, or by analogous extension from concepts we apply to human beings.

---

2 Aquinas stopped working on the third part of his *Summa Theologica* after this incident. For a brief summary of what little is known about this see Bourke (1965), pp. 192–4.

To see how this works, let us start with what we know about ourselves and the things around us. In everything in our experience, essence and existence are distinguished. That is to say, *what* a thing is is distinguished from *that* it is. So according to Aquinas, you and I have the essence or form of humanity, but our individual existence is another matter. Humanity would exist even if you and I did not, and our existence adds something to humanity. Neither one of us is identical with humanity. Each of us is a combination of the form humanity and a particular bunch of matter. That has a number of consequences that arise from the Aristotelian metaphysics Aquinas accepted:

– You and I have properties that are not part of humanity itself because of our matter.

– We are less than a perfect instantiation of the form humanity because of our matter.

– Matter is what individuates. It is what distinguishes one human being from another. So you and I are different individuals.

– Matter is the source of potentiality. What we are potentially is given by the form that all human beings share, but you and I are not actually all that is given by our form.

– Since change is movement from potentiality to actuality, we change.

– Since time is the measure of change, we are temporal.

– We have defects.

– We have parts.

Now start with the conclusion of Aquinas' Third Way, according to which a necessary being exists. If a *necessary being* is a being that cannot not exist, then *its essence is to exist*. Unlike you and me, the essence or form of this being is the same as existence. Its existence is not distinct from its essence. So, as Aquinas argues, God is his essence (I, q. 3, art. 3) The parallel would be if you were identical with humanity itself. God's being is identical with his essence (art. 4), so for God you can deny all of the above consequences that apply to you:

– God does not have properties over and above his essence, which is existence.

– God is the perfection of his essence, which is being. God is *pure form*, which means he has no matter. God has *no body*.

– Since God is pure form and matter is what individuates, there is only *one God*.

– Since potentiality comes from matter, God has no potentiality. God is *pure actuality*.

– Since change is movement from potentiality to actuality, God is *unchangeable*, and since time is the measure of change, God is *timeless*.

– God has *no defects*.

– God has no parts. God is *simple*.

The property of simplicity is more radical than it sounds since it means more than that God has no material parts. Aquinas thought it includes having no distinction at all among the divine attributes. All distinctions within the divine nature, such as the distinction between unchangeability and pure form, are distinctions useful for our comprehension, but are not distinctions that correspond to the reality of God's nature.

If God has no body, then God can have no states that require a body. Although there are states such as love which Aquinas says are intellectual appetites requiring no bodily substrate, he followed Aristotle in taking the position that most emotions do require a body, so God does not have any of these emotions. Perfection also requires that God is *impassible*, which means God is unaffected by anything outside of himself.

Aquinas accepted the neo-Platonic idea that being = goodness. Evil is a privation of being, a point to which we will return in Chapter 7. So given that God is pure being, God is also *pure goodness*. God has all perfections. Since knowledge and power are perfections, God is *omniscient* and *omnipotent*.

What about divine freedom? Human freedom of choice has assumed enormous importance in the modern era. The problem that human free will seems to be threatened by divine foreknowledge will be the topic of Chapter 5. We consider that a serious problem because we think free will is valuable, and we closely associate free will with personhood. So the issue of God's freedom is connected with divine personhood. As I mentioned above, we can't expect to learn who God is from the philosophical analysis of the attributes of First Cause or Necessary Being, but there might still be arguments *that* the First Cause is a person, even though analysis cannot reveal who God is. The concept of a designer adds to the concept of a First Cause intentional consciousness, so the Design Argument comes closer to arguing for the existence of a divine person than the Cosmological Argument does. The conclusion of the Ontological Argument can plausibly include personhood if the most perfect being would have to be worthy of worship,[3] and if we also think

3   Brian Leftow (2005) argues that a perfect being would have to be worthy of worship.

that a being is not worthy of worship unless it is personal, as I noted above. Finally, the Cosmological Argument argues that the universe does not exist out of necessity, that its existence is contingent. If its existence is contingent, its existence depends upon some necessary being, which means that the necessary being might have existed and the contingent world might not have. That can be interpreted to mean that the nec-essary being chose to create the world. If so, we have a case that all three arguments point to the existence of a personal being who acts in a non-necessary fashion in creating the world. This suggests at least a measure of freedom in the deity with respect to the creation.

We now have the beginning of a linking argument connecting the conclusions of the three classical arguments for theism. Aquinas' derivation above begins with the conclusion of the Cosmological Argument and arrives at the property identified by the Ontological Argument via the equation of being and goodness. So if the necessary being of the Cosmological Argument is pure being, and if being = goodness, the necessary being is pure goodness, which is the property identified by the Ontological Argument. In my opinion, the conclusion that the nec-essary being is also a designer of the universe requires the subsidiary conclusion that the necessary being is a person. The argument given in the above paragraph makes the personhood of the necessary being of the Cosmological Argument plausible. To get the further conclusion that the designer, the necessary being, and the greatest conceivable being are all the same person requires an argument that there can only be one such being. There are a number of different ways to give such an argument. As we have already seen, Aquinas maintains that multiplicity comes from matter, so if the necessary being is pure form, there can only be one such being. It can also be argued that certain perfections, such as omnipotence, are necessarily instantiated in a single being. I see no reason to conclude from the Design Argument that there is a single designer, so it seems to me that linking arguments have to begin with one of the other two arguments. I will leave it to interested readers to pursue the various avenues by which the conclusions of the three classical arguments can be linked together.

Before concluding this section, let us return to the point that the properties attributed to God through these arguments are not done so literally. We have an idea of what it is for an intelligent being to be a causal agent from our experience of our own agency, and the same thing applies to our experience of being a designer. But there is an enormous difference between the way we produce something and the way it is done by God. According to Aquinas, when we take concepts from our experience, we can only apply them to God in one of two ways: by negation, or by analogy. Attributes like timelessness are in the first category; attributes like goodness and agent causality are in the second category. This means that our knowledge of God in the Thomistic view is not wholly negative. There *is* something right about saying that God is pure goodness, pure being, First Cause, and so on for many other attributes.

Some philosophers and theologians have extended the negative approach to the divine attributes much farther than Aquinas. John Hick's pluralist philosophy is an influential contemporary example. Hick carries the apophatic tradition as far as he can in order to explain the diversity of world religions. According to Hick (1995) the ultimate reality, which he calls the Real, is beyond conceptual categories. Nothing can be truly attributed to the Real except purely logical categories:

> A qualification has to be made to the idea of the Real *an sich* as the ultimate reality that is ineffable in that it transcends our human thought forms. This is that purely formal statements can be made even about the ineffable – such as, for example, that it is ineffable! But this is a logical triviality. We cannot attribute to the Real *a se* any intrinsic attributes, such as being personal or non-personal, good or evil, purposive or non-purposive, substance or process, even one or many, though the limitations of our language compel us to speak of it in the singular rather than the plural. For example, we are not affirming that the Real is impersonal by denying that it is in itself personal. This polarity of concepts simply does not apply to it, and likewise with the other polarities. Our system of human concepts cannot encompass the ultimately Real. It is only as humanly thought and experienced that the Real fits into our human categories. (p. 50)

Hick's view of the Real has attracted attention mostly because of its perceived usefulness in explaining why many different religions seem to produce persons who are equally moral and equally justified in their religious beliefs. We will return to Hick's pluralism in Chapter 9, but for the purposes of this chapter I think it is worth noticing that this theory pushes to the limit an approach that has a very long history, supported by conceptual difficulties in applying properties to a transcendent entity, and underwritten by the experiences of many mystics.

The conclusion that human beings cannot grasp what God is like in his true nature is the price for rejecting the anthropomorphic view of the deity that necessarily imposes limits on divinity.

4.3   Puzzles within the Traditional Attributes

The coherence of the traditional conception of God outlined in the preceding section is threatened by a number of historically important puzzles about the attributes of God. Some of these attributes seem to be inconsistent with others, and some of them seem to be inconsistent with personhood. I am putting personhood in a different category than an attribute for reasons that will hopefully become clear in the next section. Being a person is not like being omniscient, omnipotent, perfectly good, pure form or timeless. Being a person is not having a quality that is *attributed* to a being. A person is in a unique ontological category that makes it such that qualities may be attributed to it, but it is not attributed to something else. We will return to what a person is when we get to the doctrine of the Trinity in the next section, but for the purposes of this section, I think it is sufficient to observe that being a person (or persons) is not a negotiable claim about God in Judaism, Christianity, or Islam. If forced to give up personhood or one of the attributes on the list discussed by Aquinas, there is no doubt that the attribute would go.

I will briefly review a list of puzzles about the attributes. For most of them I will not discuss the various ways out of the problem that have been suggested by medieval or contemporary philosophers since the relevant literature is enormous, but I will propose my own method to resolve some of them.

4.3.1   Puzzles about timelessness

As we saw in Chapter 1, the view that God is timeless can be traced to the pre-Socratic philosopher Parmenides and is carried through much of Greek philosophy. Timelessness is logically connected with unchangeability, and unchangeability is connected with perfection. Both connections are worth attention. The Aristotelian idea that time is a measure of change seems to make the unchangeable identical with the timeless, but although timelessness does seem to entail unchangeability, it is not clear that the converse holds. It might be possible that a temporal being is unchangeable in its intrinsic properties, although the change of things around it would make it change in its relational properties. The idea that perfection entails unchangeability can also be disputed. Arguably, if a being is perfect, any change would make it less than perfect, but perhaps there is more than one way to be perfect, so change need not entail a reduction of perfection. A different reason for thinking that God is timeless is the idea that time itself is contingent, a creation of God. If God created time through the creation of a material universe, then presumably God would have to be outside of time in order to create it. However, timelessness has some interesting problems.

1. Can a timeless God know what time it is? A. N. Prior (1959) argued in his paper "Thank Goodness That's Over" that there is a difference between what you know when you knew yesterday that a dreaded event was coming the next day, and what you know after it is over. If there really is a difference in what you *know*, not just in how you feel about what you know, then a being for whom there is no tomorrow and no yesterday could not know the difference, and therefore, could not know everything.

2. The conception of God as timeless assumes that a being outside of time can create a temporal world and continue to affect it. But that is using causal language for a relation between a timeless being and temporal events. How is that possible? It is usual in modern philosophy to apply causal language only to relations within time. If a cause can be outside of time and its effect in time, the nature of the relationship between the two cannot be the one we usually associate with cause and effect.

3. Even if a timeless being makes sense, some philosophers argue that it would not be a person. We think of persons as beings who are dynamic, change through time, and have interactions with other persons. Each person has a particular perspective on the world that is uniquely theirs, what we loosely call a personality. It seems that a timeless being would not have a personality.

4.3.2   Puzzles about perfect goodness

Perfect goodness is one of the most central of the traditional attributes, and is *the* central attribute used in the Ontological Argument. But perfect goodness can be interpreted in more than one way. To be perfectly good might mean to be unsurpassably good. Alternatively, it might mean purely good, having no evil in it. If perfect goodness is part of God's essence, then not only is God perfectly good, but God *cannot* be less than perfectly good. If it is also true that a perfectly good being never chooses evil, then if perfect goodness is essential to God, God cannot choose evil. This latter property is called *impeccability*. But impeccability raises several issues of consistency with other divine attributes.

1. It looks like an impeccable being is not omnipotent because he cannot do something that even you and I can do: a wrong act.

2. An impeccable being appears to lack morally significant freedom. If God cannot choose between good and evil, then God is free only in the morally trivial sense of being able to choose among goods. This puzzle leads to another:

3. If God cannot choose between a good and an evil, how is God good in the moral sense? Don't we call persons good when they choose good but could have chosen evil instead? This puzzle might indicate that the concept of essential *morally* perfect goodness does not make sense. An essentially perfect being would have no choice, but if his goodness is moral as opposed to the kind of goodness beings do not choose, like beauty, then he would have to have a choice.

4. Perfect goodness when combined with omnipotence seems to lead to the conclusion that there is no evil. Yet obviously evil exists. Notice that this is not a problem with impeccability, nor is the problem limited to *perfect* goodness, since even an extremely good but not quite perfect being would presumably be motivated to prevent at least most of the evils we have in this world.

4.3.3   Puzzles about omnipotence

It is not clear that omnipotence can be defined in a way that is not self-refuting. This is the moral of the well-known Paradox of the Stone. Can God create a stone too heavy for him to lift? If he can, then there is something he cannot do: lift the stone. If he cannot, then again there is something he cannot do: create the stone. Many writers on omnipotence agree that God cannot do the logically impossible, like square the circle, but creating something too heavy for one to lift is not in that category, since it is something that many humans can actually do. It doesn't help to say that an omnipotent being can do anything possible for *that being* to do, since that trivializes omnipotence. What's more, there are lots of possible things God can't do that involve no paradox in the description, such as evil things. As already observed, omnipotence appears to conflict with impeccability. There are other things God can't do. For example, God can't destroy himself.

Aquinas attempted to solve this problem by saying that many alleged "powers" are not actually powers (*Summa Theologica* I, q. 25, art. 3). The power to do evil is not a power, nor is the power to destroy oneself. The ability to make oneself go to a lower level of being is not a power if we think of power as something good. For example, the ability to make yourself forget something you know is not a power. The ability to starve yourself is not a power. The ability to make yourself morally inferior is not a power. The ability to make yourself ugly is not a power.

4.3.4 Puzzles about omniscience

An omniscient being is all-knowing, but what does it mean to be all-knowing? Is it sufficient to know the truth value of all propositions? Perhaps, but what distinguishes one proposition from another? The first puzzle about timelessness mentioned above is the problem that if there are things that can only be known from a certain temporal perspective (e.g., "Tomorrow is the day of the test"), then a timeless being cannot know these things. A related problem is whether a timeless being can know what certain things feel like – the touch of fur, the sound of music, the smell of roses. These sensations seem to require not only temporality, but having a body. In addition, there is the problem that the objects of knowledge may not be neutral to the subjects that have the knowledge. There may be things we know that are person-specific. You know what it is like to be you. Is it even logically possible that anybody else can know what it is like to be you? If not, then nobody can be omniscient.

The final puzzle I will mention is that if there are truths about the contingent future, then omniscience entails knowledge of the contingent future. If divine omniscience is essential, then God's foreknowledge is infallible. What God believes about the future is not only true, it *cannot* be false. But if it cannot be false, then what God believes cannot be other than what he believes it to be. If God believes that you will tell a lie ten months from now, you cannot do otherwise than tell that lie when the time comes. So infallible foreknowledge seems to be incompatible with human free will. Notice that the standard formulation of the problem assumes that God is in time, not that God is timeless. This problem will be the topic for Chapter 5, and I will argue that the timelessness of God does not solve the problem.

I have just presented a bewildering array of puzzles about the divine attributes. Many philosophers have been undaunted, arguing that each one can be answered in a way that preserves all of the traditional attributes as well as the religious conviction that God is personal. Others have been persuaded that the classical conception of God must be altered. Sometimes the argument for altering it is supported by appeal to the biblical portrayal of God, which arguably is not much concerned with maintaining the high metaphysical view of the attributes that so enthralled the Greeks. My own view is that it is not too difficult to preserve most of the traditional view, assuming it is desirable to do so.

To see the way I propose doing that, let us go back to the reason for attributing various attributes to God. Whether we start with the concept of a necessary being or with the concept of a perfect being, the attributes discussed above are only entailed if they are contained within the concept we start with. My own preference is to start with the concept of a perfect being, or that than which nothing greater can be conceived. Various attributes are said to be entailed by the concept of perfect being, including omniscience and omnipotence. But as we saw above, this leads to puzzles such as the problem that omnipotence seems to be incompatible with perfect goodness. How are we to think about this? Take an internally inconsistent concept like a square circle. Call it SC and call perfect goodness PG. SC entails square. SC entails circle. Square is inconsistent with circle. Hence, SC is inconsistent. Analogously, if PG entails impeccability and PG entails omnipotence, and impeccability is inconsistent with omnipotence, then PG is inconsistent. But PG differs from SC. It is obvious that SC entails both square and circle, and everybody knows the definitions of square and circle. In contrast, it is not obvious that PG entails both impeccability and omnipotence, and even if it does, the definitions of impeccability and omnipotence are not straightforward.

Usually discussion focuses on the definition of omnipotence since the vagueness of omnipotence makes it the more likely culprit. Why would we think that PG entails omnipotence? Presumably because we think that omnipotence is a perfection, a good property to have. But now the vagueness of the concept of omnipotence becomes critical, and we see that Aquinas was on the right track in what he says about the power to do evil. In any sense of omnipotence in which an omnipotent being can destroy itself, do evil, or create a stone too heavy for it to lift, omnipotence is not entailed by perfect goodness. However, if omnipotence *is* entailed by perfect goodness, it should not be defined in a way that is independent of goodness. At least, that is what I propose.

Let us see how this proposal permits us to resolve puzzles under 4.3.2 and 4.3.3 above. If an attribute entailed by perfect goodness should not be defined in a way that is independent of goodness, omnipotence is perfectly good power. Omniscience is perfectly good knowledge. Divine freedom is perfectly good freedom, and so on. An omnipotent being therefore does not have the power to do evil. What about perfectly good freedom? Is the freedom to choose evil a good thing or a bad thing? We think it is a good thing in ourselves, but it is not obvious that it is a good thing in the deity.[4] So I think this approach can resolve the first three puzzles under 4.3.2, but notice that it does not help with the problem of evil because it is plain to almost everybody that a being with as much power as it is good to have would have the power to prevent evil. This problem is so important that it will get a chapter of its own, Chapter 7.

The puzzles under 4.3.4 are harder to resolve using this method than the ones in 4.3.2 and 4.3.3, since I don't think we are ambivalent about whether it is a good thing to know the future. Ironically, this is a case in which we are pretty sure it would not be a good thing for us, but most of us think it would certainly be a good thing for the deity. The foreknowledge problem will therefore get its own chapter. What about the first puzzle under 4.3.4, the problem that an omniscient being would be expected to know what it is like to have the experiences that arise from your own subjective take on the world? This problem does not have the extensive literature of the others, and all I will say about it is that it is not obvious that God does not have the ability to see through your eyes and mine. This possibility raises interesting issues about personal identity, but I will not venture into those issues here.

That leaves the puzzles about timelessness under 4.3.1 above, which have a substantial literature. Timelessness is doubly hard to grasp

---

4   I discuss the puzzles about impeccability in Zagzebski (2004), ch. 6. For an excellent book-length discussion of whether God is free, see Rowe (2004).

because not only can it only be grasped by negating the concept of time, but the concept of time itself is extremely difficult. Physicists tell us time is much different from what ordinary people think it is, both in terms of its relation to space, and in terms of its shape. (Whatever that is, it is probably not linear.) A timeless being clearly is transcendent in a very strong sense, so if there is such a being, that raises serious questions about how it can be both transcendent and yet immanent in the created world. Since these issues probably cannot be adequately addressed without venturing into theology, I will not go farther in this book.[5] However, I think that the Christian doctrine of the Incarnation is important in resolving the puzzles about timelessness. When a timeless and immutable deity becomes incarnate, he acquires the properties of a human being, including temporality and changeability.

As I mentioned, there are many contemporary philosophers and theologians who reject some or all of the classical picture of God and offer alternative conceptions of the deity. An alternative that has received a lot of attention in the twentieth century is the way of Process Philosophy, deriving from Alfred North Whitehead in the early part of the century, and developed in the interesting work of Charles Hartshorne in the later part of the century.[6] Some day, perhaps during this century, a new, grand metaphysical picture will be developed by somebody, and when that happens, I think we can confidently predict that it will be used to develop a new conception of God. Maybe there will even be a philosopher as great as Plato or Aristotle, whose metaphysical categories will supplant all that went before. It is worth considering, however, how we should think about that in advance. To what extent should we embrace what seems obvious to us as philosophers for ten years, 100 years, or 3,000 years? We should beware of falling into a trap identified by the contemporary philosopher Hilary Putnam (1997), who argues that "trying to assimilate God to one or another philosophical

---

5   There is a large literature on the question of God's relationship to time, and it is frequently technical. However, for readers interested in pursuing this debate, Ganssle (2001) provides an excellent and fairly accessible introduction.

6   Whitehead (1929) is his key work. Hartshorne published many works. See the entry on Hartshorne in the *Stanford Encyclopedia of Philosophy* (Dombrowski 2005). David Basinger's (1998) entry on Process Theism in the *Routledge Encyclopedia of Philosophy* contains a good bibliography. Basinger recommends Cobb and Griffin's *Process Theology: An Introductory Exposition* (1976) as a very accessible introduction.

construct, whether the construct be Platonic, or Aristotelian, or Kantian, or Whiteheadian, or what have you, is like trying to improve the appearance of gold by covering it with tinsel . . . Metaphysics is, so to speak, too *superficial* to be of help here" (p. 185). The best Christian metaphysicians have always agreed.

4.4 Divine Personhood

At the beginning of this chapter I mentioned that it is not obvious that it should be first settled *that* a being exists before settling on *what* the being is and *who* that being is, if it is a person. Think about the way you get to know a person. Finding out who a person is usually occurs at the same time as finding out that the person exists. Sometimes you learn that a person exists before meeting her personally, but even then, you usually are simultaneously getting to know her indirectly through stories, photographs, or descriptions of her. Suppose you receive a letter from a person you did not know existed. Would you first determine whether the person exists before finding out who the person is through the letter? Possibly you would if there was some reason to think that the existence of the person was particularly problematic, but there is no reason to think that establishing the existence of a person is always logically prior to establishing that the person has communicated with you. But suppose the person appears to be of a radically different kind than anything in your experience. Wouldn't it then be reasonable to ask first whether persons of that kind exist before asking whether you have received a letter from such a person?

Sandra Menssen and Thomas Sullivan (2002) have proposed that the answer is "not necessarily." They refer to the SETI research program (Search for Extra-Terrestrial Intelligence), which involves monitoring enormous numbers of radio signals from outer space. Although natural objects emit these signals, SETI researchers look for signals that almost certainly would have to be sent by intelligent agents. Suppose, for example, that researchers discover a 1126-bit sequence corresponding to the prime numbers from 2 to 101. It would be eminently reasonable, say Menssen and Sullivan, to try to confirm the statement "Some highly intelligent life form in outer space has sent this signal" *in order to* confirm the statement "There is (or was) some highly intelligent life in outer space" (p. 333). Menssen and Sullivan use this example to argue for the falsehood of the following claim about the connection between the rationality of theism and the rationality of belief in revelation:

(P) One cannot obtain a convincing philosophical case for a revelatory claim without first obtaining a highly plausible case for a good God.

They argue that not only is claim (P) false, but the defense for the existence of God might be established in part through a convincing study of the content of communications widely acknowledged to be from God. They recognize objections to the existence of God, but argue that the evidence of revelation ought to be taken into account, and as long as the existence of God is not exceedingly improbable, the probability that there is a God, given background evidence along with the evidence of apparent revelation, can push the probability of God's existence above 0.5. Similarly, the existence of a single author of the *Iliad* was disputed in past centuries on the grounds that a work of such length could never have been composed by a single author in the absence of writing. But now that scholars are in general agreement that the hypothesis of a single author is not exceedingly improbable, it is commonly accepted that the internal evidence of the *Iliad* indicates it was authored by a single person, Homer, whom we get to know indirectly through his works.

Revelations may reveal personhood, but an important question I have avoided addressing until now is what distinguishes a person from a non-person. What does it mean to say that the Scriptures reveal a God who is a person or persons? Do we think Homer was a person only because, if he existed at all, he pretty clearly was human? What if the SETI project is a success and we discover signals that are widely acknowledged to come from intelligent agents. Would we also take them to be persons? I think we would be inclined to say yes, although we would want to find out more about them before taking a definite position. But to recognize the possibility that intelligent agents from other parts of the universe are persons is to recognize that persons need not be human.

The historical background of the Latin word *persona* is fascinating for what it reveals about the origin of the Western concept of a person and how it relates to the issue of the personhood of God. A number of scholars have argued that the word *persona* was developed in the early centuries of the Christian era as a way to explain the theology of the Trinity and the Incarnation.[7] The problem for the early Christian theologians was to explain how God can be three in one and how Jesus Christ can be one but be both God and human. It was decided that the concept of *persona* was the right concept to explain what God is three of and what Christ is one of. God is one *substantia* but three *personae*. (In Greek, God is one *ousia* and three *hypostases*.) Jesus Christ is one *persona*. Tertullian was apparently the first to use the term *persona* for each of the Father, Son, and Holy Spirit, and he coined the term *Trinitas* for the three-person Godhead. So personhood originally applied to the persons of the Trinity, and subsequently was used to apply to other beings, most especially, to human beings. The idea of a person as we use it today did not precede these debates.

If we use the doctrines of the Trinity and the Incarnation as the key to answering the question "What is a person?" we see that a person must be distinct from an instance of a nature. God is three persons in one nature, and Jesus Christ is one person with two natures. The doctrine of the Trinity is not the doctrine that there is a generic nature, divinity, which is divided among three persons in the way that there is a generic nature, humanity, which is divided among all the human beings in the world; that would be tri-theism, and there would be nothing mysterious about it. Rather, the claim is that God is one being, one instance of the divine nature, albeit in three persons. This only makes sense if a person is not the same thing as an instance of a nature. If this distinction is applied to human persons, it means that a human person is not the same thing as an instance of human nature.

Is that what we think about persons today? I think the answer is undoubtedly yes. In the first place, we do not identify a person with an instance of *human* nature since we do recognize the possibility that there are extra-terrestrial intelligent beings who would be persons. Some people think their pets are persons. Some think there are angels or other spiritual beings that are persons. My point is not that all these people are right in what they think, but that what they think is not incoherent. We do understand what somebody means when they say their dog is a person, and to understand that, we must distinguish the concept of a person from the concept of a human being. In the same

---

7   See Rudman (1997), who cites Rheinfelder (1928), p. 356, note 11. Geach (1977) makes the same point in ch. 1, "Faith," pp. 41–2.

way, we understand what people mean when they say that some human beings are not persons. For example, some people say that the human fetus is a human being, but deny that it is a person. Some say that a human being in a persistent vegetative state is not a person. Again, I want to stress that I am not endorsing their claims, but pointing out that what they say makes sense, and hence, can be debated. But it wouldn't make sense if we did not conceptually distinguish a person from a human being. The interesting and, as far as I know, generally unacknowledged origin of the distinction between person and human being is the Christian doctrines of the Trinity and the Incarnation, both of which require that person be a unique ontological category distinct from an instance of a nature.

We still have not arrived at what a person is, only what a person is not. What do people have in mind when they say their dog is a person but a human embryo is not? We have already alluded to a feature they may have in mind when we discussed the SETI program above, namely, intelligence. But it is unlikely that intelligence is either necessary or sufficient for personhood, and it does not distinguish a person from an instance of intelligent nature. Recall Aristotle's Unmoved Mover, a being that is thought thinking upon itself. Is the UM a person? That is debatable, since the UM does not act to bring about ends, has no relationship with any being outside itself, has no emotions, and is not a moral agent. Of course, we do not know in advance that all of these properties are necessary to personhood, but intuitively we shrink from calling a being a person if it has none of those qualities, and never did and never will.

Alain of Lille, a little-known twelfth-century philosopher, defined a person as "an individual distinct by reason of dignity."[8] This makes personhood a moral category, a move that became important in the eighteenth century in the moral philosophy of Immanuel Kant, and one which continues to dominate moral thinking among philosophers. But if a person is a being with a special moral status, that must be grounded in some metaphysical feature of a person he or she shares with other persons with a different nature, and which explains why some philosophers think there can be beings with a like nature but which are not persons. That metaphysical feature is something that we

8   Quoted by Aquinas (1981 [1273]) in *Summa Theologica* I, q. 29, art. 3.

associate with intelligence, emotions, relationships with other persons, and morality, but that still does not tell us what it is.

Let us look more closely at the doctrine of the Trinity. A person is distinct from an instance of a nature, and a nature is a set of qualitative properties. Can a person be anything more than an instance of a set of qualitative properties? One way to answer this question is to imagine having a complete description of all the qualities of some person and to ask whether there is anything left over. Think of someone you know extremely well, someone you love. Imagine that there is a complete description of his or her qualities – all her properties except for a property like *being her*. Is he or she anything other than all those properties put together? One reason you might say yes is that qualitative properties are always in principle duplicable. Each one can be shared by someone else. So if a person is just an instance of a huge set of qualitative properties, it is possible in principle that somebody else could have all the same properties. But that person would not be her. Of course, the probability of that happening is exceedingly low, but it is possible in principle. If so, that might indicate that a person is more than the instantiation of a list of qualities, even an extremely long list of all the qualities the person has. It would follow that there is something non-qualitative about each person that makes him or her different from every other person. A person, I suggest, is what is left over when their qualitative features are exhaustively described.

This idea exists in a rudimentary form in our culture in the idea that each person is unique. "Unique" is not the right word because it suggests that each person is one of a kind, whereas I am proposing that a person is not something that is "of a kind," not even a kind that has a single member, but is something to which the idea of a kind does not apply. The philosophical tradition that comes the closest to identifying the idea I am working towards is existentialism, and the work of Karol Wojtyła before he became Pope John Paul II.[9] The idea that a person is non-qualitatively unique would explain why we think that a person has a special dignity, and why we think that when a person dies, something of irretrievable value has been lost to the world.

Let us go back to the relationship between finding out *that* God exists and finding out *who* God is. If a person is non-qualitatively unique in

9   See Wojtyła (1979) and (1993). I have developed these ideas about personhood in more detail in Zagzebski (2001).

the way I have described, then we could never hope to get to know a person as a person, rather than as a being with certain qualities, except by acquaintance. Even then, it is very hard to say whether we can ever penetrate the non-qualitative uniqueness of another person. The problem is obviously even more difficult when the person is divine rather than human. Perhaps there are mystics who are able to make that kind of penetration, but I assume that their experience is out of the range of philosophical investigation because of its rarity and ineffability. Still, there are other forms of acquaintance that are accessible to philosophical examination. In William Alston's book *Perceiving God* (1991) he describes common experiences of God on the model of sense perception of a physical world. The Abrahamic faith traditions teach that the primary way in which the personhood of God is revealed to humankind is through revelation. The divine personality is veiled, since we discover it through the personality of the human author and that of the translators, but it is possible that the reflective reader can justifiably discover that there is a divine person behind the Scriptures, even if the unique personality of the deity is largely hidden.

The hiddenness of God is sometimes considered necessary for the plan of salvation. In *Philosophical Fragments* (1985 [1844]) Kierkegaard tells a parable of a prince who hides his royal identity in order to woo a humble maiden. Kierkegaard suggests that God is like the prince who enters history without revealing himself in his full splendor, which would overwhelm us and prevent us from responding with love rather than fear or desire for a reward. God must appear in a disguised form, just as the prince does in wooing the maiden.

In the middle of the twentieth century, there was a famous symposium at Oxford on the theme of religious belief and falsification.[10] Antony Flew (whose recent change of mind was mentioned in Chapter 2) led off with a parable that challenged theists to state the conditions under which they would give up their belief, using a principle of logical positivism that unless one can do so, one does not have a belief with any cognitive content. One of the respondents was Basil Mitchell, who presented his own parable of the situation of the Christian. The parable brings out many more complexities than the one by Kierkegaard, including concern about the apparent lack of response from God to our

10   The contents of this symposium, including the parable discussed below, were printed in Flew and MacIntyre (1964).

personal petitions and the evil in the world, and it shows that even though one can come to believe in God by starting with a personal revelation or revelation from Scripture, one does not *really* know who God is. In this parable, a country at war has been occupied by an enemy country. One night a member of the resistance meets a stranger who deeply impresses him. They spend the whole night in deep conversation. The stranger tells the partisan that he himself is on the side of the resistance, and in fact, is in command of it, and urges the partisan to have faith in him no matter what happens. The partisan is utterly convinced that the stranger has told him the truth, and he places complete trust in the stranger. They never meet again in conditions that permit them to talk privately, but sometimes the partisan sees the stranger helping members of the resistance, and he is grateful. At other times the stranger is seen in the uniform of the police handing over the patriots to the occupying power. Even then the partisan continues to trust him and believes the stranger is on their side. Sometimes he asks the stranger for help and receives it, but sometimes the stranger seems to ignore him. Through it all, the partisan continues to trust.

We can imagine many variations of this parable that bring it closer to the experiences of different religious believers. Perhaps some people never actually meet the stranger, but get a detailed report of the meeting. Others are lucky enough to meet the stranger more often. Some get cryptic personal messages. Maybe the stranger's writings are found in the language of a distant people. In all these stories it would be both natural and reasonable to use communications from the stranger to get to know him without first establishing his existence. Unlike the classical arguments of Chapter 2 and Pascal's pragmatic argument of Chapter 3, these stories reveal ways actual people can come to have faith in a person.

At the beginning of Section 4.4 we looked at Menssen and Sullivan's argument against proposition (P): One cannot obtain a convincing philosophical case for a revelatory claim without first obtaining a highly plausible case for a good God. Menssen and Sullivan maintain that the agnostic inquirer can come to believe that a revelation comes from God without first establishing that there is a God. This may seem surprising, but maybe it should be less surprising than that people come to believe there is a God on the basis of one of the classical arguments. There are remarkably few people who have been convinced by one of those arguments. On the other hand, Menssen and Sullivan's article is partly autobiographical. They were both agnostics who converted to Christianity.

Further reading

Books on the nature of God by philosophers tend to focus on generic Western theism rather than the God of a particular religious faith. An excellent exception is Richard Swinburne's book *The Christian God* (New York: Oxford University Press, 1994). Recommended books on the divine attributes include *The Divine Attributes* by Joshua Hoffman and Gary Rosenkrantz (Oxford: Blackwell, 2002), Swinburne's *The Coherence of Theism* (New York: Oxford University Press, 1993), Gerard J. Hughes, *The Nature of God* (New York: Routledge, 1995), Edward R. Wierenga, *The Nature of God: An Inquiry into Divine Attributes* (Ithaca: Cornell University Press, 1989), and Stephen T. Davis, *Logic and the Nature of God* (Grand Rapids: W. B. Eerdmans, 1983). There are numerous books on particular attributes. William L. Rowe's *Can God Be Free?* (New York: Oxford University Press, 2004) is highly recommended.

Chapter 5

Fate, Freedom, and Foreknowledge

5.1   Introduction

The idea of fate has gripped the human imagination since earliest recorded time in virtually all parts of the world, and most languages have a word for fate. In Chinese the word for fate is *ming*, in Sanskrit *daiva*, in Greek *moira*, in Latin *fortuna*. There are differences in what different peoples meant by fate and the extent to which they thought human beings are its victims, but the basic idea is that a fated event is necessitated; it cannot *not* happen. A fascination with fate is no doubt part of the human sense of vulnerability to forces beyond our control. Fate is not always bad, however, and when it is good it is usually called "destiny."

What necessitates a fated event? Some peoples equated fate with the will of a god and some did not. The Greeks thought of fate as something to which even the gods must submit. The gods could know the future, but did not create it. In the *Iliad* (900 BC) Homer portrays Zeus as saying that it was fated that his favorite, Sarpedon, would die in battle, and even he couldn't stop it. The most the gods could do was to delay the inevitable.

In the Vedic period of ancient India (around 800 BC), it was thought that the gods control the forces that determine what happen to human beings, but later the idea arose that the cycle of birth and rebirth is due to karma, the effect of one's own actions in this life and in previous lives, so the idea that humans are hostage to fate evolved into the view that humans make their own fate by their actions in this life and in past lives.

Thomas Cahill (1998) argues in his popular book *The Gifts of the Jews* that the unique contribution of the Jews to Western civilization was the rejection of the prevailing idea among ancient peoples that time is cyclical and fatalistic. He argues that the Jews viewed time as a linear narrative that would come to a triumphant conclusion in the future. There is destiny in this vision, but not unavoidable fate. Cahill's thesis may be exaggerated, since apart from the Stoics, even the Greeks, who were hyper-anxious about fate, did not think the details of human life were fated. Fate determined your span in life, your degree of fortune, and sometimes a life-altering event such as the fate of Oedipus, but there is no evidence that the Greeks thought of human life as pre-determined in every particular. Nonetheless, Cahill is correct to note that there is a difference between the way the will of the gods is carried out in human affairs according to the Greeks, and the way the divine will is treated in the Jewish Scriptures. The will of Yahweh is quite different from the will of Zeus. It is not identified with fate, nor does Yahweh have to submit to fate himself. The will of Yahweh is very clearly the will of a person who has a relationship with the Jewish people. And because of God's covenant with the Jews, it is a will that responds to what the Jews do and how they respond to him.

Compare the destiny of Abraham with the destiny of Aeneas as depicted in Virgil. Both were called by God or a god to found a new nation. In the *Aeneid* Virgil tells us that Aeneas was destined to leave Troy and found Rome. It is clear that he could do it his own way, but it is a destiny. He does not discuss it with a god or decide whether it is his destiny or anything like that. Destiny is destiny. In contrast, God calls Abraham to leave his homeland and found a new nation. He has a choice, and more importantly, he is informed by God himself of his wishes. Abraham does not learn that his destiny preceded him. So even though Abraham believed he was destined to found a new nation because of God's promise to him, his destiny was not independent of his choice.

Fatalism became important in Western philosophy with Stoicism (300 BC–AD 300). The Stoics identified happiness with willing conformity to a pre-ordained plan, and they approved of divination as a method to determine one's fate. One of the earliest Stoics, Chrysippus (*ca.* 280–*ca.* 206 BC), proposed the thesis of universal determinism. Time unravels like the unwinding of a rope (see Sedley (1998)), with each event following from previous events by the laws of causality. Contemporary determinists have the same position, although ever since Hume there has been debate about whether determinism is a form of fatalism.

Fate can be applied to particular events or to one's whole life. If a fated event is the same thing as a necessitated event, what is fated can be a non-human event, such as a storm at sea, or it can be a human act. Few people worry about the former; it is only the latter that causes distress. The source of the necessitation also varies in different forms of fatalism. Some people still impute fate to the will of God, but the types of fatalism that get the most attention today trace the source of fate either to the structure of time, the infallible knowledge of the future, or the impersonal laws of nature. What is problematic about fate is not that what is fated is bad, but that fate seems to take away our control over our lives.

There are at least two ways in which we can think of a fated or necessitated event. First, we might think of a fated event as an event that would happen no matter what anybody does beforehand. Let us call this Fate 1. This way of thinking appears in the movie *Lawrence of Arabia*, which chronicles the adventures of T. E. Lawrence, an extremely gifted leader who was obsessed with helping the Bedouin tribes of Arabia obtain their freedom during World War I. In the movie Lawrence risks his life to go back and save a man who had fallen off his camel while crossing the vast Nefud desert on their way to attack Acaba. The Bedouins plead with Lawrence not to do it, claiming that obviously "it was written" that the man's time was up. Lawrence succeeds in saving him, but later the man kills a member of a rival tribe, starting a melee, and, as the only neutral member of the party, Lawrence executes the man himself. Upon discovering that the man was the same one Lawrence had previously saved from death, a by-stander remarks, "So it *was* written."

This way of thinking may seem naive, but it probably can be found among people in almost any country. Michael Dummett (1964) reports that in London during the Blitz of World War II, some Londoners refused to take shelter during the bombing, arguing as follows:

(i) Either I will die in the bombing or I will not.
(ii) If I will die, it must happen that I will die, so there is nothing I can do to prevent it. There is no use in going to a bomb shelter.

(iii) On the other hand, if I will not die, it must happen that I will not die. Again, going to a bomb shelter has nothing to do with it.

Their idea was that either "your number is up" or it isn't. Hopefully, it is clear that their reasoning was fallacious, but if someone really believes in Fate 1, it is very hard to talk him out of it.

There are two famous stories that might also illustrate Fate 1, although part of the reason they are famous is that they are open to more than one interpretation. In both stories the belief in fate is part of what causes the fated event, and in both of them it is unclear what would have happened if the victim had not believed in fate. The first is the ancient legend of the appointment with Death.[1] In this story, the servant of a merchant goes to the marketplace at Baghdad and sees the figure of Death making what appears to be a threatening gesture towards him. The servant rushes to the merchant and begs him to lend him his horse so that he may ride to Samarra, far away from Baghdad. The merchant agrees and the servant takes off on the road to Samarra. The merchant then goes to the marketplace himself and sees Death. "Why did you threaten my servant?" the merchant asks. "I was not threatening him," replies Death. "I was just expressing surprise at seeing him here because I have an appointment with him tonight in Samarra."

The story of Oedipus has the same feature. The tragedy begins when the parents of Oedipus are told a prophecy that he will kill his father and marry his mother. Their belief in the prophecy helps to cause the prophecy to be fulfilled. They have Oedipus taken up into the hills and left to die, but he is rescued and raised by a shepherd. Later, when Oedipus learns of the prophecy himself, he thinks his parents are the shepherd and his wife, and in an effort to prevent the prophecy from being fulfilled, he flees his home, encounters and kills his real father on the road, and ends up marrying his mother, exactly as had been foretold. The issue for us, however, is what kind of fate, if any, is described in Sophocles' tragedy. If it is Fate 1, it makes no difference whether Oedipus and his parents hear the prophecy. If they are not told of it, it will still be fulfilled, only by a different causal path.

---

1   This is W. Somerset Maugham's version of the legend, which inspired the title of John O'Hara's (1953) *Appointment in Samarra*. O'Hara reprinted Maugham's version at the beginning of the novel.

Perhaps Sophocles should have written another play called *Oedipus in an Alternate Possible World* to let us know whether he believes Oedipus is the victim of Fate 1.

The second kind of fate is less extreme and appears much more often in the history of philosophy. In this sense of fate, a fated event is one that must happen, given the events that precede it, but it is not possible that those events do not occur. Let us call this Fate 2. In a deterministic world, all preceding events themselves are fated in the sense of Fate 2. As applied to the story of Oedipus, if it is Fate 2 that Oedipus kills his father and marries his mother, those events do not occur in alternate worlds in which the events after the prophecy is revealed are very different from the story in the play, but since those alternate events could not occur, Oedipus is still the victim of fate. Similarly, in the story of the appointment with Death, if it is Fate 2 that the servant will die in Samarra, clearly he won't die in Baghdad, but he is the victim of fate as long as it is Fate 2 that he flees to Samarra after seeing Death in the marketplace, and it is Fate 2 that he sees Death in the marketplace, and it is Fate 2 that he goes to the marketplace at that particular time, and so on.

If an event is Fate 1, all causal paths lead to it. A Fate 1 event occurs, no matter what precedes it. On the other hand, if an event is Fate 2, only one (or a small number) of paths lead to it, but no paths that do not lead to it are possible paths. Both Fate 1 and Fate 2 seem to be matters of fate because both seem to take away our power over what happens in the future.

In the rest of this chapter the kind of fatalism that will be under discussion is Fate 2 and it is global. That is, the thesis under discussion is that every event is Fate 2. Causal determinists, who are committed to Fate 2, sometimes claim that Fate 2 is not a form of fatalism. They claim that only Fate 1 is fatalism properly speaking because only Fate 1 is incompatible with free will. Fate 2 is compatible with free choice. Those philosophers who take the position that free will is compatible with determinism are called *compatibilists*. Compatibilists do not accept the view that Fate 2 is really a kind of fate. Those philosophers who take the position that free will is incompatible with determinism are called *incompatibilists*. They say that Fate 2 *is* a kind of fate. The theological problems of predestination and infallible foreknowledge are only problems if the incompatibilists are right that Fate 2 really is a form of fatalism. I assume that Fate 2 is a problem, whether the underlying mechanism is the foreknowledge of God, the impersonal laws of nature, or something else. The same point applies to the Calvinist doctrine of predestination, in which the mechanism that leads to being saved or damned is the will of God. If your eternal destiny is Fate 2, that is worrisome even if it is not fate in the stronger sense of Fate 1.

5.2   Logical and Theological Fatalism

The relationship between God and fate in the Abrahamic religions is interesting because God seems to be both a source of fate and a rescuer from fate. In the Hebrew Scriptures it is because of divine providence that the Israelites are saved when fleeing the Egyptians, and there are numerous places in the Psalms that refer to God sparing the people from what otherwise would be irrevocable forces for destruction. But the doctrines of divine foreknowledge and divine providence also seem to threaten fatalism. If God knows the entire future in a way that cannot be mistaken, it appears that nothing can happen differently than it does. If so, and if human freedom requires the ability to do otherwise, humans are not free. Everything that happens is Fate 2. Likewise, if everything is controlled by the divine will, then everything happens the way God determines it, and again, we apparently lack the power to act differently, so every event is an instance of Fate 2. But whereas there are nuances of the doctrine of divine providence that permit its compatibility with human freedom, the foreknowledge problem is much harder to resolve, and it has received significant attention in the history of philosophy. As with many problems in philosophy of religion, the foreknowledge issue has ramifications for much more than theology. We will not be able to explore all these issues here, but hopefully it will become apparent that the dilemma of foreknowledge and free will has implications for the nature of time, causality, the logic of necessity, and many metaphysical principles that have nothing to do with fatalism.

Arguments for fatalist conclusions are almost never used to *support* fatalism, but to show that fatalism follows from certain plausible assumptions. For this reason these arguments are often called dilemmas because they seem to force a hard choice. Logical fatalism is the problem that fatalism seems to follow from the truth of propositions about the future. Theological fatalism is the problem that fatalism seems to follow from infallible foreknowledge. Causal fatalism is the problem that fatalism seems to follow from causal determinism. In the following subsections I will discuss the parallel problems of logical and theological fatalism. I will also present a well-known argument for causal fatalism that is similar in structure to the other two, but will leave it to interested students to pursue the similarities and differences between the causal dilemma and the other two dilemmas.

5.2.1   Logical fatalism

Logical fatalism is the problem that the present truth of propositions about the future seems to entail the necessity of the future. Aristotle rejects logical fatalism in his famous Sea Battle Argument of *De Interpretatione* 9, an argument that is more notable for its confusion than for its aid in resolving the problem of fatalism. Briefly, the fatalist argues as follows:

(1) Future tensed propositions about human actions were true in the past. For instance, either it was true yesterday that there will be a sea battle tomorrow, or it was true yesterday that there will not be a sea battle tomorrow.

From (1) the fatalist infers:

(2) The future is necessary. Either it is necessary that there will be a sea battle tomorrow or it is necessary that there will not be a sea battle tomorrow.

Everyone agrees that Aristotle rejects (2), but it is by no means clear what he thinks is wrong with the fatalist's argument. Simplified the way I have presented it, there are two basic interpretations. One is that he accepts the validity of the argument from (1) to (2), but rejects (1). Ackrill endorses this interpretation,[2] but there are difficulties with it. Perhaps the most serious one is that it means Aristotle rejects the Law of Excluded Middle for future-tensed singular propositions, and this does not sound like Aristotle. And apart from the Law of Excluded Middle, there is the problem that the argument leads to conflating truth with

2   See his notes on *De Interpretatione* 9 in Aristotle (1963), pp. 132–42.

necessity. Whatever is true is necessarily true; whatever is false is necessarily false. But Aristotle distinguished truth and necessity elsewhere, so this does not sound like Aristotle either.[3]

The second interpretation is that he rejects the inference from (1) to (2), so he does not have to give up (1). The fatalist's argument is invalid. The past truth of propositions about our actions does not imply that our actions are necessitated. Terrence Irwin (1998) supports this interpretation. He says that if on Friday Socrates decides to walk and he acts on that decision on Friday, then it was true on Thursday that Socrates would walk on Friday and also true on Friday that he would act on his decision to walk, but it was not true on Thursday that he would walk whether or not he decided to. The problem with this interpretation is that Aristotle does not say the fatalist's argument is invalid. In fact, he appears to endorse it. But even worse, on the Irwin interpretation, Aristotle is simply saying that Socrates' act of walking is Fate 2, not Fate 1. But presumably the issue *is* Fate 2. It is hard to believe Aristotle would even be tempted by the view that the future is Fate 1. The Irwin interpretation simply pushes the problem back to the event of Socrates' deciding to walk, and we can run the same argument about the necessity of the decision as for the necessity of the walking.

In subsequent philosophy the so-called Master Argument of Diodorus Cronus (late fourth–early third centuries BC) became the *locus classicus* for discussions of logical fatalism. There are a number of versions of this argument, but they all identify the two key components of any plausible argument for logical fatalism: the idea of the necessity of the past, and the principle of the Transfer of Necessity. What I mean by the *necessity of the past* is expressed in the aphorism "There is no use crying over spilled milk." The idea is that the past is fixed and untouchable. It has a kind of necessity because there is nothing anybody can do about it. What's done is done. In contrast, we do not say, "There is no use crying over milk that has not been spilled yet." So this type of necessity is temporally asymmetrical. It applies to the past simply in virtue of being past, but it does not apply to the future. If the future is necessary it is because of features other than its being future, in particular, because portions of the future (or all of it, on the determinist thesis) are effects of past causally sufficient conditions. But

---

3 See, for example, *Prior Analytics* 25a28–25b25.

futurity does not make something necessary, whereas pastness allegedly does.

The second assumption needed for the argument for logical fatalism
is the *Transfer of Necessity Principle*. The most general form of this
principle is as follows: If it is necessary that H, and it is necessary that
if H then A, then it is necessary that A. An alternative version of the
principle can be formulated in terms of lack of human control: If there
is nothing anybody can do about X and there is nothing anybody can
do about the fact that if X then Y, then there is nothing anybody can do
about Y.

Short standard argument for logical fatalism

Consider any human act in the future, for example, a crime of murder. Let's call the proposition that A kills B next Saturday K. It is
commonly thought among philosophers that propositions are always
true if ever true and always false if ever false. Suppose that K is true.
If so, K was true throughout the past as well as throughout the
future. But this assumption, along with the principle of the necessity
of the past and the Transfer of Necessity, seems to lead to fatalism by
the following argument:

(1L) K was true yesterday. (Assumption)

(2L) Nobody now can do anything about the fact that K was true
yesterday. (We can't control the past)

(3L) Nobody can do anything about the fact that if K was true
yesterday, then A will kill B next Saturday. (Definition of "true")

(4L) So nobody now can do anything about the fact that A will
kill B Saturday. (2L, 3L Transfer of Necessity)

(5L) So A will not kill B freely.

Assuming that (3L) is indisputable, the ways out of this argument
seem to come down to the following choices:

The first possibility is that assumption (1L) is false. Contingent propositions about the future have no truth value. This is one of the
interpretations of Aristotle's Sea Battle Argument.

The second possibility is that the principle of the necessity of the past
is either false in general or false in the case of the past truth that a
particular event will occur tomorrow.

The third possibility is that the Transfer of Necessity Principle for the
necessity of the past is false.

All of these moves have parallels in responses to theological fatalism, but the latter dilemma admits of other responses as well. It is useful to consider the two dilemmas together, since the same move or a parallel move might be justified as a response to both dilemmas. On the other hand, it is worth noticing if a parallel response does not work for both. Another reason for comparing the two dilemmas is that historically the theological dilemma has been considered the more threatening of the two. Few philosophers have been convinced that the truth of a proposition about the future entails the necessity of the future, but many have concluded that infallible foreknowledge does entail the necessity of the future. When we look at the two dilemmas together, ask yourself if the theological one is the more serious of the two.

5.2.2   Theological fatalism

The argument for theological fatalism arises from the assumption that there is a God who knows the entire future infallibly, meaning that God knows in a way that cannot be mistaken everything that will happen in the future, including future human choices.

Short standard argument for theological fatalism
(1F) God infallibly believed K yesterday. (Assumption)
(2F) Nobody now can do anything about the fact that God infallibly believed K yesterday. (We can't control the past and we can't control God's nature)
(3F) Nobody can do anything about the fact that if God infallibly believed K yesterday, then A will kill B on Saturday. (The definition of "infallibility")
(4F) So nobody now can do anything about the fact that A will kill B on Saturday. (2F, 3F Transfer of Necessity)
(5F) So A will not kill B freely.

Those who begin by accepting both divine foreknowledge and human freedom need to find a mistake in the above argument. If they conclude that there is no mistake, they must reject either infallible divine foreknowledge or human free will in the sense of free will that is incompatible with Fate 2. There are strong motives against denying (1F). Why worship, trust, or obey a deity who does not infallibly know the future? And even if such a deity would be worthy of trust and worship, to deny divine foreknowledge seems to lead to giving up some of the other attributes discussed in Chapter 4 – absolute perfection, essential omniscience, sovereignty, and immutability. Moreover, divine foreknowledge, whether infallible or not, is mentioned in both the Hebrew Scriptures and the New Testament.[4]

However, some philosophers and theologians have been convinced by the argument above that God has to choose between having the attribute of infallible foreknowledge and permitting human beings to have free will. Perhaps God "gives up" infallible foreknowledge for the sake of creating a certain kind of creature. This is the position of the so-called "Open Theists."[5]

Many philosophers treat the argument for logical fatalism as obviously fallacious, but treat theological fatalism as a serious threat. Why do they do that? In my opinion, one reason is that it is more plausible to deny the second premise of the logical fatalist argument than the second premise of the theological fatalist argument. To attribute the necessity of the past to its being true yesterday that X will occur tomorrow sounds phony. Something's being true yesterday is not something that *happened* yesterday, like an explosion, or the spilling of milk. Normally we would not think to include in a history of yesterday that it was true then that a certain event would happen two days (or years or millennia) later, so the past truth of a proposition about the future may not have the fixity we ascribe to spilled milk. Would anybody invent an aphorism that says, "There is no use crying over the fact that it was true yesterday that you would spill your milk tomorrow?" Probably not. But past beliefs are different. They seem to be happenings as much as anything in the history of yesterday can be. A past belief is more like a past explosion than a past being-such-that-something-would-happen-two-days-hence. In respect to the second premise, then, the theological argument seems to be on firmer ground. Nonetheless, as we will see in the next section, one of the most famous solutions to the theological dilemma denies the second premise of that argument.

---

4   In Genesis 25 God reveals to the pregnant Rebecca the destiny of her two unborn sons, and Paul comments on that passage in Romans 9:17–18.

5   See Hasker (1989), Sanders (1998), Pinnock (2001), and Pinnock et al. (1994).

5.3   The Traditional Solutions to the Problem of Theological Fatalism

There are three traditional solutions to the problem of divine foreknowledge and human freedom, all of which have contemporary supporters.

5.3.1   The Boethian solution

In the sixth century, Boethius proposed a solution that denies the first premise of the argument for theological fatalism: God infallibly believed K yesterday. In the thirteenth century Aquinas adopted the same solution. What Boethius and Aquinas denied is not that God believes infallibly, and not that God believes the content of the proposition K, but that God believed it *yesterday*. Boethius maintained that God is not in time and has no temporal properties, so God does not have beliefs at a time. It is therefore a mistake to say God had beliefs yesterday, or has beliefs today, or will have beliefs tomorrow. It is also a mistake to say God had a belief on a certain date, such as June 1, 2006. As Boethius describes God's cognitive grasp of temporal reality, all temporal events are before the mind of God at once. To say "at once" or "simultaneously" is to use a temporal metaphor, but Boethius is clear that it does not make sense to think of the whole of temporal reality as being before God's mind in a single *temporal* present. It is an atemporal present, at which God has a single complete grasp of all events in the entire span of time (Boethius (1962 [524])).

Aquinas referred to Boethius in defending this solution and used some of the same analogies in explaining how an atemporal being can know all of temporal reality at once. In the circle analogy, Boethius and Aquinas compare the way a timeless God is present to each and every moment of time to the way in which the center of a circle is present to each and every point on its circumference (*Summa Contra Gentiles* I, 66). Another analogy is of an observer on a mountaintop looking down at the travelers along a road. The observer can see all the travelers at once, but the travelers do not see what is in front of them or behind them (at least, not very far in either direction).

Most objections to the timelessness solution to the dilemma of foreknowledge and freedom focus on the concept of timelessness, arguing either that it does not make sense, or that it is incompatible with other properties of God that are religiously more compelling, such as the personhood of God and divine interaction with temporal events (see Chapter 4). Defenders maintain that there is nothing incoherent in the idea of a timeless person, even a person who is able to timelessly act in a way that has effects in time. Clearly, the idea of timelessness is abstruse. It is so far from our experience that it is difficult to know whether it makes sense or not. But I do not have any objection to time-lessness itself. My objection is something else. It seems to me that the timelessness move solves one dilemma only to fall into another. An argument exactly parallel to the standard argument for theological fatalism can be formulated for timeless knowledge. If God is not in time, the key issue would not be the necessity of the past, but the necessity of the timeless realm. So rather than to use the principle: If Φ is about the past, then nobody now can do anything about the fact that Φ, the new dilemma would use the principle: If Φ is about the timeless realm, then nobody now can do anything about the fact that Φ. The first three steps of the argument would be reformulated as follows:

Dilemma of timeless knowledge
(1t) God timelessly believes K and is infallible.
(2t) Nobody now can do anything about the fact that God timelessly believes K and is infallible.
(3t) Nobody can do anything about the fact that if God timelessly believes K and is infallible, then A will kill B on Saturday (what is next Saturday to us).
(4t) So nobody now can do anything about the fact that A will kill B on Saturday (what is next Saturday to us).
(5) So A will not kill B freely.

The distinctive premise of this version of the argument is (2t). The idea is that we have no more reason to think we can do anything about God's timeless believing than about God's past believing. The timeless realm is as much out of our reach as the past. So the point of the principle of the necessity of the timeless realm is that we cannot now do anything about the fact that God timelessly believes what he believes about our future, and of course, we also cannot do anything about God's infallibility. It follows by reasoning parallel to that of the standard dilemma that we cannot do anything about what is in our future.

In spite of the fact that the Boethian solution generates a parallel dilemma, it may still be an advance in solving the foreknowledge problem because of the elusiveness of timelessness. The weakness of our intuitions about anything outside of time is both an advantage and a disadvantage of this solution. Granted, it is difficult to know if time-lessness makes sense, but for the same reason it is difficult to know whether we can trust the intuition of the necessity of the timeless realm. In contrast, the necessity of the past is deeply imbedded in our ordinary intuitions about time. Most people think it is obviously and straightfor-wardly true that we can't do anything about the past. The view that God is timeless may therefore put the theological fatalist on the defen-sive. I will return to the view that God is timeless at the end of the chapter.

The timelessness move can also be used as a way out of the problem of logical fatalism. If propositions are timeless entities, as many philoso-phers believe, and if truth is fundamentally a property of propositions, not utterances or thoughts that occur at a time, then it can be argued that the first premise of the argument for logical fatalism is false. It is not accurate to say that anything was "true yesterday." I will leave it to readers to decide whether there is a plausible dilemma of timeless truth parallel to the dilemma of timeless knowledge above.

5.3.2   The Ockhamist solution

The second solution is due to the thirteenth-century philosopher William of Ockham. This solution rejects premise (2F) of the standard argument for theological fatalism. It was revived in the recent literature by Marilyn Adams (1967), who follows Ockham in arguing that the necessity of the past applies only to the past strictly speaking, or the "hard" past. A "soft" fact about the past is one that is in part about the future. An example of a soft fact about the past would be the fact that it was true yesterday that a certain event would occur a year later. This explains the intuitive phoniness of the second premise of the argument for logical fatalism (2L). According to the Ockhamist solution, that premise is false, and the Ockhamist wants to make the same case for the second premise of the argument for theological fatalism. Adams follows Ockham in arguing that facts about God's existence in the past and God's past beliefs about the future are not strictly past because they are facts that are in part about the future. Why would something like

(2F) be in part about the future? It is because (2F), like (2L), entails that A kills B next Saturday. In other words, both (2L) and (2F) are propositions that entail a proposition about what happens in the future, and hence are propositions that are in part *about* the future.

Adams' argument was unsuccessful, since, among other things, her criterion for being a hard fact had the consequence that no fact is a hard fact,[6] but it led to a series of attempts to bolster it by giving more refined definitions of a "hard fact" and the type of necessity such facts are said to have – what Ockham called "accidental necessity" (necessity *per accidens*). One of the best-known Ockhamist proposals after Adams was made by Alvin Plantinga (1986), who defined the accidentally necessary in terms of lack of counterfactual power. For someone, Jones, to have counterfactual power over God's past beliefs, the following must be true:

CPP It was within Jones' power at T2 to do something such that if he did it, God would not have held the belief he in fact held at T1.

So take some act that Jones has the power to do or not to do, such as mowing his lawn at T2, and suppose that in the actual world Jones does mow his lawn at T2. God, being an infallible foreknower, believed at T1 that Jones would mow his lawn at T2. But according to CPP, Jones has the power to do something – not to mow – and if he were not to mow, *it would have been the case that* God believed at T1 that he would not mow at T2. If this is coherent, and Plantinga argues that it is, God's belief at T1 is not accidentally necessary; it does not have the kind of necessity the past is alleged to have in premise (2F) of the standard argument.

In evaluating this solution to the foreknowledge problem it is important to distinguish counterfactual power over the past from *changing* the past and from *causing* or bringing about the past. Changing the past is incoherent. We say something changes when it is first in one state and at a later time is in a different state. But that makes no sense as applied to the past, since it would amount to there being two pasts – the one before the change and the one after. T1 cannot happen twice, once with God having one belief and again with God having a different belief.[7] What CPP affirms instead is that there is only one actual past,

6   See Fischer (1989), pp. 35–6.
7   I think that some movies, such as *Back to the Future*, are incoherent in this way.

and therefore one moment T1, but there would have been a different event at T1 if Jones had acted differently at T2. In a different possible world Jones acts differently at T2 and God has a correspondingly different belief at T1. So CPP cannot be rejected on the grounds that it amounts to the position that Jones can change the past.

CPP also does not require backwards causation, the assumption that what Jones does at T2 causes God to have the belief he has at T1. There is much debate about the way to analyze the causal relation, but it is generally agreed that the causal relation is stronger than what is affirmed in CPP. Still, it should be admitted that, if the relation between Jones' act and God's belief on CPP is not causal, its nature is mysterious. Much more needs to be done to explain the kind of metaphysical connection that grounds the counterfactual dependency of God's beliefs on our acts.

In short, the following three claims need to be distinguished to make sense of the version of Ockham's solution supported by Plantinga:

(i) The past can be changed. T1 occurs twice. At the first T1 God has one belief; at the second T1 God has a different belief.
(ii) The past can be caused by the future. What happens at T2 is the cause of what happens at T1.
(iii) The past counterfactually depends upon the future. What happens at T1 would not happen were it not for the fact that a certain thing happens at T2.

I assume that (i) makes no sense and that (iii) differs from (ii). I think that whether (iii) makes sense should be treated as inconclusive. I will return to a variation of (iii) at the end of the chapter.

5.3.3   The Molinist solution

The doctrine of Middle Knowledge was widely accepted in the sixteenth century as a way to explain God's knowledge of the future free acts of human creatures. In the contemporary literature the version of Luis de Molina (2004 [1588]) has received the most attention. Unlike the solutions that aim only at showing that there is a false premise in the argument that infallible foreknowledge entails the lack of human freedom, Molinism provides an account of *how* God knows the contingent future, along with a strong doctrine of divine providence.

Middle Knowledge is called "middle" because it is said to stand between God's knowledge of necessary truths and his knowledge of his own creative will. The objects of Middle Knowledge are so-called counter-factuals of freedom:

If person S were in circumstances C, S would freely do X.

Middle Knowledge requires that there are true counterfactuals of this form corresponding to every possible free creature and every possible circumstance in which that creature can act freely. These propositions are intended to be contingent (a claim that has been disputed by some objectors), but they are prior to God's creative will. God uses them in deciding what to create. By combining his Middle Knowledge with what he decides to create, God knows the entire history of the world.

Here is how God knows the future on the doctrine of Middle Knowledge. First, he knows each of an infinite number of creative options. Each option includes not only the particular kind and quantity of matter he could initially create, but also the laws of nature governing that matter, and how any non-material beings are related to that world (such as how souls are connected with bodies). Everything that occurs after the initial creation is either the result of a law of nature, the free choice of a creature, or some combination of the two. By combining his knowledge of the initial creation, his knowledge of the laws of nature, and his knowledge of all relevant counterfactuals of freedom, God knows everything that would occur in the entire future history of any world he might create. He can then use this knowledge in deciding what to create.

The doctrine of Middle Knowledge is clearly very powerful. If it works, it can be used to explain both how God knows future free acts of human beings, and how God goes about choosing what to create. Furthermore, Plantinga has argued that it can be used as a way to explain why it might be impossible for an all-good and all-powerful God to ensure that the world he creates has no evil in it. Suppose that no matter what combination of creatures God creates, the counterfactuals of freedom about those creatures are such that some of them bring about evil. It is *possible* that this is true for each of the infinitely many initial creative options God has. No matter what God creates, the future history of the world that would develop from that initial creation includes evil. We will return to the use of Middle Knowledge as a way to handle the problem of evil in Chapter 7.

There are a number of objections to Middle Knowledge in the contemporary literature, but even assuming that the doctrine is defensible, how does it avoid the conclusion of the argument for theological fatalism? One of the premises of our standard argument must be false if the Molinist is right that infallible foreknowledge is compatible with human freedom, but which one? As far as I can tell, Middle Knowledge does not entail the falsehood of any premise of the argument for theological fatalism. Thomas Flint (1998), a recent defender of Middle Knowledge, rejects some of the premises of the fatalist argument in addition to defending Middle Knowledge, which suggests that the theory is neither necessary nor sufficient to avoid theological fatalism. But if combined with some other solution, it has the potential to explain God's knowledge and creative power.

5.4   Back to the Necessity of the Past

If we look at the arguments for logical and theological fatalism, we see that they have a common feature. Both begin with something allegedly in the past, affirm that the past is beyond our control, and then use a Transfer of Necessity Principle to conclude that the future is beyond our control as well. A parallel argument can be used to show that causal determinism is fatalistic. Determinism is the theory that at any point in time, given the entire previous history of the world and the laws of nature, only one sequence of future events can follow. All other futures have been ruled out. Let H = a statement of the total past history of the world. L = the laws of nature. As before, let K = the proposition that A kills B on Saturday. If K is true, determinism includes the following thesis: Necessarily $[(H \& L) \rightarrow K]$. The argument that determinism leads to fatalism is similar in structure to the arguments we have examined for logical and theological fatalism.

Short Argument that causal determinism entails fatalism
Assume H & L and assume Necessarily $[(H \& L) \rightarrow K]$.

(1C) Nobody now can do anything about H and nobody now (or ever) can do anything about L. (We can't control the past and we can't control the laws of nature)

(2C) Nobody now (or ever) can do anything about the fact that [(H & L) → K]. (We can't control the fact that the determinist thesis is true)

(3C) So nobody now can do anything about the fact that K.[8]

This argument and its many variants have generated a large literature. Interested readers may want to compare the moves used by many determinists to escape the conclusion of the above argument with those used by other philosophers to escape the conclusions of the arguments for logical and theological fatalism. Of course, relevant differences in the arguments might also have the consequence that one is valid and another invalid. But in the rest of this section I want to focus on a feature that all of these arguments share: the idea of the necessity or uncontrollability of the past.

Notice first that premises of the form "Nobody now can do anything about the fact that p" are very unclear. They might mean that p is necessary in some sense. Or they might mean to deny that any human being has causal power over whatever it is that makes p true. Or they might mean something that has nothing to do with either causality or necessity. Let's look at the difference between the necessity of the past and the non-causability of the past. If premise (2F) of the argument for theological fatalism is interpreted as affirming the "necessity" of the past, then the application of a Transfer of Necessity Principle is understandable and straightforward. That is because a Transfer of Necessity Principle is an axiom of all the axiomatized systems of modal logic (the logic of necessity and possibility). But it is doubtful that the ordinary person who says there is nothing we can do about the past means to say that the past is necessary in any sense of necessary. She may just mean to say that causes must precede their effects, and so we have no causal control over the past. But to say a past event is not causable is not the same as to say it is necessary, and to say some future event is causable is not to say it is contingent. The modes of causable and not causable do not correspond to the standard modes of necessary, possible, impossible, and contingent. For one thing, the actual past is not causable, but alternative pasts are not causable either.

8   This is a variation of the consequence argument against determinism given by Peter van Inwagen (1983).

It is too late to cause either the actual or the non-actual past. So if p is a proposition about the past, both p and not-p are no longer causable. This is disanalogous to the logical modalities, since if p is necessary, not p is impossible, and the impossible is the contrary of the necessary. Another disanalogy between necessity and non-causability is that if p is necessary, p is possible, but if p is not causable, there is no category parallel to the possible that applies to p. So the standard modalities of necessary, possible, impossible, and contingent do not correspond to the causable and the non-causable, and the logical relations between and among the standard modalities do not apply to the causable.

These considerations suggest that premise (2F) is a premise denying our power either to cause or to prevent the past. But the lack of causability of the past is not the heart of the problem; it is the unpreventability of the past that is most threatening. So (2F) should be interpreted as:

(2Fa) Nobody now has the power to prevent the fact that God infallibly believed K yesterday.

Similarly, (4F) should be amended as:

(4Fa) So nobody now has the power to prevent the fact that A will kill B on Saturday.

The transfer principle warranting the inference to (4Fa) from (2Fa) would be a transfer of unpreventability. If we let $Up = p$ is now unpreventable, the simplest such principle would be:

$$U\,p, U\,(p \to q) \vdash U\,q$$

Whether the principle can be sustained is still in dispute, but notice that if it can be, and if premise (2F) of the foreknowledge argument is interpreted as (2Fa), the only way to block the inference to fatalism while retaining God's infallible foreknowledge is to deny (2Fa). Some philosophers have been prepared to deny that premise, thereby accepting power over the past.[9]

---

9   See, for example Mavrodes (1984) and Dummett (1964).

There is still the possibility that (2F) should be interpreted neither as (2Fa) nor as an affirmation of the necessity of the past, but in some other way. Let's go back to Plantinga's version of the Ockhamist solution of section 5.3.2. Suppose that (2F) is interpreted as:

(2Fb) Nobody can now do anything which is such that if he were to do it, God would not have believed K yesterday.

(2Fb) denies Plantinga's principle CPP. As we saw above, CPP affirms neither that God's past belief can be changed, nor that a present act causes God's past belief. It does, however, affirm a counterfactual dependency of God's past beliefs on future events, but that dependency need not be causal, and I proposed that its coherence is not yet determined. Suppose that it is coherent and suppose also that Boethius is right that God's beliefs are timeless. In that case, the dependency of God's beliefs on future human acts would almost certainly not be causal, assuming causal relations hold only between temporal events. By combining the Boethian and Ockhamist views, we would then interpret (2F) of our standard argument for theological fatalism as:

(2Fc) Nobody now can do anything which is such that if he were to do it, God would timelessly believe not K.

The rest of the fatalist argument would then be recast as follows:

(3t) Nobody can do anything about the fact that if God timelessly believes not K and is infallible, then A will not kill B on Saturday.
(4Fc) So nobody now can do anything which is such that if he were to do it, A will not kill B on Saturday.

I think we can doubt (2Fc) and that (4Fc) is therefore doubtful as well, but I will leave it to readers to decide.[10]

The problem of infallible foreknowledge and human free will is a tangle of problems about time, causation, transfer principles, and the issue of whether free will requires power over alternate pasts and futures. As we have seen, there are theses besides the thesis of divine

10   I have suggested other ways to combine the Thomistic and Ockhamist responses in Zagzebski (1991a), pp. 85–96.

foreknowledge that lead to similar fatalist dilemmas; in particular, the determinist thesis and the thesis that the past truth of a proposition about the future entails the future truth of that proposition. It is possible that the features these dilemmas share will have the result that there is no way out of any of them, or perhaps a way out of one of them is also a way out of the others. But the situation might be more complicated. A solution to one may depend upon features it does not share with the other dilemmas, in which case they may have to be handled separately.

Further reading

Besides having a very long history, the dilemma of divine foreknowledge and human free will has an enormous contemporary literature. For a survey of the work in the last couple of decades, see my "Recent work on divine foreknowledge and free will" in the *Oxford Handbook on Free Will*, edited by Robert Kane (New York: Oxford University Press, 2002). For the incompatibilist position on infallible foreknowledge and free will, see William Hasker, *God, Time, and Knowledge* (Ithaca: Cornell University Press, 1989). I defend the compatibilist position in Zagzebski, *The Dilemma of Freedom and Foreknowledge* (New York: Oxford University Press, 1991). The Molinist account is ably defended by Thomas Flint in *Divine Providence: The Molinist Account* (Ithaca: Cornell University Press, 1998).

Chapter 6

Religion and Morality

6.1   Does Morality Need Religion?

Almost all religions give a diagnosis of the pitiful state of human life and a way to rectify the problem. Living a morally good life is usually regarded as part, but not all, of the remedy, so most religions teach a code of morality. They also prescribe sanctions for violating it. But if a religion shows us a way out of the human predicament, it almost assuredly informs us of the concomitant possibility of getting even deeper into trouble. But getting into trouble need not be identified with sin. Not all religions have the concept of sin, but they do have concepts that serve the same function. For example, there is the idea of *avidya* (ignorance) in the non-theistic Advaita Vedanta, a branch of Hinduism. *Avidya* is a kind of ignorance that involves not only thinking wrongly, but also desiring, feeling, and choosing wrongly. We will return to the connection between sin and wrongdoing, but it is fair to say that teaching the difference between moral right and wrong is an intrinsic feature of the way each religion attempts to deal with the human condition. From the perspective of a given religion, then, the practice of morality is a component of the practice of that religion. This suggests that religion needs morality. A more difficult question is whether morality needs religion. Is morality autonomous, or does it need religion to support it? There are at least three different respects in which morality may need religion: (1) to provide the goal of the moral life, (2) to provide the motive to be moral, (3) to provide morality with its foundation and justification. We will discuss each of these in the following sections.

Before the Enlightenment the relation between morality and religion was taken for granted, and it is still taken for granted in large portions of the world. But there is strong resistance in the modern West to the idea that morality needs religion for at least two reasons. One is the naturalistic temper of the times. As we have seen in earlier chapters, a legacy of the Enlightenment was the weakening or destruction of belief in God and a supernatural world among Western intellectuals. On the other hand, almost everyone believes that morality is important. Clearly, then, *belief* in a religion is not required for belief in either a code of moral behavior or a moral theory. Of course, that fact does not show that morality does not depend upon religion any more than the fact that belief in tables does not depend upon belief in quarks shows that tables do not depend upon quarks. But, of course, if it is a fact that there is no God or supernatural world, then it cannot be a fact that morality depends upon religion for the same reason that if it turns out quarks do not exist, tables cannot depend upon quarks. So one of the effects of the widespread rejection of theism was the attempt to defend the autonomy of morality, and the history of Western ethics since the Enlightenment can be read as a series of attempts to ground morality in something other than God.[1]

The second reason for resistance to the idea that morality needs religion is political. We live in a world of many religions, so if morality depends upon religion, upon which religion does it depend? Whether or not there is one true religion, the Western world treats religious freedom as an important civil liberty, an idea that has spread well beyond the boundaries of the West. Persons have the right to practice their own religions without interference from other individuals or the State. If morality is intrinsic to and dependent upon particular religions, it follows that individuals have the right to practice their own moralities without interference from the State. But no society can

---

1 A very interesting and compelling alternate account of Enlightenment ethics has been given by J. B. Schneewind, who argues that when conceptions of morality as obedience gave way to conceptions of morality as self-governance during the Enlightenment, the change was made primarily by religious philosophers who took for granted that God is essential to morality. One could make the same point about the rise of modern science, which was not precipitated by atheist scientists, but by religious believers who thought that God had created a natural order accessible to investigation by the scientific method. That suggests that both the autonomy of moral reasoning and the autonomy of scientific reasoning are compatible with a deeper theistic metaphysics. See Schneewind (1998), especially ch. 1, sec. 3. For the point about the rise of modern science see Jaki (2000).

accept that. Morality is a system for getting along with everyone, and that requires a sufficiently common morality to insure that a society can function. Differences in moral beliefs and behavior can be permitted within limits and within carefully circumscribed categories, e.g., some behavior within families and close personal relationships. And it is not necessary that all members of a society agree on the metaphysical basis for morality, nor need all persons in a well-functioning society have the same motives for being moral. But they must agree on a substantial core area of moral behavior, or at the very least, there must be a core morality that is recognized as having authority over all members of the society, including the recalcitrant few who resist it. In a society with no common religious authority, moral authority must come from another source.

In a liberal, pluralistic society religion is a matter of choice; a large area of morality is not. You can opt out of religion, but you cannot opt out of morality. For this reason even devout religious believers in liberal democracies generally support the search for a way to make morality independent of religion. Or to make the point more carefully, they want to say that there is an important respect in which morality is autonomous even if there is another respect in which it is not. Distinguishing the different respects in which morality may depend upon religion is therefore important.

One way to resolve the problem is to take the position of Aquinas that morality has a two-tier grounding – one in God, the other in nature. According to Aquinas' approach to Natural Law, the basic norms of morality sufficient for civil society have a foundation in human nature, and so morality is common to all human beings. The Natural Law generates norms of behavior which are accessible, in principle, by ordinary human reason. The Natural Law, however, is not ultimate. Everything outside of God comes from God, including the Natural Law, which is an expression in the created order of the Eternal Law of God.[2] Natural Law theory makes morality ultimately dependent upon God, while giving it sub-ultimate metaphysical grounding and justification in something all humans have in common. It is not necessary, although often advantageous, to refer to God's revealed word in order to know what morality teaches and why. The moral law therefore depends upon God only at the deepest level of the

2   See Aquinas (1981 [1273]), *Summa Theologica* I–II, q. 91.

metaphysics of morals. The way in which morality needs God in Natural Law theory does not threaten the functioning of societies internally nor in their relations with each other.

In Natural Law theory and in biblical ethics wrongdoing is a violation of a law. If the ultimate lawgiver is God, and God is a being with whom the agent has a relationship through the practice of religion, wrongdoing is something more than merely doing what is morally wrong. It is a sin, an offense against God. This means that the concept of sin is richer than the concept of wrongdoing. Sin makes no sense outside the context of personal and communal relationships, defined in part by narratives, and sometimes involving elaborate theological accounts. In contrast, wrongdoing is a thin concept intended to be the common denominator in a set of concepts used by atheists, Jews, Muslims, Christians, Hindus, Buddhists, Sikhs, and others. All can understand the idea of doing what is wrong even though many of them believe that every act of wrongdoing is more than mere wrongdoing. We should be wary, then, of the idea that when the Christian speaks of "sin" and the non-religious person speaks of "moral wrong," they are talking about the same thing. It is not just a matter of the Christian having distinctive beliefs about the implications and consequences of wrongful acts. I am suggesting that the concept of sin and the concept of moral wrong are different concepts, although they are not disjoint, and the Christian or Jew is able to understand what is meant by moral wrong because of their ability to understand discourse outside their religious community and the extent to which it overlaps their own. If I am right in this conjecture, the idea of moral wrong is thinner than the parallel concepts in religious moralities, but it has the advantage of permitting discourse across religious divisions as well as with people who do not find a home in any religion.

The same point applies to concepts for the goal of morality – concepts of salvation, enlightenment, or Aristotle's *eudaimonia*. These concepts also have something in common even though they are distinct. All apply to the goal of living morally. The idea of an ultimate moral goal, like the idea of moral wrongdoing, is a common denominator among a wide range of religious moralities as well as some, like Aristotle's, that are metaphysically rich but not religious. Sometimes the idea of happiness is taken as the equivalent for the idea of the moral goal. The thinnest concept of happiness is identified by Aristotle at the beginning of the *Nicomachean Ethics* (hereafter *NE*); it is simply the concept of that at which all humans ultimately aim. This concept can be thickened by a description of the content of the goal, and Aristotle's concept of *eudaimonia* is gradually thickened in the course of Book I of the *NE*, and throughout the rest of the work. Religious discourse almost always begins with a thick concept of the goal of human life, often called salvation. Salvation can be interpreted as a thickening of the goal identified by Aristotle on the first page of the *NE*, although in a different direction. So just as sin adds to wrongdoing the idea of offending God, salvation adds to happiness the idea of existing in union with God, or recognizing one's identity with the Brahman, or realizing one's Buddha-nature, and so on.

Clearly, the thinning of religious concepts like sin and salvation into non-religious moral concepts like wrongdoing and happiness is an advantage in a pluralistic society, but one of the consequences of thinning religious moral concepts is that the resulting concepts are so abstract, it is unclear that they are able to motivate an agent in her practical life. The question, "Why should I be moral?" is not obviously a trivial question, whereas "Why should I care about offending God?" is foolish to anyone who understands the context in which such a question would be asked. It seems to me that the relation between morality and motivation is a serious one in modern secular ethics because the thinning process removes the aspects of moral concepts most directly relevant to motivation.[3] This problem is perhaps most evident in the case of the concept of happiness. It is very difficult to be motivated by the mere concept of that at which all humans aim, whereas it is much easier to be motivated by the thicker concepts of salvation, enlightenment, or Aristotelian *eudaimonia*. The thinner the concept, the wider its conceptual applicability, but the price is a reduction of motivational strength.

This leads to the issue of whether there are crucial religious moral concepts that cannot be thinned. Elizabeth Anscombe (1958) argued in a famous paper inaugurating the contemporary re-emergence of virtue ethics that the concept of obligation makes no sense without

---

3   In fact, debate over the issue of whether the "Why be moral?" question is trivial may show that the concept of the moral is thinner for some people than for others. For many people the concepts of being moral, doing the right thing, and avoiding the wrong thing have an affective content lacking in the thinnest versions of these concepts. I propose a theory on the thinning of moral concepts of their motivational content in Zagzebski (2003).

a moral lawgiver, and that the only lawgiver capable of filling the role is God. One way of interpreting Anscombe's point is that the concept of moral obligation cannot be thinned; the idea of a lawgiver cannot be removed from the idea of moral obligation. Perhaps in implicit agreement with this point, some modern moral philosophers have searched for an alternative lawgiver – society or the moral agent herself. These attempts have been unsuccessful, says Anscombe, because neither society nor the agent is the right sort of thing to have the authority to be a lawgiver. To think so is to misunderstand the concept of law.[4] Of course, one can dispute Anscombe's claim that there is such a conceptual connection between obligation and a divine lawgiver, but the fact that the point arises at all suggests that it is not obvious that the thick moral concepts that developed within religious practice can be thinned without threat of incoherence.

One of the greatest challenges of the contemporary world is to find a moral discourse that can reach all the inhabitants of the earth, but one that preferably does no violence to the conceptual frameworks of the particular religions. If the concepts that are central to moral practice within the world's great religions cannot be thinned into a common set of concepts, the task is impossible. Or it may be impossible for some other reason, perhaps because it is impossible to get a common content to morality that is sufficient for the requirements for life in a pluralistic world. But it is a goal that should not be given up until its impossibility has been demonstrated. A given religion may find that some of its moral teachings are not viable for interaction with the practitioners of other religions and it may have to succumb to pressures from the outside, but that is an issue that needs to be addressed within the framework of that religion.

The philosopher of religion has a different task, since philosophy is a practice distinct from the practice of any particular religion or any religion at all. The philosophical question is whether morality can be independent of religion and, if so, what it would look like. There are important arguments that morality needs religion to reach its goal, to provide moral motivation, and to provide morality with its foundation and justification. These arguments will be examined next.

---

4   The concepts of guilt and punishment are related to the concept of law. If the former cannot be thinned, it is unlikely that the latter can either.

6.2   The Goal of Morality

One important set of arguments that morality needs religion or that moral theory needs theology is that there is a goal or point to morality, and that point is inexplicable within a naturalistic, autonomous moral theory. Within this class of arguments are the moral arguments for the existence of God. These arguments require the identification of a particular point to morality, e.g., a system of cosmic justice in which the good are ultimately rewarded and the bad are punished, or the idea that there is an end of history, a goal at which all human life aims, that human life is pointless without such a goal, and the goal is unattainable without a supernatural power. Many of these arguments are in the class of transcendental arguments, or arguments that purport to identify the preconditions for the truth of some assumption that is assumed by all parties. These arguments begin with a premise giving the content or point of morality, and the argument attempts to show that the truth of such a premise requires the truth of important religious propositions such as the existence of God or an afterlife.

The classic statement of an argument of this type was given by Immanuel Kant in his moral argument for the existence of God. Kant accepted the ancient Greek and medieval Christian teaching that all human beings necessarily seek happiness. Where he differed from his predecessors was on the relation between virtue and happiness. The Greeks and medieval philosophers agreed that there is a strong connection between the virtuous life and the happy life, although the Greeks worried about the place of good fortune in happiness, and the Christians maintained that the happiness we seek is not fully attainable in this life. Nonetheless, with some variations, they believed that the ultimate goal or end of the moral life is a unitary good in which happiness and virtue are integrated and virtually inseparable. Kant denied that. Virtue and happiness are neither conceptually nor probabilistically connected, according to Kant. They are two different ends. But since both virtue and happiness are goods, Kant argues, the highest good, or *summum bonum*, would be one in which human beings combine moral virtue with happiness and, in fact, it would be a world in which their happiness is proportional to their virtue.

With the idea of the highest good in place, Kant offers the following simple argument for theism. Morality obligates each of us to seek the good, and so it obligates us to seek the highest good. But morality cannot obligate us to seek the impossible. Hence, the highest good must be attainable. It is not attainable without a cause adequate to the effect, which is to say, unless there is a God with the power to proportion happiness to virtue. God's existence is therefore a necessary condition for the possibility of the highest good, and so it is a necessary condition for our obligation to be moral.[5]

The intuition behind Kant's argument is profound even though his description of the highest good is idiosyncratic. What may seem particularly bothersome about the argument is that Kant creates a problem for value theory himself and then argues that there must be a God to solve the problem. The ancient and medieval philosophers, among others, did not see the tension in the concept of the highest good in such stark terms to begin with, so the need to bring God to the rescue was not as glaring. Nonetheless, some of them did think that the highest good must be reachable and that it is not reachable without the existence of an afterlife. A comparison of Kant's notion of the highest good with that of Aquinas is illuminating. Aquinas accepted the Aristotelian position that all humans desire happiness by nature, that happiness is our natural end. But if we investigate what would truly fulfill the human longing for happiness, we see that it is something unattainable without God and the possibility of the enjoyment of seeing God. Aquinas's view of the ultimate human end is an extension and deepening of the view Aristotle expresses in Book X of *NE* that happiness is contemplation of the highest things.[6] As Aquinas describes it, to seek happiness is to seek the satiation of the will. To be happy is to have nothing left to will.[7] The will is satiated in the possession of reality, which, for human beings, is accomplished through an act of the intellect, an intellectual vision. The human desire for happiness is not satisfied with anything less than a total vision of reality. This vision is contained in the Beatific Vision, a vision of God in whom all things are seen.[8]

Aquinas does not construct his explanation of human happiness in the form of an argument for theism, since it appears in a part of the

---

5   Kant (1956 [1788]) *Critique of Practical Reason* pt I, bk II, ch. 2, sec. 5.
6   Aristotle (1984) *NE*, bk X, ch. 7.
7   Aquinas (1981 [1273]), *Summa Theologica* I–II, q. 5, art. 8.
8   For an interesting and accessible twentieth-century defense of the Thomistic idea that happiness is found in contemplation, see Pieper (1998).

Summa Theologica that presupposes his Five Ways at the beginning of the work. But a transcendental argument for the existence of God is implicit in Aquinas' account of the nature of happiness. The natural end for humans requires union with an eternal being who satisfies our natural craving for happiness. Without such a being the end of human living is unattainable. Either there is a God or human beings aim at the impossible by nature. So while Kant argues that morality puts an impossible demand on us if there is no God, the Thomistic argument understands nature as structured in such a way that it aims at the impossible if there is no God. The former argues that in the absence of God there is something wrong with morality, whereas the latter argues that in the absence of God there is something wrong with nature.

As we saw in our discussion of Aquinas' Fifth Way in Chapter 2, Aquinas agreed with the Aristotelian idea that nature is orderly and teleological in structure. There would be no point to the existence of natural desires unless they are capable of fulfillment,[9] and therefore the conditions for their fulfillment reveal important metaphysical truths. In contrast, modern thinkers are generally wary of drawing any conclusions from human needs and desires. If we come to believe that our natural human desires cannot be satisfied in this life, the typical response is to conclude that we should change the desires, an option that displays a remarkable degree of confidence in the power of therapy. Another alternative is to conclude that life really is absurd. This is the position of an important strand of atheistic existentialist literature which accepts the Thomistic idea that human desires and aims are irremediably thwarted without God, but rejects the premise that human desires cannot be irremediably thwarted. Albert Camus's essay "The myth of Sisyphus" (1991) is a poignant portrayal of this view of human destiny. With an admirable ability to face the consequences of his own thought, Camus gives his essay the following epigram: "Oh my soul do not aspire to immortal heights but exhaust the field of the possible." Camus's kind of atheism makes an interesting contrast with the atheism of the Enlightenment. The latter rejects the soundness of arguments for theism while attempting to keep most of traditional ethics. Camus denies God's existence, but agrees that the moral goal is impossible to reach without God, the major premise

9   Aquinas (1981 [1273]) *Summa Theologica* pt I, q. 75, art. 6, corpus.

of the moral argument for theism. The absurdity of life is his price for accepting that premise.[10]

6.3   Moral Motivation

When people in contemporary American society are asked whether morality needs religion, they usually think first of whether people need the threat of divine punishment as a motive to be moral. Judging by the response of my students, most, but not all, say no, and those who say no often feel insulted by the question. This issue is an old one. For example, the theme of the ancient Greek play *Sisyphos* (attributed to Euripides or Kritias) is that "the gods are the invention of a clever politician in order to bind people to laws which could not otherwise be enforced."[11] Notice that the link between religion and the morals of the polis is thought to be suspicious on the grounds that, if morals need the support of religion, there must be something wrong with both the religion and the morals. In a similar vein, Aristotle writes with disdain for the traditional myths and rituals of Greek society, saying that "the rest" of Greek religion other than the provable Unmoved Movers "was introduced to persuade the multitude and with a view to practical use for the laws and expediency" (*Metaphysics* 1047b1–8). It is interesting that whereas the idea that religion is necessary to motivate people to be moral has been roundly criticized for millennia, nobody objects to the idea that one of the purposes of legal authority is to motivate people to desist from killing, stealing, cheating, and so on. It is hard to object to the fact that there are many people who need a motivation outside of morality to keep them in line, even though the truly moral person does not need such a motive. Morality itself does not need law or religion. It is only immoral people who need them. But the objections above imply that if people need religious beliefs to get them to be moral, the beliefs are probably false.

The idea that religion is an illusion used to prop up civil society appears again in the twentieth century in the work of Sigmund Freud.

---

10   It is interesting that Camus retains many features of traditional morality, including the traditional sense of justice, in his novels *The Plague* and *The Rebel*. He is not a moral nihilist.

11   See Burkert (1985) p. 247.

In *Civilization and Its Discontents* (1962), Freud argues that civilization protects us simultaneously from nature and our own fears at the cost of repressing our instincts through the institution of morality. Religious beliefs form an important part of the myths that civilized society needs to sustain it. Few people would put up with the repression of their sexual and aggressive desires were it not for the fact that they get compensation from the same system that represses them. Civilization is therefore a mixed blessing. In Freud's later work *The Future of an Illusion* (1961) he judges religion more severely. He maintains that religion has its origin in psychological needs that make it a matter of wishful thinking, but also permit human beings to accept morality.[12] The theory is partly intended to explain the origin of religion, and also to identify motives for religious belief that still function. There are basically three needs that religious beliefs satisfy:

(1) The need for defense against a cold, cruel nature.
(2) The need to be reconciled to fate, in particular, death.
(3) The need to be compensated for the restrictions that civilization imposes upon us.

In the modern world the last function is more important and the first function less important.

What do religions teach that fulfill these needs?

(1) There is a divine providence that cares for us and gives us a higher purpose that does not leave us helpless in the face of the more powerful forces of nature.
(2) Death is not the end, but a beginning of a new life.
(3) There is a cosmic justice in which the good are rewarded and the evil punished.

Freud (1961) calls these beliefs "illusions, fulfillments of the oldest, strongest and most urgent wishes of mankind" (p. 38). He says "We call a belief an illusion when a wish-fulfillment is a prominent factor in its motivation, and in doing so we disregard its relations to reality, just as the illusion itself sets no store by verification" (p. 40). An illusion,

---

12 Freud's idea that religion arises out of psychological needs continues the nineteenth-century approach of Feuerbach in *Lectures on the Essence of Religion* (1967).

according to Freud, is not the same as a delusion. The latter contradicts reality, whereas an illusion is completely unrealistic, but not impossible. He gives as an example of an illusion the belief of a young girl that she will marry a prince. According to Freud, belief in a Messiah is in that category.

It is critical to Freud's argument that religious belief is not only motivated by the desire to fulfill certain psychological needs, but is also unsupported by rational considerations. To see why he needs the latter assumption, consider another common belief in which a psychological need is a "prominent factor" in its motivation: the belief that most other people are favorably disposed towards you. Compare three cases: (1) the evidence on the whole supports the truth of the belief; (2) the evidence on the whole supports the falsehood of the belief; (3) there is no evidence one way or the other, or the evidence is mixed. If the belief is partly or largely caused by psychological need but it is true and there is evidence for it, would you judge it differently than if it is caused by psychological need and the evidence is either mixed or against it? I suspect you would. A hypothesis to explain the first case is that we are designed by nature to have certain built-in beliefs that bypass reasoning processes because the beliefs are very important for our good, even for our survival. Reasoning and the weighing of evidence take time, and we might be better off if we do not take time to evaluate the evidence before believing that other people generally have a favorable attitude towards us. This might be a case in which the most efficient mechanism for belief-formation is non-cognitive, and it is an evolutionary advantage to believe in that way. And there is just as much reason to think this mechanism would operate if the belief is true. Freud must assume, then, that the mechanism for generating religious beliefs is objectionable when wish-fulfillment plays a prominent role in motivating the beliefs because the evidence on the whole is either against the truth of the beliefs or it is non-existent or mixed.

In addition, Freud defines illusion in a way that implies that he suspects the beliefs are false. Freud says, "Of the reality value of most of them [religious beliefs] we cannot judge; just as they cannot be proved, so they cannot be refuted. We still know too little to make a critical approach to them. The riddles of the universe reveal themselves only slowly to our investigation; there are many questions to which science to-day can give no answer. But scientific work is the only road which can lead us to a knowledge of reality outside ourselves" (1961, p. 40). The objection, then, cannot be to the role psychological needs play in the beliefs, but to the lack of scientific evidence for them and the unlikelihood of their truth. He focuses on psychological needs to explain why human beings would believe what otherwise is so irrational. The irrationality of the beliefs is an assumption of the argument, not the conclusion.

The Freudian view of religion, then, is that religion is an illusion that motivates a person not only to follow the rules of morality, but to buy into the whole system of civilization, which includes making some sacrifices of the instincts for the sake of certain benefits. The illusion of religion includes the illusion of morality. Freud concludes:

> We shall tell ourselves that it would be very nice if there were a God who created the world and was a benevolent Providence, and if there were a moral order in the universe and an after-life; but it is a very striking fact that all this is exactly as we are bound to wish it to be. And it would be more remarkable still if our wretched, ignorant and downtrodden ancestors had succeeded in solving all these difficult riddles of the universe. (1961, p. 42)

6.4   The Metaphysical Ground of Morality

Western religions maintain that morality arises from God. In Natural Law theory morality rests upon God's nature. In Divine Command theory morality rest upon God's will. In the theory I call Divine Motivation theory, morality rest upon the motives that are the primary constituents of God's virtues. In each case the theory may not be committed to the idea that morality needs religion, since it is possible that, even though morality in fact derives from God, morality would exist even if there were no God. But clearly, if morality derives from God, it depends upon God in actuality whether or not morality would have existed in some other possible godless world.

Other than Natural Law theory, the principal theory of a theistic foundation for morality is Divine Command (DC) theory. In the fourteenth century Duns Scotus and William of Ockham each had a view of the ground of morality that went at least part way in the direction of DC theory, although that has been disputed.[13] The theory subsequently appears in the work of Luther and Calvin as part of the discussion of justification and predestination. Luther says:

> Therefore, why does man take pride in his merits and works, which in no way are pleasing to God? For they are good, or meritorious, works, but only because they have been chosen by God from eternity that they please Him. Therefore we do good works only in giving thanks, for the works do not make us good, but our goodness, rather, the goodness of God, makes us good and our works good. For they would not be good in themselves except for the fact that God regards them as good.[14]

The key element in DC theory, then, is that the divine will, the divine command, or in some versions, the divine preference, is the source of morality. Some contemporary forms of DC theory limit the theory to an account of right and wrong acts, not an account of moral value in general.[15] A common form of DC theory, then, is the following:

– An act is morally required (an obligation) just in case God commands us to do it.
– An act is morally wrong just in case God forbids us to do it.
– An act is permissible just in case God neither commands nor forbids it.

Since a divine command is the expression of God's will with respect to human and other creaturely acts, the divine will is the fundamental source of the moral properties of acts.

The nature of the relation between God's commands and moral requirements is an important issue for DC theorists. To say that "x is morally required" *means* "x is commanded by God" is too strong, since

13   For evidence of Divine Command theory in Duns Scotus, see *The Paris Commentary on the Sentences*, bk IV, ch. 46, and *The Oxford Commentary on the Four Books of the Sentences*, bk III, ch. 38, ques. 1. For William of Ockham, see *On the Four Books of the Sentences*, bk II, ch. 19. These selections, along with a number of other historical readings are included in Idziak (1979).

14   Martin Luther, *Lectures on Romans*, Scholia, ch. 9, reprinted in Ikziak (1979), p. 97.

15   Robert Adams explicitly limits his version of Divine Command theory to a theory of obligation, not a general theory of the good. See Adams (1999) for his most recent detailed defense of such a theory.

that has the consequence that to say "x is morally required because God commands it" is just to say "x is commanded by God because x is commanded by God," which clearly says nothing. On the other hand, to say that God's commands and moral requirements merely coincide is too weak. That is compatible with the lack of any metaphysical connection whatever between morality and God's will, and it makes DC theory uninteresting. DC theory, then, aims at something in between identity of meaning and contingent equivalence. It should turn out that God's will *makes* what's right to be right. Acts are right/wrong *because* of the will of God. A plausible version of the intended relation has been proposed by Robert M. Adams, who argues that the relation between God's commands and the rightness/wrongness of acts is akin to the relation between water and H_2O in the theory of direct reference defended by Saul Kripke, Hilary Putnam, and others in the seventies.[16] "Water" and "H_2O" do not mean the same thing. To think so is to misunderstand the importance of the discovery that water is H_2O, which was certainly not the discovery of the meaning of a word, nor a change in meaning of a word. Nonetheless, it is not a contingent fact that water is composed of H_2O. The discovery that water is H_2O is the discovery that what makes water water is its being H_2O. Being H_2O is essential to water. We think now that nothing ever was or will be water that is not H_2O even though nobody was in a position to understand that before the modern discovery of molecular structure. Similarly, the moral properties of acts could be essentially connected to God's commands even though many people are not in a position to realize the connection and perhaps nobody was at some periods of history.

In a famous question in Plato's *Euthyphro*, Socrates asks, "Is the pious being loved by the gods because it is pious, or is it pious because it is being loved by the gods?" (10a). This question has subsequently been used as a dilemma for DC theory, although Plato was using it to make a point about definition, not to refute a theory nobody held at the time. As applied to DC theory, the dilemma is this: If God wills the good (right) because it is good (right), then goodness (rightness) is independent of God's will, and the latter does not explain the former. On the other hand, if something is good (right) because God wills it, then it looks as if the divine will is arbitrary. God is not constrained by any

---

16   See Adams (1973), which was reprinted as chapter 7 of Adams (1987). The theory of direct reference originated with Kripke (1980) and Putnam (1975).

moral reason from willing anything whatever, and it is hard to see how any non-moral reason could be the right sort of reason to determine God's choice of what to make good or right. The apparent consequence is that good/bad (right/wrong) are determined by an arbitrary divine will; God could have commanded cruelty or hatred, and if he had done so, cruel and hateful acts would have been right, even duties. This is an unacceptable consequence. It is contrary to our sense of the essential nature of the moral properties of certain acts, and the goodness of a God who could make cruelty good is not at all what we normally mean by good. It is therefore hard to see how it can be true that God himself is good in any important, substantive sense of good on this approach.

To solve this problem Robert Adams modifies DC theory to say that the property of rightness is the property of being commanded by a *loving* God. This permits Adams to allow that God could command cruelty for its own sake, but if God did so he would not love us, and if that were the case, Adams argues, morality would break down. Morality *is* dependent upon divine commands, but they are dependent upon the commands of a deity with a certain nature and with a certain relationship to us. Divine commands are not arbitrary, since they are constrained by God's nature, but neither do they affirm an independent realm of obligation. They are akin to the requirements persons make of those whom they love. Lovers impose demands on those they love, but a demand only constitutes a requirement under the assumption that the lover is good and the relationship itself is good.[17]

Many other philosophers have proposed versions of DC theory, but my own preference is to look in a different direction for a way God is related to morality. My reason is not that I think that DC theory has insurmountable difficulties, but that DC theory is a kind of theory that makes morals fundamentally a matter of law, of obligation. I think that a virtue ethics is a preferable form of ethical theory, and that a virtue theory grounded in God's virtues is a better candidate to provide the metaphysical grounding of ethics than a theory grounded in God's will. In any case, I have proposed a theory in which God has a foundational role in ethics as an exemplar rather than as a lawgiver. This approach has advantages for the ethics of religions that identify

17   See Adams (1979). For a fuller account of his theological moral theory, see Adams (1999).

particular persons as paradigmatically good, as in Christian ethics, and since it permits distinct but overlapping versions for different cultures, it has advantages for the task of constructing a common morality. I call the theory Divine Motivation theory.[18]

In Divine Motivation (DM) theory, all moral properties are grounded in the motives of God. Motives are emotions, but I call an emotion a motive when it is initiating action. Motive-dispositions are components of virtues. The divine motives can be considered divine emotions, although I do not insist that they are literally emotions.[19] They are states like love and compassion. Whether or not these states are properly classified as emotions, they are motivating. God acts *out of* love, joy, compassion, and perhaps also anger and disgust. These are the states that I propose constitute the metaphysical basis for moral value. They are components of God's virtues. Given that we do not experience God directly, we identify virtues by the paradigmatic but imperfect instances of virtuous persons in our experience, and we acquire them by imitation.

The structure of the theory is exemplarist. The moral properties of persons, acts, and outcomes are defined via direct reference to an exemplar of a good person. God is the ultimate exemplar, but there are many finitely good human exemplars. Although we imitate finite exemplars, the metaphysical basis of value is God. Value in all forms derives from God, in particular, from God's motives. God's motives are perfectly good, and human motives are good in so far as they are like the divine motives as those motives would be expressed in finite and embodied beings. Motive-dispositions are constituents of virtues. A virtue is an enduring trait consisting of a good motive-disposition and reliable success in bringing about the aim, if any, of the good motive. God's virtues are paradigmatically good personal traits. Human virtues are those traits that imitate God's virtues as they would be expressed by human beings in human circumstances. The goodness of a state of affairs is derivative from the goodness of the divine motive.

18   See my book by the same name, Zagzebski (2004).
19   In philosophies influenced by Aristotelian psychology, such as that of Aquinas, emotions are thought to be essentially connected to the body and therefore do not apply to God. Personally, I see no reason to deny that emotions are components of the divine nature, but my theory requires only that there are states in God that are analogous to what we call emotions in humans in the same way that there are states in God analogous to what we call beliefs in humans.

Outcomes get their moral value by their relation to good and bad motivations. For example, a state of affairs is a merciful one or a compassionate one or a just one because the divine motives that are constituents of mercy, compassion, and justice respectively aim at bringing them about. Acts get their moral value from the acts that would, would not, or might be done by God in the relevant circumstances.

The exemplarist structure of DM theory allows versions for different religions as well as cultural traditions that are non-religious but recognize common exemplars of goodness within the tradition. In Plato and the Stoics we become like God by becoming virtuous, which means to imitate Socrates or the Stoic Sage. In Christianity Jesus Christ is both God and man, the exemplar of God in human nature. For Aristotle, the exemplar is the person with practical wisdom. Other religions have exemplars as well – the Buddhist *arahant*, the Jewish *tzaddik*, and so on.[20] If there is a God of all peoples, it would not be surprising that there is as much commonality among the exemplars of different cultures and religious traditions as is compatible with the differences in their experiences and the degree to which they have reached an understanding of the divine. In contrast, DC theory has the problem of explaining how morality can be grounded in divine commands promulgated only to a certain group of people.

Let us return to the *Euthyphro* problem for DC theory. If morality is grounded in God's commands and if God can command anything, then it looks as if God could command brutalizing the innocent, in which case brutalizing the innocent would have been an obligation. But that is unacceptable. As we saw above, Adams proposes that moral obligation is grounded in the commands of a loving God, but even though his proposal may succeed in answering the objection it is designed to address, it appears to be *ad hoc*. There is no intrinsic connection between a command and the property of being loving, so to tie morality to the commands of a loving God is to tie it to two distinct properties of God, only one of which involves commands. In DM theory there is no need to solve the problem of whether God could make it right that we brutalize the innocent by making any such modification to the theory, since being loving is one of God's essential motives. The right

20   See the prologue to Flanagan (1991) for a nice discussion of the many ways of sainthood and moral exemplariness.

thing for humans to do is to act on motives that imitate the divine motives. Brutalizing the innocent is not an act that expresses a motive that imitates the divine motives. Hence, it is impossible for brutalizing the innocent to be right as long as (i) it is impossible for such an act to be an expression of a motive that is like the motives of God, and (ii) it is impossible for God to have different motives. Assumption (ii) follows from the plausible assumption that God's motives are part of his nature.[21]

The arbitrariness problem also does not arise in DM theory. That is because a will needs a reason, but a motive *is* a reason. The will, according to Aquinas, always chooses "under the aspect of good," which means that reasons are not inherent in the will itself.[22] In contrast, motives provide not only the impetus to action, but the reason *for* the action. If we know that God acts from a motive of love, there is no need to look for a further reason for the act. On the other hand, a divine command requires a reason, and if the reason is or includes fundamental divine motivational states such as love, it follows that even DC theory needs to refer to God's motives to avoid the consequence that moral properties are arbitrary and God himself is not good. This move makes divine motives more basic than the divine will even in DC theory.

DM theory also has the theoretical advantage of providing a unitary theory of all evaluative properties, divine as well as human. DC theory is most naturally interpreted as an ethics of law, a divine deontological theory, wherein the content of the law is promulgated by divine commands. God's own goodness and the rightness of God's own acts, however, are not connected to divine commands, since God does not give commands to himself. In contrast, DM theory makes the features of the divine nature in virtue of which God is morally good the foundation for the moral goodness of those same features in creatures. Both divine and human goodness are explained in terms of good motives, and the goodness of human motives is derived from the goodness of the divine motives.

21 This is assuming, of course, that the motives of which we are speaking are suitably general. Love is essential to God, but love of Adam and Eve is not, since Adam and Eve might not have existed.

22 Aquinas (1981 [1273]) *Summa Theologica* I–II, q. 1, art. 6, corpus.

There are innumerable ways that a moral theory can be structured with a theological foundation. The dominance of DC theory and Natural Law theory in Western religious ethics is probably due to a combination of the importance of law in Western thought and a particular way of reading the Bible that became standard. Virtue ethics can have a theological foundation also, whether or not it has the specific form I have proposed here. Whether ethical theory on its metaphysical side needs religious theory is an issue that cannot be disentangled from the general question of what is required for an acceptable metaphysics. When naturalistic ethical theories are preferred to religious ethical theories, it is not because they are thought to be superior as ethical theories, but because it is thought that naturalism is superior to religion. That, of course, is not a dispute that will be resolved within ethics, but requires the project of this whole book and more.

6.5   Conclusion

The links between religion and morality are extensive and many people find them suspect. Clearly, there is a need for a common morality applicable to people of any or no religion, and it is becoming increasingly obvious that there must be a core area of morality applicable across national boundaries. The days when moral relativism was *de rigueur* are over. We can all hurt or be hurt by people on the other side of the world, most obviously through war and terrorism, and less obviously through harm to the environment and the network of global economics. If morality is a system for getting along with everyone, participation in that system cannot depend upon believing in any particular religion. And everyone must participate in morality. But as I've argued in this chapter, people can accept a common code of behavior without agreeing on the metaphysical ground of value and the source of the authority of morality, nor need they agree on the ultimate aim of human life, nor need they have the same motives to be moral. The Universal Declaration of Human Rights of 1947 was signed by forty-eight countries with widely disparate histories, cultures, and values. It would not threaten the prospects for global recognition of these rights if it turned out that morality is connected with religion in any of the ways I've discussed in this chapter.

Further reading

Even though ethical theory is a major branch of philosophy, and theological ethics is a large field, religious philosophical ethics has a much smaller literature than most of the other subjects treated in this book. There have, however, been some recent works by philosophers on religious ethics and the connection between religion and morality. I recommend William J. Wainwright's book, *Religion and Morality* (Burlington, Vt.: Ashgate, 2005). Robert M. Adams, *Finite and Infinite Goods: A Framework for Ethics* (New York: Oxford University Press, 1999) includes much more than Adams' version of Divine Command theory discussed in this chapter. For my Divine Motivation theory, see Linda Zagzebski, *Divine Motivation Theory* (New York: Cambridge University Press, 2004). For a recent introduction to Natural Law theory, see Alfonso Gomez-Lobo, *Morality and the Human Goods: An Introduction to Natural Law Ethics* (Washington, D.C.: Georgetown University Press, 2002). Also recommended is Mark Wynn, *God and Goodness: a Natural Theological Perspective* (New York: Routledge, 1999).

Chapter 7

The Problem of Evil

7.1 What Is Evil and Why Is It a Problem?

The problem of evil is a different kind of problem in philosophy than in religion, something that should come as no surprise, given the separation of philosophy from religion in the West. Philosophers are concerned with what is called the logical problem of evil, and more recently the evidential problem. The first is the problem that the existence of evil seems to be logically inconsistent with the existence of an omnipotent and perfectly good God. The second is the problem that evil seems to make it *unlikely* that there is an omnipotent and perfectly good God. Both are theoretical difficulties. Forms of the logical problem go back to the ancient Greeks, as does so much in philosophy. This problem has often been cast as an argument for atheism, particularly in the modern period.

There is another kind of problem of evil with a different historical background, epitomized in the heart-wrenching story of Job in the Hebrew Scriptures. This problem focuses on the experience of suffering and other evils within the context of the relationship between a person and God. In this form of the problem there is no question that God exists. The problem is God's motive. Why would God permit things that seem so radically unloving, so inconsistent with his other benevolent behavior? The human relationship to God in such situations might be compared to the relationship of dogs to humans. Dogs love their humans, but often find us unfathomable, particularly when we permit them to suffer for their own good, as when we take them to the vet or willfully withhold something they want. I doubt that dogs are able to think they detect a logical inconsistency in our perceived attributes, but they probably are capable of confusion and hurt. The problem here is how to understand a bond with another being which seems to reveal a motive in the other that threatens the relationship.

Which problem is harder? It might seem that the theoretical problem is more difficult because recognizing that it is either impossible or unlikely that all of a set of important beliefs are true puts strong pressure on us to give up one of the beliefs. In contrast, philosophers often think of the experiential problem as one that has little philosophical interest because it is "merely" psychological. Presumably, if the logical and evidential problems can be solved, all that's left is to learn to deal with evil, and that is not a task for the philosopher. As we will see, there are various stratagems for solving both forms of the theoretical problem, whereas the experiential problem will probably never go away, no matter how successful we are at solving the theoretical problem.

My position is that philosophers should not ignore the experiential problem of evil because there are aspects of it that directly impact the way the theoretical problem should be formulated. Even from a philosopher's perspective, the problem is not just that of why there is evil, but why there are the particular evils that there are. The bereaved parent will say that even if a good God would have a good reason to permit some children to die, that does not explain why *my* child had to die. Why is my friend left heartbroken, disappointed, and suffering from a severe illness, while others escape? Why are these particular people left homeless and starving after a major hurricane or earthquake? It might seem that God is picking on certain individuals. But a good God is presumably not just a God who cares about the general welfare; it is a God who is good *to* each and every one of his creatures. So if there is such a God, there has to be an explanation for each instance of suffering, each pain and disappointment, and each morally wrong choice. It is not enough that there is an explanation for the quantity of suffering and other evils in the world.

So the problem of evil in Western philosophy is not just a problem of how a good and powerful God would be motivated to permit evil in the quantities that occur, but why the particular evils that exist are the ones that would be permitted. The latter comes closer to the experiential problem because it demands an explanation for the actual evils in the world, including those that affect each of us personally. In this way the traditional problem of evil blends into the more general problem of what evil is, where it comes from, and how each of us should respond to the evils that affect our lives. That is a problem for everybody, not just theists.

We all experience things we take to be evil. Some evils are not caused by any human being, such as suffering due to natural death, illness, accident, or natural disaster. Other evils are brought about by intentional human acts, such as acts of cruelty, betrayal, or deception. It is usual to call evils in the first category *natural evils* and those in the second *moral evils*. Notice that this means that what we call evil covers two very different kinds of phenomena. Some students tell me that they do not call natural evils "evil," yet they almost always label natural suffering by some negative value term such as "bad."[1] In that case the problem of evil could be reformulated as the problem of bad. But, of course, re-labeling the problem does not eliminate it as long as the items in both categories are problems for the existence of a perfectly good and omnipotent being.

If there are two forms of evil, they must have something in common in virtue of which we call them evil or, alternatively, bad. But what could that be? What about suffering? Almost all natural evils are occurrences of suffering, but if you think death is an evil apart from the suffering that precedes it and the suffering of loved ones afterwards, then there must be natural evils that are not cases of suffering. Furthermore, not every case of moral evil causes suffering. Moral evils typically involve two persons – the agent or perpetrator, and the victim. If the agent deceives the victim, the victim might not suffer, but she has been mistreated. More importantly, the locus of moral evil is in the agent, not the victim. The agent is evil for intending or wanting to do harm. If there was a world where people had much evil intent but were prevented from carrying it out, that world would not be as good a world as one in which nobody ever had evil intent. There are no victims in either world, and there might not be any suffering in either world, but if you think the first world is worse, there must be evils that are not instances of suffering and in which there is no victim of the evil intent of another.

---

1 Such students have distinguished company. The early Stoic Chrysippus confined evil to moral weakness, although he allowed that natural evils are bad in some sense. See Long (1986), p. 169.

I suspect that the only thing natural and moral evils have in common is the fact that we think a good being would be motivated to prevent or eliminate them. Both are evil in virtue of the fact that both conflict with what we expect out of the motivational structure of a perfectly good being. So we are right to include both natural and moral evils in the category of things that generate the problem of evil. But because they are so different, we should not expect a solution to one kind of evil to be a solution to the other. Two different solutions may be required.

This leads to one more preliminary point. The problem of evil cannot be discussed independently of the problem of good. Of course, we do not call good a "problem," since we expect a good God to be motivated to produce a good world, but if the problem we are asking is where evil comes from and why it exists, that cannot be answered without asking where good comes from and why it exists. This issue is a general one in the metaphysics of value. My own position is that the problem of evil cannot be solved without dealing directly with that fundamental issue in the metaphysics of value, a point to which I will return.

7.2   The Logical Problem of Evil

7.2.1   Historical background

In the third century BC Epicurus presented the problem in a form that it has retained for almost two and a half millennia:

> God . . . either wants to eliminate bad things and cannot, or can but does not want to, or neither wishes to nor can, or both wants to and can. If he wants to and cannot, then he is weak – and this does not apply to god. If he can but does not want to, then he is spiteful – which is equally foreign to god's nature. If he neither wants to nor can, he is both weak and spiteful and so not a god. If he wants to and can, which is the only thing fitting for a god, where then do bad things come from? Or why does he not eliminate them?[2]

---

2   The argument has not survived in Epicurus' own writings. This statement of Epicurus' argument is reported by Lactantius in *On the Anger of God*. See Inwood and Gerson (1988), p. 64.

Epicurus was one of the few philosophers in the ancient world who used this argument to conclude that there is no god who is omnipotent and good. Epicurus' position was that the gods are uninterested in human affairs. In contrast, the early Stoics were convinced that nature is providentially ordered, and so they had to explain the compatibility of evil with divine governance. Some of the responses they made to the problem still have adherents today. In particular, they argued that everything that happens is in accordance with a cosmic providence, but particular moral evils are the responsibility of men. One of the earliest Stoics, Cleanthes (third century BC), expresses the Stoic view in his lovely *Hymn to Zeus*, a view that persisted throughout the work of later Stoicism:

> *Hymn to Zeus*
> Nothing occurs on the earth apart from you, O God,
> nor in the heavenly regions nor on the sea,
> except what bad men do in their folly;
> but you know how to make the odd even,
> and to harmonize what is dissonant; to you the alien is akin.
> And so you have wrought together into one all things that are
>   good and bad,
> So that there arises one eternal *logos* of all things,
> Which all bad mortals shun and ignore,
> Unhappy wretches, ever seeking the possession of good things
> They neither see nor hear the universal law of God,
> By obeying which they might enjoy a happy life.[3]

This hymn combines philosophical subtlety with artistic beauty, but it also raises questions. How can it be true that nothing occurs apart from the will of God "except what bad men do in their folly," while it is also true that God has "wrought together into one all things that are good and bad," suggesting that God is responsible for the bad after all? There have been many philosophical attempts to resolve this tension.

In the biblical Book of Wisdom, written in Greek about 100 BC by an unknown member of the Jewish community at Alexandria, there is a passage that makes an interesting comparison with Cleanthes' hymn:

---

3   As quoted by Long (1986), p. 181.

Indeed, before you the whole universe is as a grain from a balance,
  or a drop of morning dew come down upon the earth.
But you have mercy on all, because you can do all things; and you
  overlook the sins of men that they may repent.
For you love all things that are and loathe nothing that you have
  made; for what you hated, you would not have fashioned.
And how could a thing remain unless you willed it; or be preserved
  had it not been called forth by you? (Wisdom 11:22–5)

In this poem nothing can remain unless God wills it, yet sins are nonetheless "the sins of men." So there is a sense in which God *is* responsible for every evil, and a sense in which he is not. In subsequent history the difference has generally required distinguishing what God permits to happen and what God directly wills to bring about. This distinction is important, but it is not sufficient to solve the problem because even if God merely permits evil, there has to be some explanation for his permission, since we expect a good being to prevent or eliminate evil as far as he can. It is not enough that he does not directly bring about evil himself.[4]

By the time of the Christian era of the high Middle Ages, the attributes of God were defined in a way that made the problem of evil particularly acute. God was explicitly called omnipotent, not just powerful, and perfectly good, not just good, a creator who could have created something else instead, and there was considerable dispute over the question of whether God could have created a better world than this one. By the modern period this problem became the focus of the case for atheism. In my experience of professional philosophers, atheists almost always refer to the existence of evil as the decisive reason for disbelief in theism.

---

4 In his *Theodicy*, Leibniz distinguishes between God's antecedent will, which wills that humans always do what is good, and his consequent will, which wills to permit us to sin. According to Leibniz, God's consequent will "tends towards the production of as many goods as can be put together" and permits some evils because they are necessary for the sake of achieving greater goods (see Leibniz 1952 [1710], pp. 382–3). Aquinas (1981 [1273]) makes a similar distinction in *Summa Theologica* I, q.19, arts. 6 and 9.

7.2.2 The contemporary argument

7.2.2.1 *J. L. Mackie*

The renaissance in philosophy of religion that occurred during the last third of the twentieth century was sparked by a number of papers challenging the traditional conception of God. The seminal paper on the problem of evil was by J. L. Mackie (1955). Mackie argued that:

(1) An omnipotent and perfectly good being (God) exists

and

(2) Evil exists

are inconsistent only when supplemented with two additional assumptions:

(3) A perfectly good being eliminates evil as far as it can

and

(4) An omnipotent being can eliminate all evil.

In the subsequent literature, sometimes a further premise is added that refers to God's omniscience. You will think this premise is required if you think that an omnipotent being may not be omniscient and hence may not know of the existence of particular evils and how to eliminate them. But since no one denies that God knows of the existence of every evil and what it would take to eliminate it, this premise is not a focus of discussion whether or not it is explicitly stated.

Mackie examines several "fallacious solutions" that are worth mentioning because they are so commonly offered as ways out of the problem of evil:

(A) *Good cannot exist without evil.* Mackie points out that this move denies divine omnipotence, although the adherent of this solution probably assumes that an omnipotent being cannot do the logically impossible, and it is logically impossible for good to exist without evil. Mackie then considers the ways in which it might be true that good cannot exist without evil. Perhaps it means that good is related to evil as the great is to the small. But, Mackie objects, the great/small analogy is inaccurate because, unlike the great and the small, we think that good *opposes* evil and tries to eliminate it. Instead, good and evil might be taken as logical opposites like red and not-red. But this analogy does not work either because it makes evil merely the privation of good, not an opposing force. In any case, Mackie says he does not see why there cannot be a universe that is totally red, so if good is to evil as red is to not-red, there could still be a universe that is totally good.

A common reply is that, even though Mackie is right that it is possible for a universe to be totally good, the creatures in such a world would not *know* that it is good. If God wants us to know the difference between good and evil, evil has to exist for us to see the difference. But surely the aim of getting us to understand what evil is could be accomplished by vivid imaginative fiction, and even if a dose of real suffering is necessary, it seems unlikely we would need the amount of suffering we have in the world if the only purpose is to show us what evil is.

(B) *Evil is necessary as a means to good.* Many people have the experience of going through a period of suffering and finding that they end up a better and happier person because of it. They may then form the hypothesis that good results from evil in the end, even in those cases in which we do not see the good at the end. But Mackie objects that this response makes God subject to causal laws. Even if good *always* results from evil and outweighs the evil that precedes it, surely it would have been better if the good had existed without the preceding evil, and a God who creates the laws of nature himself could have designed the world that way.

(C) *The universe is better with some evil in it than it would be with no evil.* A fine piece of music may have some discordant notes and be a better work because of it. A beautiful garden may look better with some dead leaves on the ground. If variety in a design is good, as Leibniz argued, some components of the design will be less good than others, and some might be downright bad. So Leibniz suggested that the best world includes some evil in its parts.

According to an interesting version of this response to evil, some goods cannot exist without certain evils. What we might call first-order goods/evils are those goods and evils that do not require the existence of other goods and evils. Second-order goods are those that could not exist without first-order evils. Heroism, sympathy, compassion, kindness, and many other virtues would be in this category. There is no courage without fear, no compassion without suffering, no hope without the pain of the unknown.

This solution makes it more important to a perfectly good being to produce second-order goods than to eliminate first-order evils, and we may doubt that second-order goods are good enough to justify all the existence of pain and suffering, but more importantly, observes Mackie, first-order evils make possible not only second-order goods, but also second-order evils. Fear makes cowardice possible as well as courage. Pain makes brutality possible as well as compassion. If hope is possible, so is despair. It is useless to propose that second-order evils are necessary for third-order goods because then we get an infinite regress. If there are third-order goods, there are third-order evils, which would have to be justified by fourth-order goods, and so on.

The proponent of this solution probably stops with third-order goods. There is only one of them: free will. This leads us to the historically dominant solution to the problem of evil.

(D) *The Free Will defense.* Mackie assumes that the Free Will defense is a version of solution C. The world is better with free will and evil in it than it would be if there were no free will and no evil. Free will is therefore a good that outweighs all the evils that accompany it, both first- and second-order evils. Attempts to give a satisfactory account of free will have failed, so there is something deeply mysterious about it, but most of us have an intuitive sense that it exists, and that freedom in the morally significant sense is the freedom to choose either good or evil, right or wrong. For such choices to be possible, evil must be an option of human choice, and if we choose it, non-interference in our free agency means permitting the natural consequences of those choices to follow. So free will does seem to require evil as an option.

But is free will so good that it outweighs *any* quantity of first- and second-order evils? If so, the good of free will would have to be infinite and the bad of all the evils brought about by free creatures or necessitated by second-order goods would have to be finite. It's hard to believe that the good of free will infinitely exceeds the evil that can be done freely. Wouldn't a world of free creatures who never or almost never choose good be a worse world than one in which there are no free creatures at all? I think the answer is yes, so the proponent of the Free Will defense should not claim that any world with free will in it is better than any world without free will. But all the Free Will defense needs is the claim that *some* worlds with free will in them are better than any world without free will and that we live in one such world. In the next section we will turn to one influential version of this defense.

A natural rejoinder to make at this juncture is that even if a world with free will and evil is better than a world with no free will and no evil, the best world would be a world with free will and no evil. Mackie asks, why couldn't an omnipotent God make free beings who never will evil? He says he sees no logical impossibility in this. Presumably the idea would be that God could have created a world of creatures like the Virgin Mary who, according to Catholic doctrine, did not inherit Original Sin and never committed an actual sin in her life, although she was free to do so. If this doctrine makes sense, such beings are logically possible. But the issue is whether God can ensure that the beings he creates are like the Virgin Mary. Creating human beings without Original Sin obviously is not sufficient, since according to the Genesis story Adam and Eve were created that way but still sinned. So the issue is whether God could pick out in advance free creatures who would not sin and create just those creatures. If that can't be done, why can't it be done? And why would God create a world that is less good than many other logically possible worlds? An interesting answer to these questions is given by Alvin Plantinga in his hypothesis of transworld depravity.

7.2.2.2 Alvin Plantinga

Plantinga (1967; 1974a; 1974b) distinguishes a defense of the compossibility of (1) and (2) from a theodicy. A *theodicy* is an explanation for the existence of evil in a universe containing an omnipotent and perfectly good being. For example, a theodicy might propose that God prefers a world in which good overcomes evil to a world in which there is no evil to be overcome. Another theodicy was proposed by Leibniz, who argued that the best of all possible worlds is one that combines simplicity of laws with variety of phenomena.

In contrast, a *defense* is merely a demonstration that proposition (1) is logically consistent with proposition (2). To show that a set of propositions p and q are logically consistent, it is sufficient to find a proposition r that is logically possible (not self-contradictory) and which is consistent with p, and together with p entails q. It is not necessary to show that r is true or even plausible. For example, suppose somebody claims that the following propositions are inconsistent:

(5) God is omnipotent

(6) An omnipotent being has all powers

(7) God is unable to do evil.

A defense of the consistency of (5)–(7) might go like this. Consider:

(8) The ability to do evil is the lack of a power.

If (8) is logically possible and consistent with (5) and (6), and together with (5) and (6) entails (7), then (5)–(7) are logically consistent. Presumably the debate would center on whether (8) is logically possible. Aquinas argued that (8) is not just possible, but true (see Chapter 4). But he did not have to go that far if his aim was only to show that there is no inconsistency in the set of propositions (5)–(7).

To apply this strategy to the problem of evil, we would look for a proposition that is logically possible, is logically consistent with (1), and together with (1) entails (2). One suggested proposition is:

(3′) A perfectly good being has a morally sufficient reason to permit evil.

Is (3′) logically possible? Most discussants of this problem, including atheists, say yes. (3′) is consistent with (1), and together with (1) entails (2).[5] So (1) and (2) are logically consistent. But perhaps it is not clear that (3′) is logically possible, or perhaps its modal status is inscrutable. Plantinga has proposed another proposition to serve the function of (3′). But before explaining what it is, we need to go through some preliminaries about possible worlds.

When Leibniz said that this is the best of all possible worlds, he was thinking of a possible world as a possible object of creation. God considers all the possible worlds he could bring about and picks the one he wants. Plantinga argues that this is not the right way to look at possible worlds. A possible world is a maximal possible state of affairs. That is, for every world w and proposition p, either p is true in w or p is false in w. There are many propositions true in the actual world that God does not make true by the creation, for instance, *God exists, God is*

---

5 It may not be evident that permitting evil entails the existence of evil. If not, (3') can be suitably reworded so that the entailment is clear.

perfectly good, and many others pertaining to God himself. Since God does not bring about his own existence, God does not bring about an entire possible world in the creation, but only a part of it. What God creates he *strongly actualizes*, in Plantinga's terminology.

Suppose that part of what God brings about is the existence of free creatures, and those free creatures make some propositions true through their acts, for example, the proposition *Eve eats the apple*. There is an indirect sense in which God brings about the truth of that proposition by creating Eve and giving her free will, but Eve brings about the truth of that proposition directly. In Plantinga's terminology, God *weakly actualizes* Eve's eating the apple, and Eve *strongly actualizes* her eating the apple. What God weakly actualizes is what God actualizes through free creatures whom he creates and to whom he gives free will.

Now if God strongly actualizes certain free creatures and puts them in a world with certain physical laws and in certain physical conditions, they will act freely to bring about further states of affairs. So suppose that in one world, w1.1, God creates Adam and Eve and puts them in the Garden of Eden. They eat the forbidden fruit. So eating the forbidden fruit is a state of affairs they bring about. God weakly actualizes it by creating them and putting them in the garden. So now we have some true propositions about the world w1.1:

(A) Adam and Eve live in the Garden of Eden and have free will
(B) Adam and Eve eat the forbidden fruit.

God strongly actualizes (A) and weakly actualizes (B). But there is another proposition true in this world:

(C) If God created Adam and Eve, they would freely eat the forbidden fruit.

Plantinga says there are such propositions as (C) and they have a truth value. Propositions of this form are called counterfactuals of freedom, mentioned in the discussion of Molinism in Chapter 5.[6]

6 Counterfactuals of freedom are in the subjunctive mood, but the antecedent need not be "counter" factual because it can be true. It is therefore somewhat misleading to call these propositions "counterfactuals," but that is the standard name for them.

Other propositions true in world w1.1 follow from further counter-factuals of freedom and from propositions strongly actualized by God such as the laws of nature:

(D) If Adam and Eve ate the forbidden fruit, they would then do X
(E) If Adam and Eve do X, then y would follow

and so on.

Notice that God does not strongly actualize the entire world w1.1. God strongly actualizes a part of the world, what I call a world germ. If the actual world is w1.1, let's call the part God strongly actualizes world germ, w1. The entire history of w1.1 is a product of what God initially strongly actualizes (w1), and the counterfactuals of freedom true in w1. So another proposition is true:

(F) If God strongly actualized world germ w1, world w1.1 would be weakly actualized. Unfortunately, there is evil in w1.1.

Is there a possible world in which (1) is true and (2) is false? The answer might well be yes, but Plantinga says it won't do God any good in the creation if it is a world in which God strongly actualizes w1, because God doesn't get to decide which world will be weakly actualized if he strongly actualizes w1. God doesn't decide to make (F) true. Its truth is determined by what free creatures do.

But suppose God strongly actualized a different world germ instead. Suppose he created Adam and Eve, but did not put them in the Garden of Eden, or he changed it some way. Call this world germ w2. Let us suppose that if God created w2, the following propositions would be true:

(A') God creates Adam and Eve and puts them in the Garden of Flowers
(B') Adam and Eve do not pick the forbidden flowers.

But suppose it is also true that:

(C') Adam and Eve kill their offspring.

So:

(D′) If God created Adam and Eve, they would kill their offspring.

Let us call the world that would result from God's strongly actualizing w2 world w2.9. So another proposition is true:

(E′) If God strongly actualized w2, world w2.9 would be weakly actualized.

Suppose further that no matter what God strongly actualizes, the world that would result would have evil in it if it has free creatures in it. There might still be many possible worlds with free creatures and no moral evil, but none of them is a world that would be actualized if God strongly actualized his part of that world. No matter what the initial conditions for Adam and Eve, they do evil. And we are supposing that no matter what creatures God creates instead of Adam and Eve, they do evil also. If this is possible, Adam and Eve (and every other possible free creature) suffer from what Plantinga calls *transworld depravity*.

Now let's go back to the Free Will defense. We need to find a proposition that is logically possible and consistent with (1) and which together with (1) entails (2). So the defense is this. It is possible that there are true counterfactuals of the following form:

If God created world germ 1, world 1.1 would result
If God created world germ 2, world 2.9 would result
If God created world germ 3, world 3.4 would result
and so on,

and every world on the right side of the counterfactual contains evil. So:

(3″) No matter what God created, if it included free creatures, evil would result.

As long as (3″) is logically possible, is consistent with (1), and together with (1) entails (2), the compossibility of (1) and (2) has been demonstrated.

Presumably the world germ God chooses to strongly actualize is one that would result in a world that is at least as good as any that would result from any other world germ God could create instead. But notice that Plantinga is not committed to the claim that the actual world is the best possible world, nor is he committed to the claim that any world with free will in it is better than any world without free will in it, as Mackie interprets the Free Will defense. The counterfactuals above might turn out in such a way that w2.9 is considerably worse than many worlds without free creatures. But as long as it is possible that w1.1, the actual world, is better than any world without free creatures and is at least as good as the world that would be weakly actualized if God were to create a different world germ instead, the Free Will defense succeeds.

The Free Will defense applies only to moral evils. What about natural evils? Plantinga's defense of natural evil is that it is possible that such evils are produced by the fallen angels – devils. On this interpretation, it is possible that natural evils are a form of moral evil. All the evil in the world is the result of the free choices of free creatures.

Plantinga's account of counterfactuals of freedom raises numerous questions. Some philosophers think there are no such counterfactuals, or if there are, their truth cannot be used to explain God's creative options. But if the above account is possible, the logical consistency of God's existence and evil has been demonstrated. Most writers on the problem of evil agree with that. However, many think that if (3′) or (3″) are implausible, there is still another form of the problem of evil that needs to be addressed: the evidential problem. Even if the existence of evil does not make theism impossible, evil might still make theism improbable. We will look at the evidential problem of evil in section 7.3.

7.2.3   The metaphysics of value

Before concluding the logical problem of evil, let's go back and look at an interesting feature of the standard formulation of the problem. As we have seen, (1) and (2) are not inconsistent unless supplemented with an additional premise such as Mackie's

(3) A perfectly good being eliminates evil as far as it can.

On the most natural way to interpret (3), it presupposes moral realism, the view that good and evil are properties of acts/states of affairs independent of what anybody believes, desires, or feels. Typically, the moral realist maintains that good and evil are independent of what *human beings* believe, desire, or feel, and the anti-realist denies that. The anti-realist may think that judgments of value are projections of human feelings, or they may think value judgments are commands, or they may think that value judgments are judgments rational beings would agree to under certain conditions. In each case value is not a feature of the world; it is a creation of human sensibility and/or the rational human need to get along with others. There would be no evil and there would be no good were it not for these features of human beings. Given anti-realism, (3) is not very plausible because it is not at all clear that a perfectly good non-human being would be motivated to eliminate something that exists only as a projection of the sensibilities of human beings.

Ironically, J. L. Mackie's own view of the metaphysics of value is a version of anti-realism that is at odds with his formulation of the problem of evil. Mackie (1977) endorsed an "error theory" of value according to which good and evil are not properties of anything outside the mind, but we intend to attribute such properties to acts/states of affairs when we make a moral judgment. So all moral judgments are false, according to Mackie. It seems to follow that (1), (2), and (3) are all false. False propositions can be inconsistent, but they do not present a dilemma unless somebody believes they are true. On Mackie's position, what ought to follow is that it is possible that God exists in the same sense that the world exists, but nothing, including God, has any value properties. There is no "problem" of evil unless the error human beings make in attributing value properties is a problem, but if so, it is not a theological problem.

There is another kind of anti-realism that eliminates the problem of evil at the level of the metaphysics of value, what we might call divine anti-realism. Good and evil could be projections of *God's* motives, feelings, preferences, or will. Divine Command theory, Thomas Carson's Divine Preference theory, and my Divine Motivation theory are theories of this kind.[7] In each of these theories, God does not weigh goods and evils because good and evil are not *there* in advance of God's emotions, preferences, or will. I will describe the way I think good and evil should be understood in Divine Motivation theory, but parallel

---

7 Divine Command theory and my Divine Motivation theory were discussed in Chapter 6. For Divine Preference theory see Carson (2000).

accounts of good and evil can be given in terms of God's will or preferences.

Some things (acts, states of affairs, personal traits) are such that God is motivated to bring them about. They express the divine nature and when they exist, they give God delight. These things are good. Other things are contrary to the divine nature. God is not motivated to bring them about and when they exist, they give God pain. These things are evil. Within the class of evils some are such that it is compatible with the motives of God that they be permitted, and others are such that it is incompatible with the motives of God that they be permitted. Nothing in the latter category exists, and we probably cannot even conceive of what these things would be like. The things we call evil are those that God is motivated to permit for his own reasons, but not to bring about. Although they give God pain, they are not contrary to the motivational structure of God, all things considered.

According to this theory, God's motives cannot be explained by the goodness or evil of the objects of God's intentional states. God loves what he loves and has the other emotional attitudes he has, because of features of the object and God's relation to the object, but not because those features are good or bad. God does not respond to the good or bad of the object *per se*. Rather, God has the attitude he has because it is what it is, and it is related to him in a certain way. Because God is the perfectly good being, that attitude determines the goodness or badness of the object.

An important benefit of divine anti-realist theories is that they are not forced to play the quantity game; they need not maintain that God weighs the goods of a world, including the good of free will, against the evils that go with it. To my mind, any argument that defends evil on the grounds that good outweighs it is very fragile both because it is hard to believe that good outweighs evil in our world, and because good does not eliminate evil even when it outweighs it, a point to which I will return at the end of this chapter. According to divine anti-realism, God does not weigh anything, since the existence of good and evil and the quantity of each is not determined in advance of God's motives/reasons for creating what he creates.

Solutions of this type resolve the problem of the logical incompatibility of evil with the existence of a good God, but there is another version of the problem they do not answer. At the beginning of this chapter I said that I do not think that natural and moral evils have anything in common except that instances of both seem to be contrary to the motives of a good God. There are particular features of the world that seem, on the face of it, to be incompatible with the motives of a loving God: the suffering of a certain animal, a particular parent's loss of a child, the humiliation a particular person experiences by the act of another. Even if the divine anti-realist is right that what makes these things evil is that God permits them while hating them, we can still ask why God permits them. The fact that they are evil need not play any part in the formulation of the problem. All we need do is to point to such things and ask, "Would you expect a loving and good God to permit *that?*" Presumably the answer is no. This way of posing the problem has been used to great effect by William Rowe in his formulation of the evidential problem of evil, the topic of the next section.

7.3   The Evidential Problem of Evil

The evidential problem of evil is harder to answer than the logical problem in two ways. First, the evidential problem aims at a weaker conclusion. The conclusion of the logical problem is that the existence of the God of traditional theism is not possible, given the existence of evil. The conclusion of the evidential problem is that the existence of God is improbable, given the existence of evil. The evidential argument cannot be answered by Plantinga's strategy of finding a proposition that is logically possible, consistent with the existence of God, and which together with the existence of God entails the existence of evil. A proposition such as (3′) or (3″) may satisfy those conditions and consequently be an adequate defense of theism against the logical problem, but if (3′) and (3″) are improbable, neither will succeed in answering the objection that evil makes the existence of God improbable.

A second reason the evidential form of the problem is harder to answer is that it is usually not formulated in terms of evil in general, but points to particular examples of events that pose a *prima facie* conflict with the existence of God. William Rowe (1979) has made famous the example of a fawn slowly burning to death in a forest fire. Rowe does not claim that such an event is logically inconsistent with the existence of God, nor does he focus on general premises such as Mackie's (3). He agrees that it is possible that an omnipotent and perfectly good God would have a reason to permit the fawn to suffer such a horrible death. Nonetheless, he says, we are justified in thinking there is probably no such reason. Examine the situation carefully. Consider all angles and all probable consequences. If you think there is a small chance that some good could come from the fawn's suffering, consider that also. Taking everything into consideration, what would you say is more likely, given the fawn's suffering – that there is a God or that there is not a God? Rowe thinks it is the latter. The fawn's suffering is evidence against the existence of God even if it is not a proof of atheism. Rowe calls instances of evils like the fawn's suffering *gratuitous evils*. A gratuitous evil is one for which we are justified in believing that there are no countervailing goods that cannot be obtained without the suffering.[8]

In reply, Stephen Wykstra (1996) has criticized Rowe's argument on the grounds that it is a fallacious argument from ignorance, what he calls a "noseeum argument" (If you don't see 'em, they ain't there). The problem is that sometimes when you do not see any evidence for the existence of something, it is probable that it does not exist, but other times you are in no position to say that it probably does not exist. Suppose you look around your recently cleaned-out garage and you don't see a dog. You conclude, justifiably, that there probably is no dog in the garage. But suppose instead that you look around and don't see any fleas. You may not justifiably conclude that there probably are no fleas in the garage. The reason is that the garage would look the same to you whether there were fleas there or not. So lack of evidence for p may or may not be evidence for not p.

To take another example, suppose your spouse asks you whether the milk in the refrigerator is sour. Ordinarily, if you smell it and it doesn't smell sour, you may conclude that it probably isn't sour, but if you have a cold, you know the milk would smell the same to you whether or not it was sour. You are not justified in concluding that the milk is probably not sour. Similarly, Wykstra argues, we

---

8   Given what I said in the previous section on divine anti-realism, I think that Rowe's argument is stronger if the examples he cites are not called gratuitous *evils*. It is sufficient to point to instances such as the suffering fawn, and then ask, "Would you expect an omnipotent and perfectly good God to be motivated to permit that?" Designating them as evil shifts the discussion away from the motivational incongruity to the definition of good and evil.

cannot conclude from the fact that we do not see any reason justifying God in permitting the fawn to suffer that there probably is no such
reason, since the situation would look the same to us whether or not
there was a reason. Given the infinite difference between human cognitive abilities and divine purposes on the hypothesis of traditional
theism, there is no reason for us to expect to be aware of God's reason
for permitting suffering, even if there is one. It is even less likely that we
would be able to identify such a reason, given human faculties, than it
is for us to be able to see a flea in the garage by casually looking around
or identifying sour milk when we have a head cold.

How can we tell the difference between those situations in which
lack of evidence for something is evidence for its non-existence, and
those cases in which lack of evidence for something is not evidence for
its non-existence? As I mentioned above, Wykstra thinks the answer
has to do with what we would expect to be able to detect, given the
cognitive situation we are in and our cognitive faculties. In defending
Wykstra against Rowe, Daniel Howard-Snyder and Michael Bergmann
propose a simple principle to capture this difference.[9] I will call it the
principle of the *Requirement of Detectibility* (RD):

> When we do not have evidence for the existence of R, we are entitled to
> believe "R probably does not exist" only if it is more likely than not that
> if R existed, we would be able to detect it.

RD yields the right results for the garage situation and the sour milk
situation. You are entitled to believe there are no dogs in the garage,
but you are not entitled to believe there are no fleas in the garage,
based on the lack of evidence of each. Similarly, you are entitled to
believe that the milk is sour if you have normal olfactory powers, but
you are not entitled to believe it when you have a cold sufficiently
severe to affect your sense of smell. Applied to the evidential problem of
evil, you are entitled to believe there is no reason justifying God in
permitting evils such as the suffering of the fawn in the forest fire only
if it is more likely than not that if there was such a reason, you would
be able to detect it. But is it more likely than not that you would be able
to detect such a reason? Wykstra, Bergmann, and Howard-Snyder
say no.

9   See Howard-Snyder et al. (2001).

What should we say about this response to the evidential problem of evil? One problem is that if we take the view that it is unlikely that we'd detect a reason justifying God in permitting evil if there was one, this threatens to make theism unfalsifiable in an important way. A theory is unfalsifiable if it is compatible with all observations, i.e. incapable of disconfirmation. It is generally thought that a theory is defective if it is unfalsifiable. But there's another problem with RD. Compare the Cartesian hypothesis of an evil genius who is always fooling you about the existence of an external world with the hypothesis that there is no evil genius and there is an external world that is more or less the way you think it is. The world would look the same to you either way. But RD tells us that we are justified in believing an EG does not exist only if it is more likely than not that if an EG did exist, we would be able to detect it. But of course we would not, according to the standard skeptical hypothesis. So RD seems to pave the way for global skepticism. Readers may want to consider whether there is some variation of RD that is immune to these objections and supports the thesis of Wykstra, Bergmann, and Howard-Snyder.

7.4 Theodicy

7.4.1 Hick's soul-making theodicy

Let's go back to Plantinga's distinction between a defense and a theodicy. The former is a response to the claim that the existence of God and the existence of evil are logically inconsistent. Contemporary philosophers are in general agreement that there is no logical inconsistency, so there are defenses that succeed.[10] It is harder to demonstrate that the existence of God is not improbable, given evil, as we saw in the last section. But even harder is an explanation of the reason why a perfectly good and omnipotent God would permit evil. This is a theodicy. According to the Free Will defense, free will is a great good, the goodness of which outweighs the evils it produces in this world. As we saw in the discussion of Plantinga's version of the Free Will defense, it is not necessary

---

10 See, for example, Rowe (1979). Even Mackie (1955), in his classic statement of the logical problem of evil, admits that theists have some options for avoiding outright contradiction.

that the good of free will outweigh the evils it produces in every possible world in which there is free will, but the defense maintains that it is possible that the actual world is better than any world in which there is no free will. This defense asks us to accept the possibility that free will in our world is at least as good as the evils it produces. But why would God want such a world?

One answer has been given by John Hick in his well-known "soul-making" theodicy. Hick adds to the Free Will defense further hypotheses as to what human beings might get out of living a life in which they and other animals are so vulnerable to sin and suffering. Hick says his theodicy is in the tradition of Irenaeus rather than Augustine because it does not make the Fall a key part of the theodicy. In his book *Evil and the God of Love* Hick says he got the idea of soul-making from the poet John Keats, who said that a world of pains is necessary to "make a soul".[11] The idea is that a complete soul in the image of God cannot be made all at once. To be like God requires choice. Love also requires choice. So what God creates is not a fully mature soul in communion with God, which is impossible, but an immature soul with the potential to become a loving, freely giving creature. Sin and suffering are both part of the growing-up process. In addition to being created imperfect and with free will, it is necessary that there be an epistemic distance between us and God in order to exercise our freedom in coming to know and love God.

In this theodicy Hick does not say that freedom itself is a great good that outweighs evil. God wants a world in which eventually created persons exist in a relationship of mutual love with him. Freedom is necessary for persons to reach an end state in which they have this relationship. It is the end state that is the great good that outweighs evil, according to Hick. Freedom is a condition for that good. An automaton cannot really be loving since love that isn't free isn't real love. Unfortunately, love requires suffering and the process of soul-making inevitably includes evils, both natural and moral.

Hick (1978) says that the plan is for the development of each individual human person, not the human race as a whole, so his theodicy addresses the problem of particular evils. "God's purpose has gradually moved towards its fulfillment within each one of them, rather than within a human aggregate composed of different units of different

11   See Hick (1978), p. 259, note 1.

generations" (p. 256). The suffering each person endures is justified by the eventual salvation of that person, and Hick (2001) says that that requires universal salvation. He admits that there is a problem in combining universal salvation with the idea that the loving relationship with God is freely chosen, but he says he does not think they are incompatible.

What about dysteleological evils – severe evils that appear to be self-defeating for soul-making? Some people are so disheartened by their own suffering or the suffering of others that they turn away from God and may sink into despair. Hick (1978) answers that it is an aid to soul-making that the world contains mysteries, and the existence of unexplained suffering (gratuitous evil) is one of them. For soul-making to work, the soul-making effects of evil must not be immediately evident.[12] It is only in the afterlife that the theory will be confirmed or disconfirmed. Education will continue after death, probably in a series of lives, until the soul is perfected and brought into intimacy with God. Presumably, each soul is reincarnated as many times as it takes. So God does guarantee each created person an overall existence that is a great good to him or her on the whole.

But isn't Hick still playing the quantity game? A problem I found with the Free Will defense above is that it relies on the idea that free will in our world is so good that it outweighs all the evils it produces. Hick (1978) has a similar problem because he wants to say that "human goodness slowly built up through personal histories of moral effort has a value in the eyes of the Creator which justifies even the long travail of the soul-making process" (p. 256). So his position seems to be that the good of the end-product of soul-making outweighs whatever evils and suffering are encountered along the way. Such a claim is hard to swallow. Far preferable, in my opinion, is a divine anti-realist theory such as one of those mentioned at the end of section 7.2. These theories do not depend upon the idea that God weighs good against evil, since good and evil in creation do not exist in advance of God' motives (or will or preferences). Elsewhere I have argued that God's motives for us might be something like Hick describes.[13] He may want

---

12   See Hick (1978), pp. 333–6. For a discussion of this aspect of Hick's theodicy see the exchange between Rowe, myself, and Hick in Hewitt (1991).
13   I first defended this in Zagzebski (1991b). It has also been developed in Zagzebski (1996) and in ch. 8 of Zagzebski (2004).

a loving relationship with persons, not automatons, and free will is a necessary accompaniment to personhood. But it need not be the case that God is motivated by the *good* of free will, nor by the good of whatever free creatures do with their free will, nor even by the good of the relationship God hopes to have with free creatures. The idea of good need not enter into God's motives at all, and so he need not weigh the quantity of good against something else. God simply wants a loving relationship with other persons, and allowing persons to be persons is a condition for what he wants. What he wants is good, but he doesn't want it because it is good. Rather, it is good because a supremely good being wants it. I think, then, that combining a divine anti-realist theory with a soul-making theodicy similar to Hick's may produce a viable theodicy.

Marilyn Adams (2001) is another philosopher who argues that God guarantees to each person a life that is a great good on the whole, and this guarantee requires that there be an afterlife in which evils are defeated by participation in the divine life.[14] The idea of defeating evil rather than counterbalancing it is important. What does it mean for a good to defeat evil, not simply to outweigh it? I think it must mean at least this much: If it were possible for a creature to know ahead of time what her entire life would be like, including the earthly torments and the heavenly bliss that would follow, she would choose it. This theodicy would be vulnerable to Mackie's objections unless suffering and other evils are not *means* to the Beatific Vision, where the latter is something that could in principle be enjoyed without the suffering that precedes it. Instead, the entire life of a creature, temporal and eternal, must constitute an organic unity, one in which the temporal component is intrinsic to the eternal component, and the two components cannot be pulled apart. Suffering makes possible a certain way of participating in the divine life. Perhaps each kind of suffering makes possible a different way of participating in the divine life. A person's entire life, including the part that occurs after death, is unique, and uniquely valuable.

Of course, for this approach to be plausible, there must be an afterlife, the topic of the next chapter.

---

14 This suggests to me that there would have to be an afterlife for animals, since animals suffer too.

Jewish and Christian mystics have attested to experiences in which the self is united with the divine and in which they see the world as God sees it. Some interpret this as a foretaste of the world to come. Mystics describe these episodes in terms that are both negative and extreme in their metaphysical implications. The ordinary categories of human experience do not apply, including the categories of good and evil. It is revealing that whereas the great mystics have trouble explaining their experiences in a way that is understandable to the rest of us, they have no doubt that what they are experiencing gives them a higher or truer cognitive awareness than they ordinarily have, and it is one that they would never choose to forego, in spite of its terrifying aspects.

Further reading

There are a number of excellent collections of papers on the problem of evil. See *The Evidential Argument from Evil*, edited by Daniel Howard-Snyder (Bloomington, Ind.: Indiana University Press, 1996); *God and the Problem of Evil*, edited by William Rowe (Malden, Mass.: Blackwell Publishers, 2001); and *The Problem of Evil*, edited by Robert and Marilyn Adams (New York: Oxford University Press, 1990). Plantinga's approach, discussed in section 7.2.2.2, can be found in *God, Freedom, and Evil* (New York: Harper and Row, 1974). Also highly recommended are Marilyn Adams, *Horrendous Evils and the Goodness of God* (Ithaca: Cornell University Press, 1999), and Peter Van Inwagen's Gifford Lectures, *The Problem of Evil* (New York: Oxford University Press, 2006).

Chapter 8

Death and the Afterlife

8.1   Is Death Bad?

In Tolstoy's story *The Death of Ivan Ilych* an ordinary man learns that he will soon die. Like most of us, Ivan fears death, but he is only vaguely aware of what he fears, and the fear intensifies with the growing suspicion that he has missed something important in life. Ironically, people may be more afraid to let go of life when their life has not been very good. It is sometimes said that we die as we live, and it is possible to have a good death, but, if so, we cannot say what it takes to have a good death without knowing what it takes to have a good life. According to Aristotle, it cannot be determined whether a person had a good life until after his death because a person's life can only be evaluated as a whole. Like a film or a football game, when we are partway through, we can say that it is good "so far," but the goodness of a life crucially involves the way it ends and the way its parts fit together. The ending of a life is like the ending of a movie. There is nothing bad about ending *per se*, but some endings are better than others, and what counts as a good ending partly depends upon what precedes it.

The possibility of an afterlife suggests that the significance of death is connected with the life it ends in another way. What happens to us after death may depend upon the way we lived our life. There could be a divine judgment with reward or punishment, or we could move through another cycle of reincarnation. In either case death is the moment of truth. The test is over and the grading is about to begin.

Suppose, however, that death is annihilation, the permanent cessation of all consciousness. In that case should we fear death? Some people would say that annihilation is even worse than punishment, assuming the punishment is not too severe. If you would rather live through pain than not live at all, you might for the same reason prefer to live through pain in the afterlife than to be annihilated. But Epicurus (341–270 BC) argued that that is the wrong way to look at death. In his view, the only thing good is pleasure and the only thing bad is pain. At death all pleasure and pain cease, and a person's existence is extinguished. What follows is neither bad nor good for the person who died:

> Get used to believing that death is nothing to us. For all good and bad consists in sense-experience, and death is the privation of sense-experience. Hence, a correct knowledge of the fact that death is nothing to us makes the mortality of life a matter for contentment, not by adding a limitless time [to life], but by removing the longing for immortality. For there is nothing fearful in life for one who has grasped that there is nothing fearful in the absence of life. Thus, he is a fool who says that he fears death not because it will be painful when present but because it is painful when it is still to come. For that which while present causes no distress causes unnecessary pain when merely anticipated. So death, the most frightening of bad things, is nothing to us; since when we exist, death is not yet present, and when death is present, then we do not exist. Therefore, it is relevant neither to the living nor to the dead, since it does not affect the former, and the latter do not exist.[1]

Epicurus' view continues to receive considerable attention more than two millennia after he lived. In the passage above he makes at least three assumptions: (1) The only thing good is pleasure and the only thing bad is pain (hedonism); (2) If something is good or bad for a person, it is good or bad for that person at a particular time; (3) Death is annihilation. Each of these premises has been disputed.

Consider first the hedonism of Epicurus. Perhaps there are good or bad things that do not reduce to good or bad sensations. Life might be one of the good ones and death one of the bad ones. Many philosophers, among them Christian ethicists, maintain that human life has value in itself, apart from the good or bad features of it and apart from its consequences. If so, death is a bad thing *simpliciter*; it is just plain bad. Notice, however, that even if death is bad in itself, it does not follow that it is bad *for* the person who dies, the question Epicurus was addressing. In discussing the badness of death, we should be careful to separate

1   "Letter to Menacceus," in Epicurus (1994), pp. 28–31.

Epicurus' question from the question of whether death is good or bad for the persons left behind and whether it is good or bad in itself.

But even if we are careful to focus on the issue of what is bad for the person who dies, Epicurus may still be mistaken. Aristotle thought that every living creature has a natural end, or purpose. If it dies before it has a thriving adulthood of the normal length for the species, it has failed to reach its natural end. Aristotle's position explains why we think that it is tragic for a human being to die in infancy or in the prime of life, but not tragic, although sad for the family, when a person dies in old age after a long and fruitful life. According to the Christian view of the afterlife, even the tragic deaths can end in supernatural fulfillment for the one who died, but this does not detract from the fact that premature death denies a person her natural end. On the Aristotelian picture, then, it is bad for a person to die before reaching her natural end, but it is not bad for her to die after living a long, flourishing life. Aristotle's view can explain what is wrong with Ivan Ilych. He learned he had very little time to live when he had not yet lived a fulfilling life or even found out what a fulfilling life would be like. Ivan's life had been fairly pleasant, but Tolstoy wants the reader to conclude that a pleasant life is not sufficient for a good life, which was also the view of Aristotle. On the Aristotelian view of the nature of the good life, Epicurus' conclusion is false. Death is bad for some people, but not for others.

What about Epicurus' second premise? Some philosophers argue that even if we grant Epicurus his first and third assumptions, death is usually bad for a person because the loss of a good thing is a bad thing.[2] If life is good on the whole because the pleasures outweigh the pains, it is a bad thing for that person when her life ceases. And many people also think that if a life becomes irremediably painful for some person, death is a good thing for him because it removes a bad thing. But, Epicurus, asks, *when* is death bad for the person who dies? It can't be before death, and it can't be after death. Whether your pleasant life is cut short, or death ends a long period of suffering, there is no time at which death is either bad or good for you. So if you accept Epicurus' assumption that death is annihilation, and you also think that it is bad for you to lose a good thing (or good to lose a bad thing), you seem to be forced to deny Epicurus' second premise. It might be reasonable to do that, but it is admittedly peculiar.

2   Nagel (1993).

What about the third premise? If it is false, Epicurus' argument is unsound, but notice that that may not affect the truth of his conclusion. In fact, if there is an afterlife, and the afterlife is at least as good as earthly life, death would not be bad for you except in the sense that all major transitions in a person's life involve some loss. But death could still be bad for you in the Aristotelian sense.

But even people whose lives are good in Aristotle's sense and good in every other sense as well often desire immortality. In fact, evidence suggests that the desire for immortality is close to universal. Such people might not fear death itself; it is annihilation that they fear. So if we desire immortality and if death is annihilation, death is feared precisely because it *is* annihilation. If it is appropriate to fear (or dread) what opposes something deeply and strongly desired, then it is appropriate to fear death. This is assuming that the desire itself is appropriate.

What is it we desire when we desire immortality? Some people may want to continue living on earth as they always have and never to die, but everybody knows we can't have that. What we probably want, then, is to continue to exist after death. But that can't be all we want because immortality is not just continued existence after death, it is continued existence forever. The notion of immortality therefore raises issues about the end of time like those addressed in Chapter 2 about the origin of time. Will time continue infinitely into the future? If so, is an immortal being one who exists for an infinite time in the future? If not, is an immortal being one who exists until the end of time? Alternatively, is an immortal being one who becomes timeless? As we saw in Chapter 4, the notion of the timelessness of God is a difficult one, and timelessness is even more difficult when applied to ourselves. Bernard Williams argues that immortality would be boring; eventually, we would run out of things to do.[3] His assumption is that immortality means existing for an infinite time in the future. But if we desire eternal life, where "eternal" means "timeless" rather than "everlasting," it would be so far beyond our understanding, we could hardly say it would be boring. And even if immortality is continued existence for an infinite time, there are explanations of the doctrine of heaven according to which it would be far from boring. Jonathan Edwards (1765) thought of heaven as the infinite good of an ever-increasing union with God. He

3   See Bernard Williams' essay "The Makropulos Case: Reflections on the Tedium of Immortality" in Williams (1973). Reprinted in Fischer (1993).

writes, "Let the most perfect union with God, be represented by something at an infinite height above us; and the eternally increasing union of the saints with God, by something that is ascending constantly towards that infinite height, moving upwards with a given velocity; and that is to continue thus to move to all eternity" (p. 113).

In the ancient Egyptian *Book of the Dead* (approximately 1600 BC) there is a dialogue between the spirit of the deceased, Ani, and the supreme creator, Atum (Chapter 175).[4] The dead man cannot understand eternity because it lacks the features of enjoyable and fulfilling spatiotemporal life, such as food and human love. Atum tells Ani that all the things he has associated with a good life will be superceded by the eternal contemplation of Atum's face, amounting to a communion with the presence of the creator, an interesting comparison with Aquinas' view on the Beatific Vision in heaven, an idea to which we will return. In both cases the afterlife is not described in a way we can enjoy in imagination. We are told that it will be better than anything we can now imagine, and I suppose that nobody would complain if they got something better than they imagined, but it is pretty clear that what people imagine when they desire an afterlife varies considerably.

Evidence of belief in life after death can be found among the earliest humans and perhaps even prior to the rise of *homo sapiens* (see Chapter 1). The first written evidence of belief, or rather hope, in an afterlife, may be the *Epic of Gilgamesh*, first written in Sumerian around 2100 BC. In India there arose the doctrine of Samsara, which was close to universally accepted there by the sixth century BC, although its origin is unsettled. Samsara is the condition of being stuck in a cycle of karma and reincarnation. The ultimate goal of reincarnation is *moksha*, or liberation from the round of rebirth. A form of the doctrine of reincarnation was adopted in Greece in the fifth century BC by the Pythagoreans. They believed that human beings are naturally immortal, but because human nature is flawed, we cannot attain a higher world after death without discipline. The Pythagoreans influenced Socrates, who is portrayed as believing in reincarnation in Plato's dialogue *Phaedo*, which recounts the last day of Socrates' life. In this dialogue Plato presents the first set of extended arguments in Western philosophy for life after death.

The Jews at first had a vague idea of the hereafter that they called Sheol, a kind of existence that was not an end, but neither was it what

---

4   See Faulkner et al. (1994).

most of us would consider real existence. It certainly was nothing as lofty as the unimaginably wonderful. It was more like the imaginably dreary. By the time the Greeks began to threaten the Jewish way of life, however, Jewish leaders started teaching about an afterlife that includes bodily resurrection. The Book of Daniel, written around 165 BC, says: "Many of those who sleep in the dust of the earth shall awake, some to everlasting life, and some to shame and everlasting contempt" (Daniel 12:2). At the time of Jesus the Pharisees taught life after death, whereas the Sadducees disputed it, so the issue was a topic for debate.[5] Christians adopted the idea that the soul will be reunited with the body at the end of time, and later the Muslims did as well. So belief in a bodily resurrection is common to the three Abrahamic faiths, and belief in some form of afterlife is an important part of the teachings of the religions of most people in the world. The descriptions of the afterlife, however, differ considerably.

8.2   Immortality and Personal Identity

8.2.1   The philosophical approach to immortality

Plato thought that life after death could be demonstrated by philosophical argument. Aquinas' position was more modest. He thought that reason supports but does not demonstrate our post-mortem existence. Today's philosophers are even less optimistic about philosophical arguments for an afterlife. Generally those who write on this topic are satisfied with addressing the question of whether life after death is metaphysically *possible*. What philosophy can provide is answers to the question: What makes you at some time in the future the same person you are now? Some well-known answers to that question seem to make survival of death impossible, so there are philosophers who think that the issue of whether there is an afterlife can be settled in the negative at the first step.

Why is there so much focus on the question, "What makes a person at one time the same person as at a later time?" Western philosophy

5   Contemporary Jews do not have a settled view on the afterlife, but consistently take the line that our focus should be on this life rather than on the rewards of a hereafter.

interprets the issue of immortality as the issue of whether a certain person who exists now (for instance, you) is identical with a certain person who will exist after that person's biological death. The first step in answering this question is to propose conditions for the persistence of persons over time. We know that objects of all kinds change while remaining the same object. For example, your car remains the same car after you have the oil changed, buy new tires, get a dent in the fender, and then have it fixed. You continue to exist when you gain or lose a few pounds, change your hair color, or even have a leg amputated. So changes in the properties of a thing do not necessarily mean that the thing no longer exists. Some changes, however, do have that consequence. If a star explodes, presumably it goes out of existence. When a plant dies and its dead leaves and branches are used for mulch, the plant no longer exists. Still other changes are harder to classify. If a prince turns into a frog, does the prince – the individual who was a prince at a certain time, still exist? If the answer is unclear, that is because the difference between changes that are compatible with the continued existence of a thing and changes that make the thing exist no longer is unclear. The issue for the present discussion, then, is what changes you can undergo while remaining in existence. Obviously losing your body is a very big change. Is it like a star exploding or is it like losing your hair?

According to metaphysical materialism, a human person is identical with a certain body. A body is a certain configuration of entities described by physics as it would be ultimately developed. Assuming that the body follows predictable laws of nature, then at some time in the future it goes out of existence permanently. If so, to ask whether the person exists after her body goes out of existence is just to ask whether the body exists after the body goes out of existence permanently. Formulated that way, the answer is straightforwardly "no." In fact, an affirmative answer does not even make sense. Life after death is impossible.

Suppose instead that a person is a certain soul, a non-material entity enclosed in a body that is not an essential component of the person. In that case, to ask whether the person continues to exist after his body ceases to exist is to ask whether the person's soul continues to exist after his body ceases to exist. The answer might be "yes." This was the position defended by Plato in the *Phaedo*.

There is a third historically important position that is more complicated. According to Aristotle, a human being is a certain bunch of matter informed by a soul that is the form of the human species. (This theory is commonly called hylomorphism, from the Greek *hyle*, which means "matter," and *morphe*, meaning "form.") Your body is the material component of you that persists in existence with gradual changes of the matter over time. So in order for the person who exists next year to be you, the body of that person must be the same body as the body of the person that was you five years ago, and in addition, the soul of that person must be the same as the soul of that person five years ago. On this account of the nature of a human person, to ask whether a person exists after the body goes out of existence is to ask whether the same body and the same soul will exist after the body goes out of existence. Most Aristotle scholars say that Aristotle's position was that this is not possible. Suppose, however, that the death of the body does not lead to the *permanent* cessation of its existence. If it is possible that the same body can exist again, and if the same soul can come together with the same body at some point in the future after death, then the person would exist again after death. This was the position of Aquinas.

We will also consider a fourth position, that a person is neither a body nor a soul, but is a stream of conscious states unified by memory. To be the same person next year as you were five years ago is to have (most of) the same memories you had five years ago, in addition to memories acquired in the intervening years. This was the position of John Locke (1632–1704). On this view, for you to exist after your death, it is necessary and sufficient that there be a being existing after your death who has most of the memories you will have at death.

We have, then, four different views on the identity of the human person, each of which yields a different way to approach the question of whether it is possible for a person to survive the death of her body: (1) Same person = same body; (2) Same person = same soul; (3) Same person = same soul + same body; (4) Same person = same memories.

8.2.2   The nature of a human person and afterlife

1. In the *Phaedo* Plato argued that a person is identical with a non-material soul housed in a body that is not itself a component of the person. Immortality follows from the nature of the soul itself. The soul partakes of the eternal realm, has no parts, and is naturally indestructible because it cannot fall apart. In contrast, the body is made up of

components that come apart at death. It is fragile and corruptible, whereas the soul is pure and simple. Plato defines death as the separation of the soul from the body. Continued existence of the soul after death is not only possible, but also required by the nature of the soul.

A somewhat different view of the non-material soul was defended more than 2,000 years later in a famous argument by Descartes, who argued that the possibility of the existence of the non-material mind (thinking substance) apart from the body can be proven by the fact that we can clearly and distinctly form the idea of the thinking thing we call "I" existing without our body or in any extended substance:

> First, I know that all the things that I clearly and distinctly understand can be made by God such as I understand them. For this reason, my ability clearly and distinctly to understand one thing without another suffices to make me certain that the one thing is different from the other, since they can be separated from each other, at least by God . . . For this reason, from the fact that I know that I exist, and that at the same time I judge that obviously nothing else belongs to my nature or essence except that I am a thinking thing, I rightly conclude that my essence consists entirely in my being a thinking thing. And although perhaps (or rather, as I shall soon say, assuredly) I have a body that is very closely joined to me, nevertheless, because on the one hand I have a clear and distinct idea of myself, insofar as I am merely a thinking thing and not an extended thing, and because on the other hand I have a distinct idea of a body, insofar as it is merely an extended thing and not a thinking thing, it is certain that I am really distinct from my body, and can exist without it. (Descartes 1993 [1641], *Meditations* VI, 78)

Avicenna proposed a very similar argument in the eleventh century. He argued that anyone who doubts the substantiality of the soul has only to conceive of himself as created fully formed, all at once, but perceptually and consciously isolated from all external objects, including even his own body and the organs of his senses:

> Then he should consider whether he could still affirm the existence of his self. No doubt he could – and without adding to it any of his limbs or internal organs, not his brain, or heart, or guts – or anything external. In fact, he could hypothesize the existence of his self without length, breadth, or depth. And if in such a state it were possible for him to imagine such a thing as a hand or other organ, he would not imagine it as a

part of himself or a condition of his existence . . . Therefore the self the existence of which he affirmed must be his uniquely, despite the fact that it is arithmetically distinct from the body and the organs the existence of which he did not assume. (Goodman 1969, p. 562)

Many philosophers have thought that an argument similar to the one given by Descartes and by Avicenna demonstrates two things: (1) You are identical with a non-material substance (soul or mind), and (2) It is possible for you (the non-material substance) to exist in separation from your body. Few would claim that that argument shows that the soul does *in fact* continue to exist after death. Even so, most philosophers think that the view that the person is essentially an immaterial substance makes afterlife much more likely than the view that a certain body is what makes a person the person that she is. So life after death has generally been associated with belief in a separable soul.

The idea that there is a separable soul has a long history, both in Eastern and Western philosophy, but it is widely rejected these days among Western philosophers. There are a number of reasons for skepticism about the existence of a soul, but the primary one is probably the view that there is no good answer to the question, "What makes a soul at one time the same soul as at a later time?" The worry is that we wouldn't know how to identify souls in the afterlife, and in fact, we don't even know how to identify souls in this life. We always use a body, together with features of memory and personality, to identify persons. If souls are imperceptible, they are useless in identifying persons.[6] The objection, then, is that we do not have an answer to the epistemological question "How do we know that a soul at one time is the same as a soul at another time?" But whether or not we have an answer to that question, it does not follow that there is anything wrong with the metaphysical position that it is sameness of soul that constitutes sameness of person. We know what we mean by a soul as long as we understand Plato, Avicenna, and Descartes. The issue of how we identify souls is a distinct question.

---

6   A well-known statement of this objection appears in John Perry's (1978) *A Dialogue on Personal Identity and Immortality*. One of the main characters of the dialogue, a woman who is fully conscious but painlessly dying from a motorcycle accident, claims that if we don't know how to identify a soul as the same soul from one point of time to another, then there is a problem with the *concept* of a soul (p. 17).

Even in cases in which we clearly understand what an object of a certain kind is – say, a chair, a car, a computer – there can be cases in which we cannot tell whether or not it is the same chair (car, computer) as before. If my car is completely rebuilt and most of its parts replaced, I might not be able to say with any confidence that it is the same car I had to begin with, but that does not mean that I lack the concept of a car, nor does it mean that there is no such thing as being the same car from one point of time to another. But it does mean there is a problem with "drawing the line" between one car and another. This is relevant to the issue of an afterlife because the changes a person undergoes at death might be drastic enough that it forces us to draw a line between the changes I can undergo while remaining me and changes that make me go out of existence, possibly replaced by a different object. Notice, however, that the philosopher who claims that a person is a soul has an easy time with this question, since the soul presumably undergoes very few changes at death.

2. Suppose next that a person is identical with a certain body. What makes you *you* is the fact that you have the same body throughout your existence. You are the same person at age 70 as at age seven because you have the same body at age 70 as at age seven. On this view, obviously a body is not whatever is made up of particular molecules since your body has none of the same molecules at age 70 as at age seven. But it is reasonable to say that the body remains the same throughout your lifetime because it is a living organism that maintains an organic unity throughout the natural and predictable changes it undergoes. If you are identical with a body rather than with a soul, then the question, "What makes your body at time t1 the same body as at time tn?" becomes crucial because a body clearly undergoes drastic changes at death, resulting in what at least appears to be the disappearance of the body entirely. It seems, then, that if you are a body, you will cease to exist either at death or soon thereafter.

It may seem reasonable, then, that materialism rules out an afterlife, but some philosophers have argued that that conclusion is too fast. Even if you are identical with a certain body, they claim, it is still possible for you to exist again after death because there can be gaps in the existence of a given body. To see why this might be possible, suppose that your computer is taken apart and put back together again after a lapse of time. Is it the same computer you had before? Many people would answer yes and would also say that your computer did not exist during the time when it was scattered parts. Or consider the prince who turns into a frog and then turns back into a prince. Is the pre-frog prince the same as the post-frog prince? If you answer in the affirmative, then you have to choose between saying either that the frog *is* the prince, or saying that the prince went out of existence for a while, coming back into existence when the frog changed species. I can see how a plausible argument could be given for the second option. If so, your body could fall apart and then be put back together again after a lapse of some hundreds (or thousands) of years, and it would be you.

But there are further problems with this view because it is very unlikely that all the particles that make up your body at death are available for reassembly hundreds or thousands of years later. Those particles have in the meantime become components of the bodies of other creatures, including other human beings. For this reason, some philosophers have argued that it is not necessary that you have *any* of the same particles in your resurrected body as in your body at death for the same reason that it is not necessary that you have any of the same particles in your 70-year-old body as in your seven-year-old body. What is necessary is that the body have a certain configuration, a functional relationship among all the components of the body that is identical to the one you had during life.[7] The primary objection to this possibility is that it results in a replica of your body, not the very same body. If God can put together a body that duplicates the material configuration you had during life, with all the functional properties your body had during life, then God could do it two, three, or any number of times. But it is not possible that all those bodies are identical to the body you had during life because it is not possible that two bodies are identical with one. If you are identical with a particular body, then, what makes something your body has to be something that is not duplicable.

3. A third possibility is the view of John Locke that a person is a stream of conscious states held together in the memory. You are like a river that loses some of its water as it flows, but gains water from tributaries. The river downstream is the same river as the one upstream because there is a continuous flow from one to the other, even though the portions of water are not identical at two different points on the river. According to Locke, conscious states connected in the way

7   See Olen (1983) for an argument for the possibility of life after death based on a functionalist view of the human person.

portions of water are connected in a river are what make you you, not a mysterious substance, whether material or non-material. You would be you as long as you have a consciousness that continues what you had yesterday even if, by some unexplained accident, the substance of which you were composed yesterday differs from the one of which you are composed today. In short, Locke maintains that you do not go where a material body or a non-material soul goes; you go where your memories go.

This view also permits gaps in time. You can be unconscious for a period of time, but as long as you wake up with a continuation of the same consciousness you had when you fell asleep, it is still you who wakes up, no matter how much time has gone by in the interim. This possibility makes the river analogy harder, but we might say that a river can dry up at one point and the same river can continue at a farther point, although this is more problematic for rivers than it is supposed to be for stretches of consciousness. On this view, you can live again after death if it is possible for you to wake up at some time after death with the same memories you had at death.

There are some problems with this view of personal identity. Just as rivers can branch off into two distinct streams, consciousness can also. If you are whoever it is who wakes up with the memories you have now, what if two people wake up with the same memories? You cannot be two distinct persons, but the memory criterion does not rule that out. Furthermore, you might think that there are unconscious states that are part of you, such as unconscious desires, but the memory theory of identity does not include these states. In addition, your values and commitments may be essential to you now and determine that your future states of consciousness can only go in certain ways, like a river that can flow in some directions but not others. This point does not falsify the memory theory of identity, but it would require that it be amended.[8]

4. The fourth possibility is the Aristotelian/Thomistic view that you are a combination of matter and form. You are a form (soul) that informs a body. A human being is a composite of the material and non-material. For you to exist in the future is for the same soul to

---

8 Shoemaker and Swinburne (1984) provide a more detailed, but still accessible, introduction to various theories of personal identity. They discuss dualism, body theories, Locke's memory theory, as well as some more recent theories that attempt to improve on Locke.

inform the same body you had during life. According to Aquinas, this is what happens at the resurrection. This view inherits many of the complications of both the view that you are a soul and the view that you are a body. One feature of Aquinas' position that seems particularly problematic to me is that he accepted Aristotle's position that you and I have the same qualitatively identical form (the form of humanity), and the difference between us is due to the differences in our matter. Readers may want to consider the implications of this position for personal identity over time, but what I want to do now is to sketch out a variation of the Thomistic position that I think is coherent and has some chance of explaining how it is possible for you to exist at some time after your bodily death.

A quasi-Thomistic theory of personal identity
You have a soul (form) that is a particular. It is unique to you, although it is very similar in powers and capacities to other human forms. It is irreplaceable and non-duplicable. Your form can exist apart from a body, but in a greatly impaired state, since it needs the sense organs of the body to get experience and to gain knowledge. Your soul informs a bunch of matter during life and your form makes the matter it informs a living organism. Your living body just is whatever bunch of matter is informed by your form. At death your body dies and then ceases to exist, while your soul exists in a defective state. Perhaps you are unconscious when in this state. At the resurrection your form informs some matter again. The matter informed by your form at the resurrection is the same body as the one you had during life because it is matter informed by the same form. It is not necessary that your body be composed of the same material particles at the resurrection as at death any more than it is necessary that your body at age 70 have the same particles as at age seven. What makes a resurrected body the same body as the pre-mortem body is the same as what makes a body at age 70 the same body as at age seven: it is matter informed by the same form. When your soul informs some matter, the resulting body has a certain configuration determined by your form. So when you are resurrected, your body has the same general appearance and functions in a way that is recognizably your own. If memories and personality traits are properties of the soul (form), then the newly resurrected informed body would have the same memories and personality traits as during life. If there is anything unique in the way you think and

experience, that also would be an aspect of your resurrected self. Your resurrected body cannot be duplicated because your form can only inform one bunch of matter at a time, and a form cannot be duplicated.

The principal difference between my theory above and the theory of Aquinas is that on my theory a human form is the unique instantiation of an individual essence, so it is non-duplicable, unlike a form such as humanity that is shared by all human beings. The form, not the matter, individuates the person. In this respect the theory is more Platonic, but the function of the body is like that described by Aquinas rather than Plato.

This theory has advantages over the more common theories of personal identity. It fully respects the ordinary intuition of the uniqueness of persons, the idea that each person is fundamentally and necessarily different from every other human being, and indeed, fundamentally different from every other being in existence. A person cannot be duplicated, even in principle. If there is a human soul, the source of individuality must be something about the soul, not the matter of which the human body is composed. The latter can be duplicated, split, and continuously changes. The theory gives a straightforward answer to the question of what makes a human body at one time the same as at another time, while avoiding the puzzles that arise from theories of bodily identity that allow the body to be duplicated or split. The primary objections to my theory are the same as the objections to any theory of a persistent, non-material soul. I have already said that I do not find the epistemological objection persuasive, but readers will want to consider other objections to the existence of a soul.[9]

8.3   Arguments for Life after Death

8.3.1   Philosophical defense of an afterlife

As mentioned above, contemporary philosophers give almost all their attention to the thesis that life after death is possible rather than to

---

9 Readers interested in dualism may want to look at Swinburne (1997) and Smythies and Beloff (1989).

arguments that it is actual. Even religious philosophers who believe in an afterlife typically say that it takes a miracle to keep a person in existence after death or to bring her back into existence after a period of non-existence.[10] Nonetheless, there have been some arguments in philosophical history for life after death. We have already considered one of them, Kant's argument that morality does not make sense unless we postulate a God and an afterlife in which the good are rewarded and the bad punished (Chapter 6). A more straightforward argument for an afterlife can be given if we begin with the assumption of God's existence.

Suppose that there is a God who is perfectly good, a loving creator of the entire universe. What would such a God desire for his creatures? It is obviously impossible to answer such a question in any detail, but it does seem reasonable that God would want his creatures to be fulfilled in the natures with which he endowed them. Aquinas argued that in a universe governed by a benign being, natural desires must be capable of satisfaction (*Summa Theologica* I, q. 75, art. 6, corpus). God might also want to have a satisfying relationship with those creatures. So he would want his creatures to be as happy as they are capable of being, to have their natural desires satisfied, and possibly he would want to have a permanent relationship with some of those creatures for his own sake as well as for theirs. If human beings naturally desire immortality, it would follow that immortality can be achieved. Immortality for some creatures would be required if God desires a permanent relationship with those creatures.

Assuming that God wants human beings to be happy, what would that happiness consist in? Aquinas maintains, like Aristotle, that the natural end of human beings is happiness, but unlike Aristotle, he interprets that desire as an obscure awareness in each person that their ultimate goal is union with the supreme good. In this respect Aquinas is closer to the Socrates of Plato's *Symposium*, where Socrates defines love as the desire for the perpetual possession of the Good, and the Good is an eternal Form outside the realm of human life (206a).[11] Since for Aquinas, the supreme good is God, it follows that human beings

---

10   See, for example, van Inwagen (1978).
11   Socrates actually says that love is desire for the perpetual possession of Beauty (*to kalon*). Many scholars believe that Plato equated the Form of Beauty and the Form of the Good, but others dispute that interpretation.

have a natural but obscure desire for union with God, the supernatural end for which all human beings were created. This occurs in the Beatific Vision, which Aquinas describes as the intuitive vision of God in his essence. Since a finite intellect cannot grasp an infinite being by its own powers, supernatural help enhances the human intellect to make the vision possible. God is both the ultimate end of the human intellect, and the ultimate end of human desire. The secondary object of the Beatific Vision is knowledge of the beings and events of creation seen through the divine essence in which all things are known. Aquinas does not stress the joy of personal relationships in heaven, but his student Giles of Rome speculated that the saints form a heavenly *societas perfecta* in which they experience the happiness of human relations.[12]

8.3.2   Empirical evidence for life after death

People in the contemporary world tend to be much less impressed with philosophical arguments than with empirical evidence for an afterlife, in particular, so-called near-death experiences (NDEs). These are experiences of people who either were very close to death, or, in some cases, met the criteria for clinical death, but revived to recount their experience. Raymond Moody's *Life After Life* (1976) raised public awareness of this phenomenon and led to a number of intriguing scholarly studies of NDEs.

Descriptions of NDEs are remarkably similar. Although there are some variations in the reports, and they vary in their completeness, researchers have identified the core elements of a normal, complete NDE. Kenneth Ring (1980a) did a study based on interviews of over a hundred people who had come close to death, and found that while not all of them had NDEs, many did. According to Ring, a core experience includes each of the following stages: 1) a sense of peace and well-being; 2) separation from the body; 3) entering a dark void or tunnel; 4) seeing a bright and beautiful light; and 5) entering a beautiful world that seems to be the origin of the light. Each progressive stage is less frequent. Of the people Ring interviewed, 60 percent experienced stage 1, 37 percent stage 2, 23 percent stage 3, 16 percent stage 4, and 10 percent stage 5. Among those who progress to stage 5, some report

12   McDannell and Lang (1988).

meeting relatives and/or a Being of Light. Some people also undergo a "life review" during which they view a summary of their life and must then choose whether to stay or return to their earthly life. The remarkable similarities among the reports demands explanation.

Large numbers of people have had such experiences, and they seem to be widely distributed in the population. They are not limited to certain types of people such as people with religious beliefs or people who have prior knowledge of NDEs. Neither age, sex, nor marital or economic status increases the likelihood of having an NDE. Children have later reported having NDEs when they were younger than one year old (Ring and Valarino 2000, chap. 4).

Are NDEs evidence for life after death? Many who have had an NDE themselves strongly believe that they are. They say that they died, and yet continued to have conscious experiences; they even separated from their body and viewed it from above. This would appear to provide not just evidence, but direct proof that conscious life continues after bodily life has ceased. Skeptics object that it is not clear that those who have had NDEs were dead. For example, Karl Jansen argues that "the NDE can never be evidence for life after death on logical grounds: death is defined as the final, irreversible end, and anyone who 'returned' did not, by definition, die" (Bailey and Yates 1996, p. 267). In offering this objection, Jansen defines death in a way that rules out the possibilities of surviving death and returning from death. These possibilities should not be ruled out *a priori*; it seems that Jansen's definition begs the question.

NDEs would provide strong evidence that consciousness continues after death if there was evidence that (1) the person who had the NDE was dead according to an accepted medical definition of death, and (2) had the NDE during the time in which he or she was dead. Habermas and Moreland (1998, pp. 160–1, 193–7) report evidence of NDEs occurring while the subject has a flat EEG, although Kastenbaum (p. 258 in Bailey and Yates 1996) argues that NDE studies have not provided strong evidence for either (1) or (2).

What would it take for NDEs to provide evidence for conscious existence beyond death? The phenomenon of NDEs needs to be explained, and one explanation is that they offer us a glimpse into the nature of continued existence after bodily death. The key question, then, is whether this, or some other alternative explanation, does the best job of explaining the facts about NDEs. Many alternative explanations have been proposed. One suggestion is that NDEs are brought about by cerebral hypoxia (oxygen deficiency) or anoxia (absence of oxygen), which are known to produce hallucinations (Rodin 1980).[13] However, critics of this interpretation have responded that these conditions do not produce hallucinations that have the kind of clarity characteristic of NDEs. They have also pointed out that some people have NDEs without having cerebral anoxia.[14] So this explanation cannot account for a feature of NDEs (their clarity) or for certain cases (those that don't involve anoxia).

Many other explanations, both natural and psychological, have been proposed.[15] Some researchers such as Kenneth Ring argue that there are features of NDEs that cannot be explained by any of the proposed natural and psychological explanations, while others are unconvinced.[16] But those who take a scientific approach to human consciousness ought to investigate this evidence carefully, for the possibility that NDEs are evidence for consciousness after death calls into question the materialistic account of the relationship between brain and consciousness discussed in section 8.2.

8.4   Afterlife and the Problem of Evil

Many traditional theologians have thought that a resolution of the problem of evil requires a doctrine of the afterlife in which all the evils of the world are redeemed. What does it mean for suffering to be redeemed? What does it mean for justice to be done to the victims of injustice? What does it mean for the sinner herself to be redeemed? One proposal is that all the sufferings of the world and all the moral evils of the world are superseded in an eternity in which the good are rewarded and the evil punished. But this answer will not satisfy those people who think

---

13   Rodin had something like a near death experience himself and says, "it was one of the most intense and happiest moments of my entire life" (1980 p. 260). Following the experience he says he believed he had been dead, but he now believes his experiences were delusions brought about by anoxia.

14   These criticisms are raised by Ring (1980b), Sabom (1980; 1982), and Stevenson (1980).

15   Good summaries of these are presented in the introduction to Bailey and Yates (1996) and in Zaleski (1987), ch. 10.

16   See chaps. 2–4 of Ring and Valarino (2000).

that a perfectly good God would not want evil to exist at all, and so it should not be necessary to redeem it. They say a perfectly good being would create a world of heaven on earth, a world of no suffering, no moral evil, and no need for a redemption.

I think that an intellectually humble person should admit that we really do not know *a priori* what a perfectly good being would be motivated to do. But those who practice a particular religion have the right to consult their own sacred texts, and by doing so we might be able to make a reasonable inference about the motivations of a perfectly good God for creatures such as ourselves. In the case of Christianity, it can be argued that we see from the Scriptures that God wants a world in which good eventually triumphs over evil. The story begins with human beings living in a state of natural happiness, followed by a freely chosen fall, and then a long period in which God brings the world to a supernatural end in which good is triumphant. A good God is motivated to bring about an historical process in time, not an end without a preceding period of suffering and struggle. This is not something known *a priori*, but is revealed through a combination of Scripture, theological reflection, and actual events in history. If the motivations of a perfectly good God determine what is good and bad, and if God's motives bring about or at least permit a sequence of events in which evil occurs but is eventually overcome, then we should humbly accept the conclusion that that is a good history.

But even if a story of human history in which good triumphs over evil is a good one, there is still the question of whether the story is a good one from the point of view of each individual, including those individuals who bear a greater share of suffering or injustice. What about the unfortunate people who are born with biological defects, suffer much, and die young? What about a baby tortured and killed by an invading army? In a famous passage in Dostoevsky's *The Brothers Karamazov*, Ivan tells his brother Alyosha that even if all is reconciled by God in eternity and a child's torture is redeemed, the child's mother should not accept it (1976 [1879], p. 226). The past cannot be undone, and some evils can never be forgiven. No one should accept injustice done to someone they love, no matter what happens afterwards, even if the victim accepts it.

I find Dostoevsky's lament very insightful. It is true that we can never rewrite the past. If a terrible thing happened, it cannot be undone, so whatever forgiveness and redemption are, they do not erase history.

If redemption solves the problem of evil, it cannot be because there is a grand scheme in which good triumphs over evil in creation as a whole. It seems to me that if there is a solution to the problem of evil, then each event in time has to be redeemed. Each disappointment, each misunderstanding, each instance of human or animal pain, each frustration, anxiety, or fear has to be redeemed. And what it means to be redeemed is at least this much: If it were possible for the creature to know ahead of time what living through a life in need of redemption would earn it in the end, that creature would choose to live that life. Each creature would be motivated to live his or her entire life from beginning to end. This is what I meant by defeating evil at the end of Chapter 7. What I would say to Dostoevsky is that he is right that the child's torture is not redeemed unless it is redeemed from the point of view of the mother. So redemption must include something else: If it were possible for a creature to know ahead of time how their loved one's life would go from beginning to end, he or she would accept it. But where I think Ivan is mistaken is in his assertion that the mother could never accept her child's torture, no matter how the subsequent story of her child's life goes.

Can there be such a story? I think that the answer is yes only if there is an afterlife for each individual who suffers evil. At the end of Chapter 7 I noted that the idea of defeating evil seems to require an afterlife for animals and all sentient beings. Not many philosophers have defended an afterlife for animals because it is not part of the religious tradition of the West, but as long as animal suffering is a problem, not just because it adds to the quantity of evil in the world, but because it is a problem for the relationship between the Creator and the suffering animals, then it seems to me that it is reasonable to hope for an afterlife for animals.

The issue of whether there is an afterlife and, if so, what it is like, is not a primary philosophical question. By that I mean that it is a question that cannot be answered without answers to a series of previous questions such as whether there is a God, how God relates to human creation, and what the natural end of human life is like. Different religious traditions answer these more basic questions in different ways, and their answers to the questions about an afterlife differ accordingly. In contrast, the empirical studies of NDEs attempt to make the question of an afterlife a primary question. This approach is disputable, as we have seen, but it has the advantage of accessibility to a much wider range of people than arguments that depend upon a particular religious tradition.

Great literature is also accessible to a wide range of people, and Tolstoy's powerful short story *The Death of Ivan Ilych* has fascinated and bothered readers, who see themselves in the story's protagonist, for well over a century. We all want to know how the story ends because we think that its ending might foretell the way we ourselves will die. When Tolstoy wrote the story, he obviously had not yet experienced dying, nor, as far as I know, had he ever had a near-death experience. But at the conclusion of the story we get Tolstoy's conviction – or perhaps it is a just a hope – of what the death of a man like Ivan Ilych might be like.

"And death . . . where is it?"

He sought his former accustomed fear of death and did not find it. "Where is it? What death?" There was no fear because there was no death.

In place of death there was light.

Further reading

There is not a large literature by philosophers on life after death, although philosophers who write on the mind/body problem sometimes discuss the implications of their position for an afterlife. Recommended collections of readings include *Soul, Body, and Survival: Essays on the Metaphysics of Human Persons*, edited by Kevin Corcoran (Ithaca: Cornell University Press, 2001), and Paul Edwards' anthology *Immortality* (Amherst, N.Y.: Prometheus Books, 1997), which includes a number of readings by historically important figures. John Martin Fischer's anthology *The Metaphysics of Death* (Stanford: Stanford University Press, 1993) focuses on the issue of whether death is a bad thing, with a number of responses to Epicurus, discussed in the first section of this chapter.

Chapter 9

The Problem of Religious Diversity

9.1 Introduction

Unlike the other chapters of this book, the topic for this chapter has a short history, and the explanation for that is interesting. Before the modern era in the West, the multiplicity of religions was not perceived as a problem for participation in a particular religion. That is because different religions did not compete for the allegiance of a particular person. The pantheon of gods of one ancient group of people were not rivals of the gods of other peoples. The same point applies to American Indian religions. The indigenous peoples of North America obviously recognize the diversity of what we call religions, but it is not a problem for their own belief because each religion is identified with a particular way of life, a way of life *for* a given group of people, and Indian languages have no word for religion. Each language has a word for the way of life their people follow, which includes religious beliefs and practices, but it also includes many other culturally distinctive practices. So for a Navajo to adopt the Hopi religion, he or she would in effect have to be come a Hopi. Since that is not an option, no Navajo would think of the existence of the Hopi as a problem for the Navajo way of life. This also explains why conversion to Christianity was a problem for the sense of identity of American Indians.

Before the diversity of religions can be perceived as problematic, then, religion must be distinct from the society in which one is born and in which one lives, so it is possible to choose one religion over another. Recall that in Chapter 1 I mentioned that these are the conditions that make conversion possible. Christianity was not tied to a particular culture or ethnic group, but proclaimed itself to be a religion for all peoples, and that made conversion a new historical phenomenon, according to Nock (1998). But the conditions that make conversion possible also make the diversity of religions a problem. If one is faced with a choice, one has to have grounds to choose one over another.

The problem of diversity is heightened if different religions offer competing answers to the same question. Some of the main questions that can be answered differently by different religions are the questions of this book: Is there a God? If so, how many gods are there? If there is one God, what is God like? What does God expect of me? What will happen to me after I die? The emergence of monotheism created a new kind of conflict because not only did it force a choice with polytheism, it also made metaphysical claims that conflicted with the claims of ancient philosophies. When there is doctrinal conflict, it is impossible that both doctrines are true, and this raises the issue that perhaps one's own belief in a given doctrine is false.

In spite of the fact that conflict in belief leads to the obvious conclusion that somebody is making a mistake, the perception of conflict did not lead to the recognition of a problem for one's own belief for many centuries. People simply responded by saying, "We are right, and since they disagree with us, they must be wrong." And some people still take that line. But there are two historical changes since the Western Enlightenment that make it very difficult to take that line in good faith. One is that Europeans became directly acquainted with other religions on a large scale. Throughout the Middle Ages Christianity and Islam were adversaries. Clearly, neither side thought of the other as a realistic option for themselves, nor was there much understanding of Asian religions among either one. Christians and Jews rarely saw each other as an intellectual option, and Jews were more often persecuted than treated with sympathy. But with large-scale trade and travel in the modern period, people began to discover as much wisdom, goodness, intelligence, and integrity among the people practicing other religions as among those practicing their own. It is very hard to dismiss people you admire as just plain wrong. At the least, you need an explanation for their mistake, if they are making one.

A second reason for a change in response to religious diversity was philosophical. During the Enlightenment, the perception of the world in the West changed dramatically. Philosophers began to give up the idea that I can treat my own point of view as epistemically privileged just because it is my own. The general attraction to egalitarianism in this period was reflected in the attraction to intellectual egalitarianism, a position strongly endorsed by John Locke.[1] The idea is that all normal human beings are roughly equal in the capacity to get knowledge. Aside from the fact that some have acquired greater expertise or have greater access to information in some fields, there are no epistemic elites. The conclusion is that I am not being epistemically honest if I treat my own subjective viewpoint as privileged. Locke combined his egalitarianism with optimism about the human ability to get knowledge, but there is a pessimistic interpretation that also comes from the Enlightenment. According to this interpretation, subjective points of view are equally bad ways to get the truth. All of them are limited and distorted, so it does no good to replace your own perspective with someone else's perspective, one that is equally limited and distorted. What *is* superior is the viewpoint of an impartial observer, a being without culture or history or personal preferences. If we could imagine what the world would look like from the standpoint of such a being, we would have the most objective description of reality we could get, and that perspective would be superior to the one we have.

There have been numerous attacks on the superiority of the impartial viewpoint in the post-modern period, but it continues to attract philosophers because when we find it in operation, such as in physics or in mathematics or in the much more modest form it takes in the rule of law, we value it. On the other hand, we know that there are many disagreements in belief that cannot be resolved from such a perspective. But that does not make the subjective perspective any better. We know that there is more than one such perspective, and if you accept epistemic egalitarianism, there is no reason to think one is any better than another. So if disagreement cannot be resolved by an impartial, objective viewpoint either, then the conscientious seeker of truth seems to be left without a way to resolve the matter of what to believe in cases of irresolvable conflict. Let me call this the Enlightenment worry: *Irresolvable disagreement over a belief threatens the conscientiousness of the belief.* Since one of the most important areas in which there is irresolvable conflict is in the area of religious belief, many philosophers and ordinary people find that belief in a particular religion has been intellectually undermined.

---

1   For a discussion of Locke's egalitarianism, see Richard Foley (2001), pp. 89–92.

However, it is difficult to consistently take the line that irresolvable disagreement about a belief is threatening to it. First, if we feel threatened by disagreement, it must be because we are egalitarian enough to think that such disagreement makes our own beliefs less likely to be true, and so we should withhold belief in such cases. But if we do that, we may be depriving ourselves of beliefs in an important domain, thereby guaranteeing that we will not get the truth in that domain. By doing that, we deny ourselves important elements of a desirable life. People who do not have beliefs in important domains, who turn away from ultimate questions, tend to be shallow people.

There is another reason why it is difficult to consistently maintain that irresolvable disagreement threatens our own beliefs. The truth is, most of us are not epistemic egalitarians. In particular, I don't think many of us worry about disagreements with people whom we do not admire. If you believe acts of terrorism or genocide are wrong (by whatever definition you want), I doubt that you think the conscientiousness of your belief is threatened when you find out there are people who disagree, even though you are not likely to resolve the conflict by talking it over with them. If you think that it is a bad idea to devote your life primarily to acquiring money and fame, I doubt that it will bother you to find out that there are people who think the contrary. If you think it is important to do a good job in your role as a student, a neighbor, an employee, or a friend, it won't threaten your belief if you find out that not everybody thinks that way. Nor should it. What really bothers us, I think, is that we recognize admirable people among those who believe differently than we do about certain things and we observe that the beliefs of such people may conflict with each other. It is not really irresolvable disagreement that threatens us, but irresolvable disagreement among people we admire and between people we admire and ourselves. This is why sympathetic contact with other cultures is so important in generating the problem of this chapter. Even if we reject intellectual egalitarianism, we cannot honestly reject the view that there are intellectually admirable people who think differently than we do.[2]

---

2 Much of this section has been adapted from the beginning section of my paper "Self-trust and the diversity of religions" (2006).

9.2 Exclusivism and Inclusivism

The most common position on religious diversity among Christians until approximately the middle of the twentieth century was exclusivism: There is only one true religion – mine – and nobody who practices any other religion can be saved. This view is *exclusivist* in two senses. First, it is exclusivist about truth, since it maintains that the doctrines of only one religion are true. Of course, this view needs to be qualified because the teachings of every religion evolve over time even if the central teachings remain the same, so even from a perspective internal to a given religion, various prohibitions can change, such as eating meat on Friday among Catholics, and the teaching of a religion about other religions can also change, just to take some obvious examples. So exclusivism about truth needs to be clarified by reference to central doctrines, and the way to do that can be fairly complicated. How would we determine the set of central Christian doctrines? Does it include only the content of one of the creeds of the early Church? If so, which one? Does it include all the Hebrew and Christian Scriptures? Does it include documents of Church councils? Does it include the writings of prominent theologians? The answer to the last question is undoubtedly no, but the question is not silly and it shows the complexity of the position. Of course, exclusivism about truth does not commit a person to denying that other religions teach many truths. It is only when the teachings of other religions conflict with the teachings of one's own that exclusivism is relevant. Notice finally that exclusivism is the position that only one religion teaches the truth in its central doctrines, but exclusivists always add that that religion is their own. I've never heard of anyone who maintained that only one religion teaches the truth, but it is somebody else's religion that does so.

The position above is exclusivist in a second sense as well. It is exclusivist about salvation. Salvation or something comparable can be attained only in the way a certain religion says it can be attained. For religions that require belief, an individual has to believe in the doctrines of a particular religion in order to be saved. In the Christian form of salvation exclusivism, this means that only Christians can go to heaven. There are also forms of salvation in other religions and views that are exclusivist about the form of salvation they teach. For example, Buddhists teach that nirvana can only be reached by following certain practices. Exclusivism about salvation is obviously quite severe, and it is the first form of exclusivism to be rejected by many Christians.

Exclusivism about truth, and perhaps also about salvation, has sometimes been defended by an account that explains why the believers in a particular religion are epistemically privileged. Alvin Plantinga (2000a) defends exclusivism about truth in Christianity by arguing that it is part of Christian doctrine that the Holy Spirit has given the gift of Faith in God to some people and not others. And surely Plantinga is right that, if there is a God, God could give a special gift to some people. If so, it would follow that the reason for diversity among religions is that some people are epistemically privileged in their religious beliefs and some are not.

Those who practice other religions may have their own story about why they are right and others are wrong. In the BBC video series *The Long Search* (Montagnon and Eyre 1977), Ronald Eyre asks a Buddhist woman whether she thinks he must have done something wrong in a former life, since he was born a Christian in England. She looks embarrassed and after a pause says yes, he must have. So both the Christian and the Buddhist can make use of explanations internal to their respective religions to explain the fact of religious diversity and to defend exclusivism about truth and perhaps also exclusivism about salvation. The Buddhist woman's story is that non-Buddhists brought their fate upon themselves by their actions in a former life. Plantinga's story is that the Holy Spirit freely gives grace to some and not others. If we reject these stories, I doubt that it can be on grounds of intellectual egalitarianism, since, as I've said, I doubt that very many of us are intellectual egalitarians anyway.

Exclusivism about salvation is not as common among Christians now as it was a half century ago. In a famous 1962 paper called "Christianity and the non-Christian religions," the Jesuit theologian Karl Rahner developed the idea of the "anonymous Christian" as his response to the challenge of religious diversity.[3] Rahner argues that the healthy element in each person, that which has been healed and made holy, is the fruit of the grace of Christ, even though the person may not be

---

3 See Rahner (1966). The essay has also been reprinted in Hick and Hebblethwaite (1981), a nice collection of essays by Christian theologians about the problem of religious diversity.

consciously aware of himself as saved through Christ. This *inclusivism* about salvation is curiously similar to the view of one of the first Christian theologians, Justin Martyr (died 165), who turned to philosophy in a search that he found unsatisfying and finally ended in his conversion to Christianity. He then began to teach that Christianity was the culmination of all true philosophies and that Greek philosophy was a preparation for the coming of Christ. It was the divine Word or *logos* that had enlightened Socrates and other Greek philosophers who were able to see the errors of paganism, Justin claimed. Those in the pagan world who lived according to the divine *logos* within them were unconscious Christians. Even earlier than Justin, an inclusivist view is implied in the Acts of the Apostles 10:34–5, where Peter says, "I begin to see how true it is that God shows no partiality. Rather, the man of any nation who fears God and acts uprightly is acceptable to him."

In recent decades numerous papal documents refer to the salvation of non-Christians. But that position is combined with the view that the redemption of humankind is centered in Christ, a position that combines inclusivism about salvation with exclusivism about truth. As Pope Paul VI put it, the great world religions are not equally true, but "they carry within them the echo of thousands of years of searching for God, a quest which is incomplete but often made with great sincerity and righteousness of heart."[4] Similarly, the Dalai Lama says in his book *Ethics for the New Millennium* (1999) that religion is medicine for the human spirit. Different medicines are efficacious for persons in different cultures and conditions. But when it comes to the truth of the metaphysical claims of the various religions, there we simply have to part company, he says, and treat that as the internal business of each religion. We each think of our own religion as the sole mediator of truth, yet we should recognize that other religions can be salvific (pp. 226–7).[5]

---

4 Quoted by Arinze (2001) p. 162.
5 However, the Dalai Lama also believes that, even though other religions might be useful in the path to liberation, it is only within Buddhism that liberation can be accomplished. Harold Netland (2001) reports that in the Bodhgaya interviews, the Dalai Lama stated, "Liberation in which 'a mind that understands the sphere of reality annihilates all defilements in the sphere of reality' is a state that only Buddhists can accomplish. This kind of *moksha* or *nirvana* is only explained in the Buddhist scriptures, and is achieved only through Buddhist practice" (p. 218). See also Dalai Lama (1988).

An imaginative expression of this combination of exclusivism about truth with inclusivism about salvation appears in C. S. Lewis's novel *The Last Battle* (1956), one of the volumes of his *Chronicles of Narnia*. In the story, a Calormene soldier by the name of Emeth (whose name means "truth" in Hebrew) is accepted into heaven despite the fact that he worshiped the false god Tash.

> But the Glorious One bent down his golden head and touched my fore-head with his tongue and said, Son, thou art welcome. But I said, Alas, Lord, I am no son of Thine but the servant of Tash. He answered, Child, all the service thou hast done to Tash, I account as service done to me. Then by reason of my great desire for wisdom and understanding, I over-came my fear and questioned the Glorious One and said, Lord, is it then true, as the Ape said, that thou and Tash are one? The Lion growled so that the earth shook (but his wrath was not against me) and said, It is false. Not because he and I are one, but because we are opposites, I take to me the services which thou has done to him, for I and he are of such different kinds that no service which is vile can be done to me, and none which is not vile can be done to him . . . Beloved, said the Glorious One, unless thy desire had been for me thou wouldst not have sought so long and so truly. For all find what they truly seek. (pp. 164–5)

There is a third kind of exclusivism, exclusivism about rationality. This kind of exclusivism is much stronger than exclusivism about truth. The exclusivist about rationality maintains that the teachings of only one religion are rational. It is irrational to believe the teachings of any other religion in so far as they conflict with the teachings of the one that is rational. In my experience, religious people who have thought about religious diversity and who try to be as fair-minded as pos-sible typically deny this form of exclusivism even when they accept exclusivism about truth. So they combine exclusivism about truth with inclusivism about rationality. They say, "Our beliefs are true and the beliefs of other religions are false in so far as they are incompatible with ours, but the beliefs of many other religions are still rational. The people who practice those religions are justified in believing what they believe, given their circumstances. If we had been born in their cir-cumstances and had their experiences, we would probably believe what they believe."

It is hard to fault this position since it seems to go as far as possible in the direction of being understanding and non-judgmental, while not compromising one's commitment to one's own beliefs. But there is a problem in combining exclusivism about truth with inclusivism about rationality. One of the main reasons we want to have rational beliefs is that we think there is a close connection between rationality and truth. What makes it a good thing for humans to be rational is that it puts us in as good a position to get truth as we can get. There is a close correspondence between rationality and truth. But suppose there are nine religions, each of which has a different and incompatible teaching on the origin of the universe. At most one of these theories can be true. But are they all rational? Presumably we would want to say yes, assuming that there are no significant differences in intelligence, sensitivity to religious experience, and intellectual and moral virtue among the adherents of the different religions. But if we say that all nine of these beliefs about the origin of the universe are rational, then clearly rationality in this case does not make it likely that a person gets the truth – less than one chance in nine, and so we cannot maintain that what makes rationality a good thing is that it makes it likely that we are going to get the truth. It appears, then, that combining exclusivism about truth with inclusivism about rationality forces us to conclude either that rationality is not really such a good thing, or if it is a good thing, its goodness cannot come from its close connection to truth. I call this the problem of the gap.

Notice also that it does not help to opt for none of the nine, but to adopt some scientific theory on the origin of the universe that conflicts with all nine – for example, the theory of physicist Alan Guth that the universe came from nothing (discussed in Chapter 2). Even if such a theory satisfies the same conditions for rationality satisfied by the nine religions, its rationality does not put it in a better position to be true as long as there are many competitors, each of which is rational.

Of course, we should not exaggerate the extent of the problem of the gap. There *are* classes of belief for which we think there is a close connection between rationality and truth, but those beliefs do not help solve the problem of religious diversity because they are beliefs in which we can realistically expect agreement. And there are probably some religious beliefs in this category. For example, the belief that compassion is good is an almost universal belief, a point stressed by the Dalai Lama (1999). And if we move to a sufficiently high level of generality, we can find agreement about some of the most fundamental religious beliefs – e.g., there is something wrong with the human condition, and when we are in contact with ultimate reality there is the possibility for both profound moral improvement and a higher level of consciousness. But belief at the level necessary for agreement is very thin, and unless we are content to ignore all but such thin beliefs, the fact that particular religious beliefs conflict with the beliefs of others remains a problem.

So religious diversity poses a problem for both religious believers and non-believers. No matter what we believe, we face a problem in our understanding of rationality. If we retain our beliefs because we judge that they are rational, and also judge that the conflicting beliefs of the atheist and of other religions are rational, we cannot maintain that the rationality of each such belief makes it likely to be true. It appears that we have no reason to think that one rational belief is preferable to a conflicting rational belief on the grounds that it is rational. The most we can say is that the rationality of a belief makes it preferable to an irrational alternative. Rationality may be more truth-conducive than irrationality, but one rational belief may not be preferable to another with respect to truth-conduciveness. On the other hand, if we give up our beliefs on the grounds that their rationality is not closely connected to getting the truth, we are forced to say that both atheists and believers in all of the world's major religions should give up their beliefs. That seems to force us into agnosticism, but if we take that option, we are forced to admit that we have given up any chance of getting the truth about a very important matter, an issue that directly impacts the desirability of our lives.

As far as I know, the problem of the gap has never been fully resolved. But in the next two sections I will propose two ways to resolve or avoid it.

9.3   The Pluralism of John Hick

An influential perspective on religious diversity is the theory of John Hick, who for some time has promoted a position about the comparative value of the major world religions he calls pluralism.[6] Hick maintains that all the major religions are salvific in that they all offer a

---

6   John Hick has defended this view in many places. See Hick (2004) for his fullest treatment of the subject. For a more concise summary, see Hick (2000).

path to radically transform human persons from self-centeredness to reality-centeredness, a life centered in ultimate reality. Each religion has something analogous to Christian saints, who are the models for this transformation. The fruit of transformation is a life of love and compassion, and Hick proposes that, since we have evidence that all the great religions are productive of a life of love and compassion, we should conclude that they all offer genuine paths to salvation. Hick thinks that the metaphysical conclusion we ought to draw from this is that the salvific ground in ultimate reality is the same in all religions. Hick then uses Immanuel Kant's distinction between the noumenal and phenomenal worlds to explain how so many religions can all be in touch with the same ultimate reality.

Kant argued that it makes no sense to think that we can know the noumenal world, or the world as it is "in itself," independent of our capacity to experience it. What we can know is the world of possible experience, the phenomenal world. That world is necessarily connected to the ways in which it presents itself to our experience, through intuitions of space and time, and through the concepts that permit us to make judgments about it, such as the concepts of cause and of substance. Similarly, Hick argues that we cannot experience God/ultimate reality as he/it is in itself directly any more than we can experience the world of things-in-themselves according to Kant. All we can do is to experience ultimate reality through the experiential and conceptual forms that each culture has developed. Each religion is a different phenomenal manifestation of the one ultimate reality. And like Kant, Hick maintains that phenomenal reality is as real as it's going to get for us; it is not an illusion. It is the only way we humans can experience the world. So the Hindu world, the Christian world, the Muslim world, and the Buddhist world are distinct phenomenal worlds that are related to the world of reality-in-itself in the same way the world of ordinary human experience is related to the world of things-in-themselves.

There is an important difference between Hick and Kant. What Kant means by the phenomenal world is the world as it has to be in order to be experienced by human beings, and so there is only one such world. It is the world of trees, animals, chairs, and all the other objects of our experience that have spatial and temporal relations to each other and are potentially affected by our actions. But Hick cannot make the parallel claim about religious phenomenal worlds, since he maintains that there are as many of them as there are religious traditions. But he *can* say that ultimate reality cannot be experienced except through cultural forms, so each religion is a different lens through which ultimate reality is experienced. We are not equipped with a particular religious lens by nature the way we are equipped with Kant's conceptual categories, but we have to have one lens or another. The Muslim world, the Hindu world, the Buddhist world, and the Christian world are all phenomenally real worlds on a par with the reality of trees, houses, and animals in Kantian metaphysics.

Notice that Hick's pluralism solves the problem of the gap. All the great world religions are true in the sense that they all put human beings in contact with religious phenomenal reality. Of course, if you insist that a belief is not true unless it puts a person in contact with noumenal reality, the world of things-in-themselves, then all the world religions are false. But according to Hick, there is no more reason to complain about the lack of contact with noumenal reality in the religious realm than there is to complain about the lack of contact with things-in-themselves in Kant's metaphysics. The problem of the gap is solved, then, because all the great world religions are both rational and true in the sense just explained.

Hick does not think that every doctrine of every religion can be explained in this way, however. There are two types of religious teachings that do not fit the Kantian model. The doctrine of creation *ex nihilo* and the doctrine of reincarnation are examples of what Hick calls trans-historical truth claims. If one religion teaches that the supreme being created the entire material world out of nothing and another religion teaches that the material world is eternal, they cannot both be right and their differences cannot be explained by reference to different religious phenomenal worlds. If one religion teaches that after death you are reincarnated, and another religion teaches that your body will some day be resurrected and rejoined with your soul, and a third religion teaches that you will be annihilated as an individual person but assimilated into something else, one of these religions may be right and the others wrong, or maybe one is more right than another, but something is going to happen to you after death. It cannot be all three.

Some religions also make historical claims that cannot be explained on the Kantian model. Either Jesus raised Lazarus from the dead or he didn't. Either there was an empty tomb on Easter morning or there wasn't. Hick says that the grounds for these beliefs ought to be the same as the grounds for any historical belief if they are taken literally. Some of these beliefs are false and disputes about them cannot be resolved by reference to the pluralism of phenomenal worlds. But even if they are not literally true, they may be true as myths. A true myth evokes the response of transforming a person into one who is reality-centered, whereas a false myth does not. Hick thinks that the Incarnation is an example of a true myth.

Hick's position on religious diversity has many defenders and many detractors. I want to mention just three problems with it. First, if Hick truly means that each phenomenal world is a real one, then, as George Mavrodes (2000) has argued, he is a polytheist. Perhaps the charge of polytheism is not quite fair because Hick is a phenomenal polytheist and a noumenal mono-something (not "theist" because he is not willing to call the ultimate reality "God"). But on the noumenal level Hick is committed to the most negative of negative theologies: We cannot say that the ultimate reality is personal or impersonal, one or many, temporal or timeless, God or being itself. So Hick's position appears to be a combination of polytheism and negative theology. Neither of these positions may be very appealing, although, as we have seen in previous chapters, there is a strong strain of negative theology among the mystics who say that we cannot hope to know what God is really like, only what he is not.

A second problem involves the kind of belief that is justified if one accepts Hick's pluralism. Pluralism seems to threaten religious commitment. Christians who become convinced that Christianity is no more true than Hinduism are bound to interpret that as weakening the connection they thought obtained between Christian doctrine and the truth, and the same point applies to the convictions of Hindus, Muslims, Buddhists, and others. To wholeheartedly embrace a particular religion is to think of that religion as giving one a superior understanding of the nature of the universe and one's relationship to that universe than one would have had without it. This is particularly important for those who think that the universe had a personal creator who providentially guides the temporal world, hears prayers, and responds to them. To be told that the idea that I have a relationship with a personal God is no more true than the idea that there is an impersonal force of unknown qualities which may or may not relate to me at all is to be told that my faith is groundless, or at least, such a reaction is eminently understandable.

202

Third, Hick's separation of salvific beliefs that are phenomenal manifestations of ultimate reality from historical beliefs and trans-historical beliefs about the origin of the universe and the afterlife is not compatible with the central teachings of some religions. In Christianity, for example, beliefs about ultimate reality include historical beliefs about the Incarnation, the Redemption, and the Resurrection. These historical beliefs cannot be separated from the theological beliefs that on Hick's account are about phenomenal reality. Hick's pluralism, then, extends only to a limited subset of the beliefs of major religions and, as Hick is aware, some religions would not accept the way in which he distinguishes those beliefs that are religiously important from those that are not.

9.4   Self-trust and Religious Belief

The problem of the gap between rationality and truth arises from a perspective external to the self. We look at our beliefs the same way we look at the beliefs of others and we think that from that perspective nobody has a privileged epistemic position. That follows if we assume that the external viewpoint is committed to intellectual egalitarianism. If one religion is rational, so are they all, barring special reason to think some of them are untrustworthy. But then there are no grounds for choice among them.

But how do we know what we would see from an external perspective? Maybe we would see that one religion does have a privileged connection to truth. When we say that from an external perspective all religions are roughly equal in rationality and one is no more likely to be true than another, aren't we really just admitting that we cannot figure out how to adopt the external perspective on religion? We *do* have some idea how this perspective works in physics and mathematics. We also have an idea how it works in the law and in ethics – it is the principle of impartiality. But what principle would the external observer of religion use to adjudicate among the different viewpoints on religion? Since we don't know, we assume there isn't one.

This problem is not limited to beliefs about religion. The vast majority of our important beliefs about morality and politics also suffer from this problem, as well as a host of beliefs about matters of personal interest – e.g., whether one movie is better than another, whether my alma mater is one of the most distinguished universities in the country, whether my spouse is looking good today, and so on. If we insist on adopting the external viewpoint on all our beliefs, we jeopardize many of the beliefs most important to us, including those we use in governing our lives.

We might think the problem does not arise when the belief is about an unimportant matter, but that is not the case. Suppose that I recall reading somewhere that coffee is very high in anti-oxidants and I encounter another person who believes that coffee has no such benefit. Suppose also that there is no reason to think one of us is an expert in this area and no reason to think one of us did a more careful reading of the news reports and any relevant follow-ups. If I evaluate my beliefs from an external viewpoint, I will withhold belief in whether coffee is high in anti-oxidants, and I might be willing to do that because it is not likely to have a significant impact on my life. But is it obvious that I should automatically trust another as much as myself? If I do, even though many of the beliefs I would have to give up are unimportant, the *quantity* of beliefs I would have to give up is very important. The conclusion is that if we evaluate our own beliefs the same way we evaluate the beliefs of other people, we are bound to end up with skepticism about all but a very few beliefs – not enough to base a worthwhile life upon.

Many philosophers these days are attempting to put the challenge of skepticism aside and get on with the business of living a life, which includes accepting with confidence the beliefs needed to live a life with energy and purpose. Doing that requires a substantial degree of trust in oneself and the forces that have shaped one into the person one is. As Richard Foley (2001) has argued, any normal, non-skeptical life will have to include a significant degree of self-trust in our intellectual faculties, procedures, and opinions (p. 99). The reason is that any defense of our most fundamental faculties, procedures, and opinions will make use of those same faculties and opinions. For example, we test a memory by perception, we test one perception by another perception, we test much of what we believe by consulting other people, so we use beliefs about them to test other beliefs, and so on. We cannot get outside of the circle of our faculties and opinions to test the reliability of the faculties and opinions taken as a whole; we have to trust them.

Foley argues that self-trust logically commits us to trust in others. He begins by defining three positions with respect to trust. The first is *epistemic universalism*. According to the epistemic universalist, the fact that someone else has a belief gives me some reason to believe it. The reason may be outweighed by other reasons; nonetheless, the fact that another person has a certain belief is a mark in favor of its credibility. What Foley calls egoists and egotists reject univeralism. The *epistemic egoist* maintains that the fact that someone else has a belief is a reason for me to believe it only if I have evidence that the person is reliable, that is, I have evidence that her beliefs are reliably calibrated with truth in the domain in which she is making the claim. The most extreme position identified by Foley is *epistemic egotism* (p. 86). Epistemic egotists maintain that it is never rational to grant credibility to the opinions of others simply because it is their opinion. The only legitimate way for someone else to influence my beliefs is through Socratic demonstration. Anyone who wants to convince me of her belief must demonstrate to me that, given what I already believe, her opinion is one I ought to adopt, but it is never reasonable for me to believe what someone else believes on the basis of her say-so. I might believe what somebody else believes, but the fact that she believes it ought to play no part in my reasons for believing it.

Now Foley argues that self-trust makes both epistemic egoism and epistemic egotism incoherent. Because of the social construction of belief, if we have basic trust in our own opinions and intellectual faculties, we cannot coherently withhold trust from others because in so far as the opinions of others have shaped our opinions, we would not be reliable unless they are. And this trust is not limited to people who preceded me historically. If my contemporaries were shaped by many of the same conditions that shaped me, then on pain of inconsistency, if I trust myself, I should trust them. Even though we tend to be fascinated with differences between people and we like to exaggerate them, there are many more commonalities than differences in human faculties and environment. The similarities among people all over the world at all times gives me *some* reason to believe whatever they believe, given that I have trust in myself and I am relevantly similar to them. Self-trust therefore commits me to universalism (p. 103), but notice that Foley assumes epistemic egalitarianism to get the conclusion. Self-trust, together with epistemic egalitarianism, requires me to accept epistemic universalism. Trust in myself commits me to trust others unless I have special reason to think they are unreliable. I need special reason not to trust them. I do not need special reason to trust them.[7]

Foley says nothing about religious beliefs in his book, but we can easily apply his points to beliefs in religious matters. The *religious epistemic egotist* would be a person who accepts no religious belief on the word of another. He expects a demonstration of the existence of God that uses premises he accepts himself, and he will accept the beliefs of a particular religion only if the same conditions can be satisfied for each doctrine of the religion. It is very unlikely that these conditions can be satisfied by any religion. The *religious epistemic egoist* will accept religious beliefs on the word of another, provided that there is good evidence of the reliability of the source. The *religious epistemic universalist* would grant *prima facie* credence to the religious beliefs of all other persons.

I think Foley's argument that epistemic egotism and epistemic egoism are not coherent positions, given that we have self-trust, is correct, and his argument applies to religious epistemic egotism and egoism. The grounds for having trust in one's own beliefs about religion are also grounds for trusting the beliefs of others, absent special considerations that show them to be unreliable. The position to which we are committed by self-trust, according to Foley, is epistemic universalism. But there are at least two problems with being an epistemic universalist about religion. For one thing, the argument Foley gives for universalism applies only to cases in which the belief of another does not conflict with a belief I already have, but in religious matters most of us have pre-existing beliefs that conflict with the beliefs of others. Secondly, Foley's argument for epistemic universalism assumes intellectual egalitarianism, but as I've said, I think that doctrine is highly disputable.

In spite of these difficulties, a closer look at self-trust may give us a way to handle conflict in religious beliefs. In my judgment Foley is right about that, and I think that the trust we need in ourselves includes

---

7 Foley treats the case in which I have a belief that conflicts with the belief of another differently. He argues that my belief defeats the belief of the other person because by my lights the other person has been unreliable (p. 108). Since it is trust in myself that creates in me a presumption of trust in another, then unless I have special evidence that the other person is more reliable than I am (e.g., the other person is a medical specialist and I am not), my trust in that other is defeated by my trust in myself. Notice that this makes Foley an epistemic egoist in cases in which one's own belief conflicts with the belief of another.

more than Foley mentions. An important element of self-trust is trust in our emotions. Emotion dispositions can be reliable or unreliable, and particular emotions may fit or not fit their objects. But we cannot tell whether our emotion dispositions are reliable without using those same dispositions in conjunction with our other faculties. How can we tell whether our disposition to pity is reliably directed at the pitiful, whether our disposition to disgust is reliably directed towards the disgusting, whether we reliably fear the fearsome, or admire the admirable without appealing to further emotions? We trust what we think we see when we take a hard look in good environmental conditions, and if others agree, we take that as confirmation. Similarly, we trust what we feel upon reflection when we feel admiration or pity or revulsion and we take the agreement of others as confirmation. We trust the emotion we have as an adult more than an emotion we had in the same circumstances as a child, just as we trust a belief we have as an adult more than our childish belief. So the grounds for trusting our emotions are similar to the grounds for trusting our perceptions and beliefs.

Furthermore, trust in the beliefs that lead to action requires emotional self-trust. My belief that I ought to escape a situation is often grounded in fear. The belief that I ought to help another person is typically grounded in compassion for her. The belief that I may not treat people in certain ways is grounded in respect for them. If I trust the belief, I must trust the emotion. So epistemic self-trust requires emotional self-trust. Both emotional and epistemic self-trust are compatible with revising what we trust, but it takes self-trust to trust that the process of revision is trustworthy.

One of the emotions I need to trust is admiration. Admiration is a basic emotion, one that does not have other emotions as parts, and I do not think we can explain what a basic emotion feels like. But I assume that all normal people have experienced the emotion of admiration, and so they know what it is in the same way they know what fear or love or anger is. I would describe the admirable as something like the imitably attractive. We feel a positive emotion towards the person we admire that would lead to imitating the person given the right practical conditions. To trust the emotion of admiration means to have confidence that it is appropriate to feel the kind of attraction and desire to imitate that is intrinsic to admiration. We trust our emotion of admiration for the same reason we trust our other emotions: we have no choice.

Trusting my emotion of admiration may lead me to trusting some of the beliefs of another person more than my own. That can happen when I notice that another person has the traits I admire in myself to a greater degree than I have myself, or she may form her belief in a more admirable way in the particular case than I have myself. Another possibility is that she is very much like my present self, only she has more experience, so she is related to me now the way I am related to my younger self. In such cases I can easily trust another person more than myself, either because I admire the other person more than myself and I trust my admiration, or because the other person has other elements I trust in myself in a greater degree than I have myself, e.g., she has more experience. For the same reason, I will trust some people more than other people. I do that because of the way I trust myself. It follows that intellectual egalitarianism should be rejected.

Now let us return to conflict in beliefs. Suppose that I trust my emotion of admiration in some case more than I trust a given belief I have. And suppose that the person I admire has a belief that conflicts with mine, and there is no other person I admire just as much whose belief agrees with mine. Self-trust would lead me to trust the admired person's belief more than my own. If I am able to imitate the admired person by adopting her belief without changing anything else about myself that I trust even more than I trust the person I admire, then self-trust should lead me to change my belief. That is because admiration includes imitation, given the right circumstances.

But let's consider a harder case. Suppose a person I admire and therefore trust has a belief that conflicts with one of the beliefs I have that I trust. I am then faced with a conflict within self-trust. It is because of self-trust that I trust my belief, and it is because of self-trust that I trust the emotion of admiration that grounds my trust in the other person. But even if I trust my admiration more than the belief, it still does not follow that I should change it. Admiration is an emotion that leads me to imitate the admirable person in suitable circumstances, but often the circumstances are not suitable. I can easily admire Olympic gold medal winners without having the slightest inclination to imitate them, and I can admire the belief system of a Hindu without the inclination to adopt that system for myself. The reason why I would not is the same in both cases: I can't do it. It is not compatible with the self that I am. But the more interesting question is whether I should try. Some religious beliefs are not central to our sense of self, but many of them are. Whether I should change an important religious belief is not simply determined by how much I trust the belief itself, but how much I trust the other aspects of myself that I would have to change if I changed the belief. Given the social construction of belief, trusting a belief commits me to trusting both the individual persons from whom I learned the belief, and the traditions and historical institutions upon which I depend to interpret the belief. Religious beliefs are usually connected to a network of other beliefs, emotions, experiences, institutional loyalties, and connections with many other admirable people, all of which I trust. So I can admire a Hindu for being a great Hindu and an Olympic swimmer for being a great swimmer without any inclination to imitate them. And I think that an intellectually conscientious person will often respond that way.

In the typical case, then, a person's trust in those aspects of himself that he would have to change if he converted to another religion will be greater than his trust in the way an admirable person of another religion believes in her religion. But sometimes trust in the latter can be greater, and so conversion can be compatible with intellectual conscientiousness. I think this is an important consequence of our analysis of self-trust. We should be suspicious of any account of conscientious belief that has the consequence that radical conversion is never a conscientious thing to do, and we also should be suspicious of any account of conscientious belief that requires us to give up the beliefs we have that conflict with the beliefs of others on the grounds that conscientiousness demands an external perspective on the self.

In a situation in which a choice whether to convert is made, some element of self-trust becomes the bottom line – that to which we refer in adjudicating between those elements of ourselves that pull us one way and those that pull in another direction. Lee Yearley (1993) gives a moving account of this process in himself while contemplating an enormous Buddha and imagining what it would be like to become a Buddhist. Yearley writes, "I could imagine attempting to incarnate the excellences I saw in the Sokkurum Buddha that morning in Korea. I admired them, they tempted me, and I believe I could have chosen them and remained myself. But I did not want to choose them, and I hoped that those about whom I most care would not choose them" (p. 247).

Notice Yearley does not say he didn't want to become a Buddhist because he thinks his Christian beliefs are true and Buddhist beliefs are false. Presumably, he *did* think that, but that is not sufficient to explain why he would not become a Buddhist. As long as it was possible for him to change his beliefs, given his admiration for another religion, imitation of that religion was possible. And Yearley might have been conscientious if he did become a Buddhist on that morning in Korea. If he had trusted his admiration for Buddhism more than he trusted the aspects of himself he would have had to change if he became a Buddhist, I think he would have been a conscientious believer. But he didn't change, and his reason seems to me to show us something about the way self-trust often operates. He genuinely admires Buddhism, but he does not like the self he would become if he converted to Buddhism, nor does he want those he loves the most to adopt such a self. He does not try to find some *reason* to reject Buddhism. The bottom line is that he doesn't *like* himself as a Buddhist. He trusts that emotion, and I think he can be conscientious in doing so.

The problem of this chapter is therefore a conflict that arises within self-trust. If I trust my admiration of others with beliefs that conflict with mine more than I trust the aspects of myself from which I gain my beliefs and the traditions that support them, then it is right for me to doubt my beliefs, and perhaps change them. But there is no standpoint outside of self-trust from which I can determine which is more trustworthy – myself or others – so it can easily happen that I have full confidence in my beliefs, emotions, and their sources in family, tradition, and the historical circumstances that shape me.

Admiration may not require me to change my beliefs, but it adds something important to the dialogue between people with conflicting religious beliefs that did not exist in the pre-modern era. What it adds is the feeling that I *would* imitate them if I had grown up with a different social construction of the self. That prevents me from taking the line "We're right, so they're wrong, and that's the end of that." Of course, we think we're right, but there's more to be said. Tolerance comes not from thinking that everybody is right, but trusting that we *are* right in the admiration we have for many people who have very different beliefs, and that logically requires us to think of them as like the self I could have been if I had been raised in a different way.[8]

8 Section 9.4 is adapted from parts of Zagzebski 2006.

Further reading

John Hick presents his pluralism in detail in *An Interpretation of Religion*, 2nd edn (New Haven: Yale University Press, 2004). For more recent books on religious diversity, see David Basinger, *Religious Diversity: A Philosophical Assessment* (Burlington, Vt.: Ashgate, 2002); Paul Griffiths, *Problems of Religious Diversity* (Malden, Mass.: Blackwell Publishers, 2001); and S. Mark Heim, *Salvations: Truth and Difference in Religion* (Maryknoll, N.Y.: Orbis Books, 1995). For collections of essays, see *The Philosophical Challenge of Religious Diversity*, edited by Philip L. Quinn and Kevin Meeker (New York: Oxford University Press, 2000), and a special issue of the journal *Faith and Philosophy*, vol. 14, no. 3 (October 1997).

Chapter 10

Faith, Reason, and the Ethics of Belief

10.1 Faith and Reason in Western Philosophy

10.1.1 Introduction

At the beginning of this book I proposed that the question "What should I believe about the ultimate matters of the universe?" is *the* question at the intersection of philosophy and religion. Philosophy addresses the issue of when it is plausible or at least defensible to believe a certain answer to these questions. In comparison, even doctrinal religions understand belief as part of something else that is more important than mere belief. Religion is a practice, not an academic field, and a central component of the practice of Western religions is faith. This leads to one of the most enduring problems in Western religious philosophy: the perceived conflict between faith and reason. The conflict exists under the assumptions that both faith and reason are processes or states that generate beliefs, and that faith and reason are at least to some extent independent. So it is in principle possible for faith and reason to generate conflicting beliefs.

Faith may not be something that *produces* beliefs; instead, it may be a state that includes beliefs as a component, and these beliefs may sometimes rise to the level of knowledge. It is usual to think of faith as involving trust, commitment, and possibly passion, as well as belief or knowledge arising from a distinctive source: revelation. If so, the potential conflict is not between faith and reason, but between revelation and reason. As Francis Bacon describes this picture, "The knowledge of man is as the waters, some descending from above, and some springing from beneath; the one informed by the light of nature, the other inspired by divine revelation."[1]

If the potential conflict between faith (or revelation) and reason is a form of conflict between two sources of belief, there is nothing mysterious or even surprising about it. We face such conflicts all the time. I may seem to remember something that conflicts with someone else's memory, or I may seem to perceive something that conflicts with my memory, or I may draw an inductive inference that conflicts with a memory, an observation, or someone else's testimony. In all such cases I have to decide which of the conflicting sources of belief I trust more. And even if I trust one source more than another in general, I may not do so in a particular case. For example, I may generally trust my own perceptions more than the testimony of others, but when I first learned that modern physics shows that what seems to be a solid table is mostly empty space, I trusted the physicists more than my perception of solidity, and I did that even before I studied enough physics to understand why objects that appear solid are not solid.

There is room for error in every putative source of knowledge, even when I think the source is God. Suppose, like Abraham, I think I hear God commanding me to sacrifice my son. I know that killing an innocent child is wrong and against one of God's own commandments. Should I believe that God has commanded me to kill my child? Possibly, but couldn't I make a mistake about what I think God is commanding me to do? And isn't the fact that the command is incompatible with other things I know about God reason to think that I might be mistaken about the command? As long as this is possible, it is possible to be wrong even about beliefs one thinks are "waters descending from above." If faith is a virtue, it is not the virtue of believing whatever one happens to think comes from God.

The potential conflict between faith and reason is related to the separation of religion and philosophy, discussed in earlier chapters. I

---

1   Bacon (1966 [1605]), bk II, ch. V, sec. 1. Bacon's view on the potential conflict between faith and reason is complicated. J. R. Milton (1998) writes, "Bacon's own religious views are by no means easy to discern and have been very diversely interpreted, but one thing that is abundantly clear is that he was wholly opposed to the intrusion of religious doctrines, Christian or non-Christian, into natural philosophy; the result of allowing this to happen was a corruption of both, into a superstitious philosophy and a heretical religion" (p. 629).

have suggested that philosophy and religion are separated in the West because of the Greeks. The Greek religion gave the Greeks sacred places in which to perform rituals, and it gave them fascinating myths, but they turned to philosophy to answer the ultimate questions about the origin of the world and the nature and destiny of human beings. Christianity was shaped both by the Jewish religion and by Greek philosophy. Since reason is the method of philosophy, and faith arises within the practice of religion, the separation of philosophy and religion continues within Christianity in the perceived tension between reason and faith. The right way to believe according to the philosophers might not be the same as the right way to believe according to a religion preaching salvation rooted in faith. This issue appeared in the earliest Christian writings, continued to be debated throughout the Middle Ages, and is still one of the most important topics in philosophy of religion.

10.1.2   Traditional religious responses to Greek philosophy

The first-century Jewish philosopher Philo of Alexandria may have been the first philosopher who personally experienced the tension between faith and reason and confronted it in his writing. Philo observed the Jewish Law, but he also belonged to the learned world of Hellenistic culture, in which philosophy was highly prized, and he apparently attempted to reconcile his two worlds. When a conclusion of reason seemed to conflict with a sacred text, Philo often interpreted the text allegorically, although he also thought literal interpretations were valid.[2] Because of his influence on subsequent Christian thought, it is sometimes said that Christian philosophy begins with Philo.

Many early Christians were suspicious of Greek culture and particularly of Greek philosophy. Paul had written: "See to it that no one takes you captive through hollow and deceptive philosophy, which depends on human tradition and the basic principles of this world rather than on Christ" (Colossians 2:8).[3] In the second century Tertullian's outburst against philosophy became famous and is still often quoted:

---

2   See Borgen (1992) p. 38. Borgen says that Philo never thought that literal interpretations were invalidated by allegorical interpretations, even though the latter are more important.
3   New International Version.

"What indeed has Athens to do with Jerusalem? What concord is there between the Academy and the Church? What between heretics and Christians?"[4] According to Tertullian, once you have faith, you have what you need. Philosophy should be regarded primarily as a source of heresy. Celsus, a non-Christian of the second century, claimed that Christians say, "Let no one educated, no one wise, no one sensible draw near. For these abilities are thought by us to be evils. But as for anyone ignorant, anyone stupid, anyone uneducated, anyone who is a child, let him come boldly."[5]

In his reply to Celsus, Origen says, "That the gospel wants us to be wise I may show both from the ancient Jewish scriptures . . . and the New Testament . . ."[6] Later in his response Origen writes:

We would say to him: If you were accusing us of drawing away from philosophy those who have been previously interested in it, you would not be speaking the truth, though your argument might have some plausibility. But here you say that we draw our converts away from good teachers. Show that these teachers are different from the teachers of philosophy or those who have labored to impart useful knowledge. However, he will not be able to show anything of the kind . . . If we turn them away from teachers who instruct them in the improprieties of the Comedy and the licentious writers of iambics, and in all else which neither improves the speaker nor benefits the hearers, and who do not know how to interpret poems philosophically and to choose in each case those which contribute to the welfare of the young, then we are doing something which we are not ashamed to confess. But if you were to show me teachers who give preparatory teaching in philosophy and train people in philosophical study, I would not dissuade young men from listening to these; but after they had first been trained in a general education and in philosophical thought I would try to lead them on to the exalted height, unknown to the multitude, of the profoundest doctrines of the Christians, who discourse about the greatest and most advanced truths, proving and showing that this philosophy was taught by the prophets of God and the apostles of Jesus.[7]

---

4   See Tertullian (1870a [199]) ch. VII.
5   Quoted in Origen, *Contra Celsum* III:45.
6   Ibid.
7   Ibid., III:57–8.

Clement of Alexandria actually became a Christian through reading Plato, and he thought that the way to convert educated people was to show them that philosophy prepares the way for the New Testament, going so far as to suggest that Greek philosophy was a revelation to the Greeks just as the Old Testament was a revelation to the Jews.[8] Both are preparatory to the revelation of Christianity. Clearly, he did not think philosophy conflicts with Christian belief any more than the Old Testament conflicts with the New.

Other scholars of the Hellenistic period were converted to Christianity via philosophy. One of them is Justin Martyr, discussed in Chapter 9. In his *Dialogue with Trypho*, written in Rome in the second century, Justin recounts his two-day conversation in Ephesus (or Caesarea)[9] with the distinguished Jew, Trypho. Early in the dialogue Justin says:

> I will tell you . . . my personal views on this subject. Philosophy is indeed one's greatest possession, and is most precious in the sight of God, to whom it alone leads us and to whom it unites us, and in truth they who have applied themselves to philosophy are holy men. But, many have failed to discover the nature of philosophy, and the reason why it was sent down to men; otherwise, there would not be Platonists, or Stoics, or Peripatetics, or Theoretics, or Pythagoreans, since this science is always one and the same.[10]

Justin continues by presenting one of the earliest first-person accounts of a conversion to Christianity.

In *Guide to the Perplexed*, the twelfth-century Jewish philosopher Maimonides, writing in Arabic, argued that when reason leads us to a conclusion that conflicts with the Hebrew Scriptures, Scripture ought to be interpreted allegorically. In the same century Averroes argued that Aristotle can be reconciled with Islam, a view that influenced Aquinas' view that Aristotle can be reconciled with Christianity. Averroes says, "truth does not oppose truth; rather it agrees with it and bears witness to it,"[11] and Aquinas makes a similar remark (*SCG* I, 7). But Averroes seems to go farther than Aquinas in the way he defends

---

8   See his *Miscellanies*, bk I, ch. V; cf. bk I, ch. II and *Exhortation to the Heathen*, ch. VI. Both the *Miscellanies* and the *Exhortation to the Heathen* are reprinted in Clement (1867).

9   Justin (2003), p. xii.

10   Justin (2003), ch. 2.1.

11   Averroes (2001 [1180]) p. 9.

philosophy. The former maintains that when reason and revelation (the Qu'ran) appear to conflict, revelation should be interpreted allegorically, although sometimes he seems to suggest that truth comes in two forms, a philosophical form and a religious form. Oliver Leaman writes:

> In many of his works, and especially in his Fasl al-maqal (Decisive Treatise), he [Averroes] argues that the highest form of demonstrative reasoning cannot clash with the principles of religion. He claims here that philosophers are best able to understand properly the allegorical passages in the Qu'ran on the basis of their logical training, and that there is no religious stipulation that all such passages have to be interpreted literally. Where demonstrative reasoning appears to conflict with the sense of Scripture, then those capable of demonstration (the philosophers) know that the passages must be interpreted allegorically so as to cohere with the demonstrative truths. Philosophers should be careful when they do this not to offend the religious sensibilities of the less sophisticated, in sharp contrast with the practice of the theologians. The latter frequently interpret such passages so crudely that they either throw doubt on religion itself, or threaten the pursuit of philosophy by raising doubts in people's minds concerning the orthodoxy of the conclusions reached by the philosophers. Language should be seen as a sophisticated vehicle for communicating information to different categories of audience. Religion is a means for the easy comprehension of the majority of the people, and where a hidden meaning exists it is up to the philosophers to discover it and keep it to themselves, while the rest of the community must accept the literalness of Scripture.[12]

Like Averroes, Aquinas thought that reason and revelation cannot conflict, but he was unwilling to say that potential conflict should be resolved by interpreting Scripture allegorically or that there are "two truths," one for the sophisticated philosopher, the other for the simple believer. There are religious truths that can be discovered by natural reason and these are "Preambles to the faith." But there are also truths that go beyond reason and which are learned by revelation. It takes faith to accept these truths, and faith is not just for the uneducated. In the first category are the existence of God and his main attributes. In the latter category are truths about the Fall, the Redemption, what will

12   Oliver Leaman (1998) p. 643.

happen after our death, the Trinity, and particular beliefs about the relationship between God and humankind. Aquinas thought it must be possible to learn the truths in the first category by natural reason, since Plato and Aristotle had done so. The truths in the second category go beyond the limits of reason, and they require faith, but Aquinas insisted that nothing in the second category is opposed to reason.

Furthermore, Aquinas argues that even though it is possible to come to know the truths in the first category by reason, it is better to know them by faith, and all Christians should accept them by faith even when they can also support them by reason. In *Summa Contra Gentiles* he argues that if these truths were left solely to human reason, there would be three awkward consequences:

(1) Few people would possess the knowledge of God since few have the education, talent, and time to do so.

(2) Those who are able to discover these truths for themselves can only do so after a long period of time.

(3) Reason mixes falsity with truth. That is why philosophers argue so much. If we want certitude about divine things, we must get that by faith (*SCG* I, 4).

In the following chapter Aquinas gives a number of reasons for thinking it is appropriate for human beings to believe matters that human reason is unable to investigate. He cites Aristotle in support of his position:

> There was a certain Simonides who exhorted people to put aside the knowledge of divine things and to apply their talents to human occupations. He said that "he who is a man should know human things, and he who is mortal, things that are mortal." Against Simonides Aristotle says that "man should draw himself towards what is immortal and divine as much as he can" . . . He also says in the *De caelo et mundo* that when questions about the heavenly bodies can be given even a modest and merely plausible solution, he who hears this experiences intense joy. From all these considerations it is clear that even the most imperfect knowledge about the most noble realities brings the greatest perfection to the soul. Therefore, although the human reason cannot grasp fully the truths that are above it, yet, if it somehow holds these truths at least by faith, it acquires great perfection for itself. (SCGs I, 5.5)

But how do we know that what we believe by faith is not foolish? Aquinas replies that the "secrets of divine Wisdom" have been revealed to men "by fitting arguments," supported by miracles (SCG I, 6.1). The argument that miracles permit a believer to distinguish between the reliability of their own Scriptures and the reliability of the sacred texts of other religions can be found in much earlier writings, including Justin's *Dialogue with Trypho*.[13]

In Chapter 7 Aquinas insists that although the truth of the Christian faith surpasses the capacity of reason, reason is not opposed to the truth of the Christian faith:

> For that with which the human reason is naturally endowed is clearly most true; so much so, that it is impossible for us to think of such truths as false. Nor is it permissible to believe as false that which we hold by faith, since this is confirmed in a way that is so clearly divine. Since, therefore, only the false is opposed to the true, as is clearly evident from an examination of their definitions, it is impossible that the truth of faith should be opposed to those principles that the human reason knows naturally. (SCG I, 7.1)

But suppose someone offers arguments against a revealed truth. Aquinas replies that these arguments must be either probable (less than certain) or sophistical, and he ends the chapter by declaring that *it must be possible to answer them* (SCG I, 7.7, emphasis added).

According to Aquinas, then, the truths in the second category – those that cannot be demonstrated by reason, but must be accepted by faith – are reasonable in at least two senses: (1) They are not opposed to reason; and (2) They are supported by miracles which accompany the revelation of Christ, and which have been worked through the saints as confirmation of the faith. (SCG I, 6.3)

In the seventeenth century, Locke made the reasonableness of assent to revelation depend upon the reasonableness of belief in miracles. Locke (1979 [1689]) argues that the prophets were reasonable to believe they had a revelation from God because God provided miracles as signs that the revelation was from him. And he argues that they were given the power to perform miracles in order to show those with whom they shared the revelation that it was from God.[14] Hume's famous attack on

---

13 See Justin (2003), ch. 7, para. 3.
14 *Essay Concerning Human Understanding*, bk IV, ch. XIX.15. See also Locke's *Discourse of Miracles* (Locke, 1958 [1702]).

the justification of belief in miracles[15] was consequently interpreted as an attack on revealed religion. The assumption is that the justification for belief in revealed religion depends upon the justification for belief in miracles. In contrast, many Christians maintain that their faith arises from the power of the Word itself and its ability to transform their lives; it does not depend upon the occurrence of miracles, if the latter is a violation of a law of nature. But others maintain that evidence of the intervention by God in nature confirms the divinity of the source of revelation, and evidence of miracles is also evidence of the truth of beliefs distinctive of a particular religion. Notice that on the latter position, the evidence of the occurrence of miracles gives *rational* support to beliefs that are held on faith.

10.1.3   Belief in miracles

Whether or not it is reasonable to believe in revealed religion only if it is reasonable to believe in miracles, it is interesting to consider whether belief in miracles is ever justified. By a miracle I mean an extraordinary event brought about by God for the purpose of giving a message to human beings. The most philosophically interesting case is one in which the event is not only extraordinary, but violates the laws of nature.

Hume's argument that it is never rational to believe that a miracle has occurred focuses on weighing the reliability of the testimonial source for the occurrence of the miracle against the extremely low probability that the event occurred.[15] The problem is that the probability that the testimony is false is higher than the probability that the miracle really occurred, even when the source is otherwise highly reliable. No human being's testimony is as reliable as a law of nature, and so it is not rational to believe such testimony. The falsehood of the miracle report can be explained in a number of different ways. Throughout history, reports of miracles have not been confirmed by a sufficient number of credible witnesses, nor have most of them occurred in circumstances in which fraud can be ruled out. Furthermore, human beings are naturally credulous, and we like to hear and to believe stories about marvelous occurrences. Hume finds it illuminating that reports of miracles are much greater among what he calls "ignorant and barbarous

---

15   See his "Of Miracles," sec. X of Hume (1975 [1748]).

nations" than among those of us who live in "the enlightened ages" (p. 119). So it is highly probable that a given piece of testimony about a miracle is false. In any case, he comments, the alleged miracles that favor one religion are contradicted by the alleged miracles favoring another, so reports of miracles cannot be used to defend belief in one religion over another.

Hume may be accepting the *possibility* that a miracle occurs, but he maintains that it is never rational to believe that one has occurred because the evidence will always favor the non-occurrence of the miracle. Assuming that this is his point, it means that *if* a miracle ever occurred, the laws of rationality would deprive us of ever knowing or justifiably believing that it had occurred. But presumably a miracle would be an important event, something worth knowing. The very fact that it is extremely improbable is part of what makes it important. If we only align our beliefs with the degree of prior probability that they are true, we could never believe anything that we judge is extremely unlikely. We would not only be prevented from believing in the occurrence of miraculous events brought about by God, but we arguably would be prevented from believing anything that would radically alter our previous ways of understanding the laws of nature. This forces us into a strong form of conservatism in our view of the world.

In contemporary philosophy, some philosophers have used Bayes' theorem of probability in formulating and evaluating Hume's probabilistic argument against the rationality of belief in miracles. John Earman (2000) has argued that testimonial evidence can make an alleged miracle A more probable than not as long as the prior probability of A on the background evidence K is greater than 0. The assignment of a probability value crucially depends upon background data. So a set of other beliefs determines how probable it is that some testimony is true. One's background beliefs include a view of the world as a whole that may or may not make room for the supernatural. If there are reasons to believe in a supernatural realm in advance of the testimony of miracles, that makes them more probable. If God's existence is part of the background data, we might expect God to pay attention to his creation, and we might also expect him to want to reveal himself to his creatures. That makes the likelihood of miracles much greater than if there is no personal God.

In Chapter 9 we investigated Foley's notions of an epistemic egotist, an epistemic egoist, and an epistemic universalist, and his argument that the first two are incoherent positions, given the need for self-trust and the similarity among people all over the world at all times. Readers may find it interesting to consider where Hume would fall in Foley's classifications.

He is clearly not a universalist. He is like an egoist in that he demands evidence of the reliability of the testifier before believing the testimony, but he uses his own calculations of the prior probability of a miracle and weighs that against the reliability of the testifier. Since the testifier always loses, he seems closer to egotism in his argument on the rationality of belief in miracles.

10.2   Reason and the Ethics of Belief

10.2.1   The varieties of reason

It is probably obvious that the alleged conflict between faith and reason cannot be resolved without a clarification of the nature of faith and how revelation generates beliefs, but it also cannot be resolved without a clarification of the nature of reason and how it generates beliefs. Does reason by itself produce beliefs? Such beliefs, traditionally called *a priori*, have been thought to constitute some of the most trustworthy of all beliefs. Philosophy itself is usually considered an *a priori* discipline. When medieval philosophers worried about a conflict between faith and reason, they usually had in mind a conflict between something they thought they learned by revelation – for instance, that time had a beginning – and something they thought they could figure out by philosophical reasoning, such as the Aristotelian position that time had no beginning. In the modern era, however, philosophy has had much more modest pretensions. Few philosophers believe that philosophy by itself teaches us much that is interesting about ourselves or the world. Philosophy has to be supplemented with something else – personal experience, empirical data, or traditions that may be left unstated. Nowadays, the conflict between faith and reason is less likely to be perceived as a conflict between religious belief and philosophy, and much more likely to be perceived as a conflict between religious beliefs and empirical data/theories, such as the theory of evolution. The idea of reason is vague, and that vagueness has permitted the faith/reason divide to take on very different forms in different periods of history.

During late antiquity and the Middle Ages, the faith/reason conflict was a conflict between religion and philosophy. That was partly, but only partly, because science in the ancient and medieval world was part of philosophy. Today the conflict is much more likely to reduce to a conflict between religion *and* philosophy, on the one hand, and science, on the other. This is not to say that there are fixed boundaries between fields, but there *are* boundaries and the boundaries can be crossed. Suppose somebody claims that nothing exists but the physical world, the world investigated and described by natural science. That is a metaphysical claim, a claim in philosophy. It is not something that can be either confirmed or disconfirmed by scientific evidence. So if someone thinks that that claim has been confirmed by modern physics, he or she is making a mistake. Suppose instead that someone claims that we know from Genesis that the earth is only a few thousand years old, and that that belief is impervious to empirical evidence. Again, I think the person is making a mistake. But whether or not I am right in the examples I have given, it is clear that there are differences in ways of knowing, and the way we come to get knowledge in philosophy differs from the way we come to get knowledge in natural science, and both differ from the way we come to get knowledge from revelation. Whether there is anything in the last category is an important question, but it is also an important question whether we can come to know things in either of the other two categories. Some celebrated twentieth-century philosophers thought that we cannot know anything non-trivial in philosophy, and the most important Western philosopher of all – Plato – thought that we cannot know anything empirically.

In philosophy since at least Locke, a particular model of how we ought to go about getting beliefs has acquired prominence – the idea that we ought to proportion our beliefs to the evidence. The idea of evidence is also vague, and it can be broadened or narrowed to suit the one who is using it. If evidence includes any reason for a belief, then to say a belief ought to be based on evidence is to say nothing of substance. Does an experience count as evidence? Does a feeling of trust in one's source? How about intuition? In recent philosophy evidence has been interpreted narrowly as empirical data, and reason has been interpreted narrowly as the drawing of inferences (following carefully prescribed rules) from the former. The narrow view of reason is understandable, given that many atrocities have been committed in the twentieth century in the name of reason, but the narrow view of reason also brings with it a severe limitation on what human beings are permitted to believe. Ironically, in public life we are permitted to believe almost anything without having to answer for it to others, yet we also live in an era in which the ethics of belief as taught by philosophers is extremely rigorous. The view that became *de rigueur* in the modern era is generally called evidentialism.

10.2.2 Evidentialism

In the seventeenth century Locke (1979 [1689]) claimed that we ought to proportion our beliefs to the evidence. In the nineteenth century, W. K. Clifford (1901 [1879]) turned Locke's dictum into a principle of moral responsibility, creating a new field called the ethics of belief. Clifford thought that it is irresponsible to believe anything upon pragmatic grounds such as those supported by Pascal and Kierkegaard (see Chapter 3), and if we believe on insufficient evidence, we are wronging humankind. In an oft-quoted declaration that has become famous as much for its passion as for its sense, Clifford says, "It is wrong always, everywhere, and for anyone to believe anything upon insufficient evidence" (p. 175). The problems with this claim are worth noting, but it is also worth noting that behind its exaggerated bluster it hides an important truth.

Clifford begins his essay "The ethics of belief" with an example of a shipowner who sends his ship full of emigrants to sea, believing without evidence that the ship is seaworthy. When the ship goes down at sea, the shipowner is guilty of the deaths of the passengers, even if his belief is sincere. The shipowner had no right to believe that the ship was seaworthy, given that he had not had the ship inspected. Furthermore, Clifford argues, it makes no difference if the belief is true. Even if the ship had been sound after all, "The man would not have been innocent, he would only have been not found out" (p. 165). The soundness of the ship would have been a lucky break for him, but his intellectual rashness still would have been unjustified.

It is clear that Clifford is talking about a moral wrong. He says that believing upon inadequate evidence is "sinful," and "it is stolen in defiance of our duty to mankind" (p. 172). One reason it is wrong is that beliefs lead to acts and acts have consequences. Other people's lives may be at stake, as in the ship example. But Clifford does not make his evidentialist claim depend upon the fact that beliefs lead to acts.

224

He says that even if the ship had stayed in port, the belief would have been wrong because we owe it to ourselves and to each other not to be stupid. "The danger to society is not merely that it should believe wrong things, though that is great enough; but that it should become credulous, and lose the habit of testing things and inquiring into them; for then it must sink back into savagery" (p. 174).

So the reasons why it is wrong to believe upon insufficient evidence are these: Your beliefs lead to acts, and your acts have consequences. Other people rely upon you to believe upon sufficient evidence, since their acts might be based on your beliefs. And even when you keep your belief to yourself and do not act on it, if your belief is not justified by evidence, you lose the habit of forming beliefs on evidence. So even though a particular unjustified belief may not have immediate bad consequences, it turns you into an idiot, a savage.

I have three objections to Clifford: (1) The evidentialist principle is a principle of conservatism. It is a principle governed more by the desire to avoid falsehood than by the desire to get truth. (2) On Clifford's principle, you should not believe the principle itself. (3) The principle would make the vast majority of our beliefs wrong.

The first point comes from William James (1897) in "The will to believe." James argues that the passion to get truth is distinct from the passion to avoid falsehood, and the two passions lead to different strategies in the formation of belief. To see why, let's consider an analogy. Suppose you are digging for gold because, presumably, you like gold, but you dislike fool's gold. In addition, let's assume that there are advantages to having real gold, and disadvantages to having fool's gold. Let's also assume that you know that there is a lot of fool's gold in the same region as the real gold. Some nuggets you dig up are clearly gold and some are clearly fool's gold, but many are hard to identify. Now what do you do when you dig? Which nuggets do you keep? If you dislike fool's gold more than you like gold, your strategy will be conservative. You can be sure of avoiding fool's gold if you put back every nugget that is doubtful. On the other hand, if you like gold more than you dislike fool's gold, you will keep more of the doubtful nuggets. So the passion to avoid fool's gold leads you to keep few nuggets, whereas the passion to have gold leads you to keep many nuggets.

Similarly, says James, if you love truth more than you hate falsehood, you will have more beliefs than if you hate falsehood more than you love truth. It is up to you how much you value truth and how much you disvalue falsehood. It is not an objective matter. But it also matters how important the truth is in the particular case. Some beliefs are about matters that cannot be settled by objective strategies of weighing evidence, yet they are about matters that are momentous. The choice whether to believe or not might also be forced. James says, "If religion be true and the evidence for it be still insufficient, I do not wish, by putting your extinguisher upon my nature . . . to forfeit my sole chance in life of getting upon the winning side – that chance depending of course, on my willingness to run the risk of acting as if my passional need of taking the world religiously might be prophetic and right" (p. 31). On the gold analogy, imagine a situation in which you cannot determine whether the nugget is real gold or not, using the tests available to you. Imagine that both keeping the nugget and throwing it back are realistic possibilities for you, and imagine that you will never get a better chance to keep it. The sooner you get it, the better. Imagine also that it is an unusually good specimen. If it is real gold, it is a winner. What should you do? Using James' reasoning, it would be rational for you to keep it, provided that your passion to get gold is greater than your passion to avoid fool's gold. It might be rational for you to take a chance on it.

According to James, religious beliefs are like that. We're never going to be able to determine on intellectual grounds alone whether they are true or false. For many people, it is realistic to believe and realistic to disbelieve (what he calls a living choice). The choice is forced because not making up your mind prevents you from getting the truth now, and if it is a truth that is momentous, you lose out. You lose out just as much by withholding belief as you do by disbelieving. He writes, "We cannot escape the issue by remaining sceptical and waiting for more light, because, although we do avoid error in that way *if religion be untrue*, we lose the good, *if it be true*, just as certainly as if we positively chose to disbelieve" (p. 30). James proposes that we are better off believing that the best things are the eternal things. He also thinks it is true that the best things are the eternal things, but he admits there is no way to determine that it is true on intellectual grounds. Believing the eternal things is like keeping a big beautiful nugget that we think is real gold when we cannot determine that it is real gold rather than fool's gold using the criteria available for telling the difference.

Now let's go back to Clifford. According to James, Clifford's evidentialist principle is not a principle governed by purely intellectual considerations. It is an expression of a certain epistemic passion, the desire to avoid falsehood. It is a conservative principle that leads to epistemic caution: When in doubt about something that cannot be settled on intellectual grounds, do not believe. But the passion to get truth is also an epistemic passion, and it leads to a more liberal strategy: When in doubt about something that cannot be settled on intellectual grounds, if it would be a really important truth if you had it and it is realistic for you to believe it, then believe.

The strategy defended by James has to be qualified because some propositions that would be momentous if true conflict with others that would be momentous if true. So other considerations may need to be brought to bear on what to believe, including a weighing of the intellectual grounds for one momentous proposition versus another, but as we saw in Chapter 9, ultimately we must fall back on self-trust, and that includes trust in our intellectual traditions and the other forces that shape us into the persons we are.

A second objection to Clifford is that the evidentialist principle is self-defeating because it cannot pass its own test. What is the evidence for the belief that it is always wrong to believe anything upon insufficient evidence? Clifford gives a couple of examples, but that hardly constitutes evidence for such a sweeping claim. Possibly he thinks of the principle as a moral norm, akin to "Respect human life," or "Tell the truth." If so, we could not expect the norm to be supported by evidence, at least not the same kind of evidence that supports factual beliefs. This raises the problem brought up earlier, that the idea of evidence is vague. Evidence might include moral intuition, such as the intuition supporting the judgment "Respect human life." But in that case it is not clear why Clifford's implied norm, "Avoid falsehood," is better than James' norm, "Pursue truth."

The third objection to Clifford is that following the evidentialist principle would require us to give up the vast majority of our beliefs. Most of our beliefs are acquired from others, without evaluation or even awareness of the reliability of the source. As we saw in Chapter 9, we have no choice but to trust ourselves, and that includes trusting our opinions, as well as our faculties, and, I added, our emotions. But, as Foley argues, we would not be trustworthy unless many other people are trustworthy, and that includes the people from whom we acquired our opinions. Foley argues that it is incoherent to take the position of epistemic egoism, that we should not trust the beliefs of others without evidence of their reliability. If so, not only does the evidentialist principle preclude the rationality of most of our beliefs, but it is a principle that is inconsistent with the self-trust that is demanded in any non-skeptical life.

The conflict between reason and faith is blunted once we see that few of our beliefs are based on a reasoning process in combination with personal observation. Most of our beliefs are acquired from others without evaluation of the reliability of the testifier, and they require a significant degree of trust in others. Recall that Locke defined faith as belief on the testimony of a divinely inspired source.[16] According to Locke's definition, faith differs from the vast majority of our other beliefs only with respect to the source of the testimony, not with respect to the belief-forming process itself. If faith is unreasonable, it cannot be because the believer forms a belief on trust. Believers ought to be skeptical about the trustworthiness of certain sources, of course, and one can raise the issue of whether faith is in that category, but that is distinct from the issue of whether faith conflicts with reason.

In spite of these objections to Clifford, I think there is something importantly true about Clifford's point. Most people have no sense of responsibility for their beliefs, and the media not only let them get away with it, but even encourage it. People can promulgate the most outrageous beliefs on the airwaves and on the internet with impunity. The fact that people believe what they believe can be entertaining, but this attitude spreads unjustified beliefs throughout the society at a rapid rate.

We need to beware of intellectual vices – traits such as intellectual carelessness, unfairness to those with an opposing viewpoint, cowardice, inattentiveness, fickleness, gullibility, and indulgence in wishful thinking. The remedy for these vices is to acquire the corresponding virtue. Wishful thinking is a particularly interesting vice because Freud claimed that it is the cause of religious beliefs (See Chapter 6). According to Freud (1961), "we call a belief an illusion when a wish-fulfillment is a prominent factor in its motivation, and in doing so we disregard its relations to reality, just as the illusion itself sets no store by verificaton"

---

16   See Locke (1979 [1689]), bk IV, ch. XVIII, sec. 2.

(p. 40). Believing in this way is surely wrong. Is James recommending wishful thinking in "The Will to Believe"? He defends belief on passional grounds in the special case in which the truth of the belief cannot be determined on intellectual grounds and the content of the belief is momentous, living, and forced. It seems to me that Jamesian belief does not satisfy Freud's definition of an illusion, but is it nonetheless a case of the vice of wishful thinking? Presumably the desire that a belief be true can play some causal role in believing without making a belief vicious. But cases *are* vicious. Where do we draw the line?

There are many fanciful tales in St. Bede's history of early Christian England, written in the 8th century. In one story we are told how the monk Paulinus visited King Edwin in northern England to persuade him to accept Christianity. After a time the king was willing to accept the new faith, but first he called a meeting of his council and asked each in turn what he thought of the new doctrine. One of the advisors rose and said,

> This is how the present life of man on earth, King, appears to me in comparison with that time which is unknown to us. You are sitting feasting with your ealdormen and thegns in winter time; the fire is burning on the hearth in the middle of the hall and all inside is warm, while outside the wintry storms of rain and snow are raging; and a sparrow flies swiftly through the hall. It enters in at one door and quickly flies out through the other. For the few moments it is inside, the storm and wintry tempest cannot touch it, but after the briefest moment of calm, it flits from your sight, out of the wintry storm and into it again. So this life of man appears but for a moment; what follows or indeed what went before, we know not at all. If this new doctrine brings us more certain information, it seems right that we should accept it. (Bede 1969 [731], pp. 184–5)

On what grounds was King Edwin's advisor recommending that they accept Christianity? Does he think that they should follow the Christian religion even though they cannot know whether it is true? If so, is there anything wrong with that? Or does he think they should accept Christianity as true because Paulinus speaks with a kind of authority he trusts? What is the desire that the belief satisfies? It cannot be mere curiosity. It is more like wonder. What should the king do if his advisors give conflicting advice? How important is it that he get advice, given that he has already been convinced by Paulinus?

These are very difficult questions, and it is not easy to draw conclusions from individual cases, whether the case is Clifford's shipowner or King Edwin of England. Just as there are difficult moral choices, there are also difficult intellectual choices. We have no assurance that intellectual virtue is any clearer than moral virtue. I think that the best we can do intellectually is to imitate the people we admire intellectually, just as the best we can do morally is to imitate the people we admire morally. In the previous chapter I suggested that trusting our emotion of admiration is an important component of self-trust. In the concluding section of the book, I would like to return to self-trust and its implications for the potential conflict between faith and reason.

10.3   Faith, Reason, and the Self

In Chapter 9 I argued that the challenge of religious diversity arises from the potentially conflicting demands of self-trust. We cannot live a non-skeptical life without trust in our faculties, the opinions we have acquired from others, our emotions, and the traditions that shape us. Most of what we learn is by imitation of others, and the emotion of admiration is the emotion we use to distinguish those worth imitating from those that are not. Those we admire most might have beliefs that conflict with our own beliefs. When we become aware of that, we have no way to determine what to do except by examining the self and deciding which aspects of the self we trust more – those we would have to change if we changed our beliefs, or our emotion of admiration. Given the nature of the self, it is not surprising that most of the time it is the former, but it is possible to take the latter route, and so conversion is possible. Conversion depends upon self-trust because we cannot rationally change one part of the self without trusting another.

Both reason and faith require self-trust. Reason is allegedly our highest faculty, and perhaps it is, but it is not invincible. Reason can falter, even in logic, mathematics, and certainly in metaphysics. We trust it, not because reason comes with a guarantee of getting us truth, but because we have no choice. And if we trust it more than other faculties, that is only because we continue trusting it when we are thinking as hard as we can. Self-trust is not trust in whatever we happen to believe or feel, but trust in what we believe or feel upon reflection. When we reflect upon our beliefs, we are aware of our beliefs as objects, and it is because of the human capacity for self-reflection that we are able to revise our beliefs. By "self-reflection" I mean the act or state of awareness of our own conscious states and the internal processes by which we revise them. We are conscious of the world, and we are conscious of ourselves being conscious of the world. If we are conscious of God, we are also conscious of ourselves being conscious of God. It is because of the human capacity for self-reflection that we are able to critically examine and sometimes amend our beliefs, emotions, and many other aspects of the self. But because it is always the self that does the critical examination and revision, we need self-trust even when we are at our most self-reflective.

Faith requires self-trust as well. All the components of faith – conviction of the truth of particular doctrines, trust in the source of revelation, commitment to a particular way of life – are components of the self that are subject to critical examination and revision. I think it would be fair to say that blind faith is faith that is not open to self-reflective scrutiny. It should not be trusted any more than we should trust blind reason or blind memory or blind perception. An important question is that of how critical self-reflection changes that upon which we reflect. Reflecting upon our experiences and reasoning about our beliefs and their connections leads to giving up or altering some beliefs and retaining others, perhaps even believing some of them with greater conviction than before.

It is possible for an unreflective belief to be strongly held, but it is not deep. What reflection does is to attach beliefs to other beliefs and to other parts of the self. At the end of the *Meno* Socrates says that what makes knowledge more valuable than mere opinion is that it is tethered. In contrast, opinion is like the statues of Daedalus (legendary statues that walked):

> If no one ties them down, [they] run away and escape. If tied, they stay where they are put . . . If you have one of his works untethered, it is not worth much; it gives you the slip like a runaway slave. But a tethered specimen is very valuable, for they are magnificent creations. And that, I may say, has a bearing on the matter of true opinions. True opinions are a fine thing and do all sorts of good so long as they stay in their place, but they will not stay long. They run away from a man's mind; so they are not worth much until you tether them by working out the reason . . . Once they are tied down, they become knowledge, and are stable. That is why knowledge is something more valuable than right opinion.

What distinguishes one from the other is the tether. (*Meno* 97d–98a, trans. W. K. C. Guthrie)

Plato thought his doctrine of recollection explained the process by which a belief is tethered and becomes knowledge, but it seems to me that what ties a belief down is that it survives critical reflection and acquires many connections to other beliefs, emotions, and experiences. The depth of a belief is measured by the degree to which it is tethered. It has little to do with the strength of the belief. What I would like to propose is that Plato's distinction between knowledge and mere true opinion has a parallel in two kinds of faith. Faith without critical reflection lacks depth because it lacks a tether. It can be given up with little difference to the self, and for that reason is not as valuable as faith with a tether.

Depth of any aspect of the self is gained by critical self-reflection, but the latter can be frightening because it sometimes destroys parts of the self before rebuilding them. As al-Ghazali (1994 [1108]) wrote of his own awakening:

> There is certainly no point in trying to return to the level of naive and derivative belief (*taqlíd*) once it has been left, since a condition of being at such a level is that one should not know one is there; when a man comes to know that, the glass of his naive beliefs is broken. This is a breakage which cannot be mended, a breakage not to be repaired by patching or assembling of fragments. The glass must be melted once again in the furnace for a new start, and out of it another fresh vessel formed (p. 26).

It seems to me that in this passage al-Ghazali is describing the process of becoming a larger as well as more unified self. The self grows as we gain experience and acquire more beliefs, more complex values, and more subtle emotions. We become a larger self, a more significant self, when our emotions are more refined and more carefully targeted.

At the beginning of this book I said that I think philosophers of religion pay too much attention to religious beliefs and not enough attention to religious emotions. The scope of a person's emotions is not only determined by her experiences, but by the traditions that show her a way to interpret those experiences. Every religion has distinctive emotions expressed in its works of art and its narratives, and no philosophical treatment of religion will be more than superficial if it does not include a genuine appreciation for the emotions that partially constitute a particular religious tradition. These emotions dispose a person to interpret her experiences in ways characteristic of her tradition, and they permit her to grow emotionally in distinctive ways. Imagine a creature who never eats who then decides to write a treatise on food based only upon watching the performance of TV chefs and listening to the raves of their audience. Without the experience of eating in the manner and style promoted by the chef, one does not really understand what is going on. I think the parallel point applies to religious emotions, which like all except our most basic emotions, are learned through the experience of living in a certain environment. That capacity often outlives belief in the doctrines of a given religion and enlarges the self even when a person no longer accepts her former religious beliefs.

Sometimes we may not permit ourselves to have certain emotions because we cannot believe that a certain emotion can be appropriate for the circumstances. For example, Christians teach that we may not like the emotion that goes with seeing ourselves as the fit object of the wrath of another, much less as the fit object of the wrath of a vastly superior being. And it is even harder to see ourselves as the fit object of wrath of a vastly superior being who also loves us. It is difficult to permit ourselves to have the emotion that accompanies seeing ourselves as the recipient of gifts so great, we can never hope to adequately express gratitude. Ironically, it takes humility to allow oneself to be so important to someone else. To do so makes one vulnerable; vulnerable persons allow themselves to be more significant.

The emotions I have mentioned are Christian, and I mention them because they are the ones with which I am most familiar. The distinctive emotions of other religions make a different growth of self possible. When philosophers evaluate religious beliefs, they tend to evaluate the beliefs independent of the emotions that ground or support them. This is understandable since philosophers are usually operating outside a religious tradition. But it puts us in the same position as the viewer who attempts to evaluate a chef's creations without tasting the food, and that is a severe disadvantage.

The virtue of philosophy is purity of mind. We trust it because we trust that the mind is by nature directed at truth. The virtue of religion is eagerness of spirit. Philosophy of religion can easily miss some of the most important features of religion because the philosophical urge tends to temper eagerness. But philosophy is also humble, and one of the many lessons we have learned from the philosophers studied in this book is that philosophy often critiques itself. The critical self-reflection we find in a well-integrated self is also a feature of the field of philosophy. The best we can do as philosophers of religion is to think as hard as we can about the issues of ultimate importance to human life, while never losing the eagerness of spirit that drove us to ask the questions in the first place.

Further reading

Paul Helm's *Faith and Reason* (New York: Oxford University Press, 1999) is an excellent selection of historical readings, including ancient and medieval sources on the relationship between faith and reason. A classic of the movement that became known as Reformed Epistemology is *Faith and Rationality*, edited by Alvin Plantinga and Nicholas Wolterstorff (Notre Dame, Ind.: University of Notre Dame Press, 1983). For a collection of Catholic responses to Reformed Epistemology, see my *Rational Faith* (Notre Dame, Ind.: University of Notre Dame Press, 1993). Nicholas Wolterstoff's book *John Locke and the Ethics of Belief* (New York: Cambridge University Press, 1996) is an important historical study of the first major philosopher to make the ethics of belief a significant field. The relationship between reason and emotion and its bearing on religious belief does not get much attention, but a noteworthy exception is William Wainwright's *Reason and the Heart* (Ithaca: Cornell University Press, 1995), which uses the work of John Henry Newman, Jonathan Edwards, and William James to argue for the importance of our passional nature in seeing the force of reason. For a detailed and insightful study of the relationship between emotion and religion, see *Emotional Experience and Religious Understanding* by Mark R. Wynn (New York: Cambridge University Press, 2005).

Bibliography

Adams, M. M. (1967) Is the existence of God a hard fact? *Philosophical Review* 76, 492–503.

Adams, M. M. (2001) The problem of hell: a problem of evil for Christians. In Rowe (2001), 282–309.

Adams, R. M. (1973) A modified divine command theory of ethical wrongness. In Outka and Reeder (1973), 318–47.

Adams, R. M. (1977) Kierkegaard's arguments against objective reasoning in religion. *Monist* 60, 228–43.

Adams, R. M. (1979) Divine command metaethics modified again. *Journal of Religious Ethics* 7, 66–79.

Adams, R. M. (1987) *The Virtue of Faith*. Oxford University Press, New York.

Adams, R. M. (1999) *Finite and Infinite Goods: A Framework for Ethics*. Oxford University Press, New York.

Alston, W. (1991) *Perceiving God: The Epistemology of Religious Experience*. Cornell University Press, Ithaca, N.Y.

Anonymous (1983) *The Cloud of Unknowing*, trans. I. Progoff. Dell, New York.

Anscombe, G. E. M. (1956) Aristotle and the sea battle. *Mind* 65, 1–15.

Anscombe, G. E. M. (1958) Modern moral philosophy. *Philosophy* 33, 1–19.

Anselm (1965 [1078]) *St. Anselm's Proslogion*, trans. M. J. Charlesworth. Clarendon Press, Oxford.

Aquinas, T. (1955 [1265]) *On the Truth of the Catholic Faith. Summa Contra Gentiles*, trans. A. C. Pegis. Image Books, Garden City, N.Y.

Aquinas, T. (1981 [1273]) *Summa Theologica*, trans. Fathers of the English Dominican Province. Christian Classics, Allen, Tex.

Arinze, F. A. (2001) The church and interreligious dialogue. *Logos* 4, 156–77.

Aristotle (1963) *Aristotle's Categories and De Interpretatione*, trans. J. L. Ackrill. Clarendon Press, Oxford.

Aristotle (1984) *The Complete Works of Aristotle*, 2 vols., ed. J. Barnes. Princeton University Press, Princeton.

Bibliography

Athanassiadi, P. and Frede, M. (eds.) (1999) *Pagan Monotheism in Late Antiquity*. Clarendon Press, Oxford.

Augustine (1950 [427]) *The City of God*. Modern Library, New York.

Averroes (2001 [1180]) *The Book of the Decisive Treatise Determining the Connection between the Law and Wisdom; and, The Epistle Dedicatory*, trans. C. E. Butterworth. Brigham Young University Press, Provo, Utah.

Bacon, F. (1966 [1605]) *The Advancement of Learning*. Reprinted in: *The Advancement of Learning and New Atlantis*. Oxford University Press, London.

Bacon, F. (1985 [1625]) *The Essayes or Counsels, Civill and Morall*. Harvard University Press, Cambridge, Mass.

Bailey, L. W. and Yates, J. L. (1996) *The Near-death Experience: A Reader*. Routledge, New York.

Basinger, D. (1998) Process Theism. In Craig (1998), vol. 7, 716–20.

Bede, V. (1969 [731]) *Bede's Ecclesiastical History of the English People*, ed. B. Colgrave and R. A. B. Mynors. Clarendon Press, Oxford.

Boethius (1962 [524]) *The Consolation of Philosophy*, trans. Richard Green. Bobbs-Merrill, Indianapolis.

Borgen, P. (1992) Philo of Alexandria. In D. N. Freedman et al. (eds.), *The Anchor Bible Dictionary*, vol. 5. Doubleday, New York, 333–42.

Bourke, V. J. (1965) *Aquinas' Search for Wisdom*. Bruce Publishing Co., Milwaukee.

Buckley, M. J. (1987) *At the Origins of Modern Atheism*. Yale University Press, New Haven.

Buckley, M. J. (2004) *Denying and Disclosing God: The Ambiguous Progress of Modern Atheism*. Yale University Press, New Haven.

Burke, E. (2001 [1790]) *Reflections on the Revolution in France*, ed. J. C. D. Clark. Stanford University Press, Stanford.

Burkert, W. (1985) *Greek Religion*, trans. J. Raffan. Harvard University Press, Cambridge, Mass.

Byron, G. G. (1979) *"In the Wind's Eye": 1821–1822. Byron's Letters and Journals*, vol. 9. Belknap Press of Harvard University Press, Cambridge, Mass.

Cahill, T. (1998) *The Gifts of the Jews: How a Tribe of Desert Nomads Changed the Way Everyone Thinks and Feels*. Nan A. Talese, New York.

Cahn, S. M. and Shatz, D. (eds.) (1982) *Contemporary Philosophy of Religion*. Oxford University Press, New York.

Camus, A. (1991) The myth of Sisyphus. In *The Myth of Sisyphus and Other Essays*, trans. J. O'Brien. Vintage Books, New York.

Cargile, J. (1982) Pascal's wager. In Cahn and Shatz (1982), 229–36.

Carson, T. L. (2000) *Value and the Good Life*. University of Notre Dame Press, Notre Dame, Ind.

Casey, M. (2004) *Fully Human, Fully Divine: An Interactive Christology*. Liguori/Triumph, Liguori, Mo.

Bibliography

Cicero, M. T. (1979) *De Natura Deorum; Academica*, trans. H. Rackham. Harvard University Press, Cambridge, Mass.

Clark, K. (1969) *Civilisation*. Harper and Row, New York.

Clarke, S. (1998 [1705]) *A Demonstration of the Being and Attributes of God and Other Writings*, ed. E. Vailati. Cambridge University Press, Cambridge.

Clement (1867) *The Writings of Clement of Alexandria*, vol. 1. In A. Roberts and J. Donaldson (eds.), The Ante-Nicene Christian Library, vol. 4. T. and T. Clark, Edinburgh.

Clifford, W. K. (1901 [1879]) *Lectures and Essays*, 2 vols. The Macmillan Co., New York.

Cobb, J. B. and Griffin, D. R. (1976) *Process Theology: An Introductory Exposition*. Westminster Press, Philadelphia.

Collins, J. (1967) *The Emergence of Philosophy of Religion*. Yale University Press, New Haven.

Copleston, F. (1962) *A History of Philosophy*, vol. 2, Mediaeval Philosophy, pt II. Image Books, Garden City, N.Y.

Corwin, M. (1983) From chaos to consciousness. *Astronomy* 11, 15–22.

Craig, E. (ed.) (1998) *Routledge Encyclopedia of Philosophy*. Routledge, New York.

Craig, W. L. (1979) *The Kalam Cosmological Argument*. Barnes and Noble Books, New York.

Craig, W. L. (1980) *The Cosmological Argument from Plato to Leibniz*. Barnes and Noble Books, New York.

Craig, W. L. and Sinnott-Armstrong, W. (2004) *God?: A Debate between a Christian and an Atheist*. Oxford University Press, New York.

Dalai Lama (1988) *The Bodhgaya Interviews: His Holiness the Dalai Lama*, ed. J. I. Cabezon. Snow Lion Publications, Ithaca.

Dalai Lama (1999) *Ethics for the New Millennium*. Riverhead Books, New York.

Dawkins, R. (1996) *The Blind Watchmaker*. W. W. Norton, New York.

Dawkins, R. (1997) Is science a religion? *The Humanist* 57 (1), 26–9. Available online at http://www.thehumanist.org/humanist/articles/dawkins.html.

Descartes, R. (1993 [1641]) *Meditations on First Philosophy*, trans. D. A. Cress. Hackett Publishing Company, Indianapolis.

Dole, A. and Chignell, A. (eds.) (2005) *God and the Ethics of Belief: New Essays in Philosophy of Religion*. Cambridge University Press, Cambridge.

Dombrowski, D. (2005) Charles Hartshorne. In E. N. Zalta (ed.), *The Stanford Encyclopedia of Philosophy* (Winter 2005 edition). Available online at http://www.plato.stanford.edu/archives/win2005/entries/hartshorne/.

Dostoevsky, F. (1971 [1871]) *The Devils*, trans. D. Magarshack. Penguin Books, Baltimore.

Dostoevsky, F. (1976 [1879]) *The Brothers Karamazov*, trans. C. Garnett, rev. and ed. R. E. Matlaw. W. W. Norton and Co., New York.

Bibliography

Dummett, M. (1964) Bringing about the past. *Philosophical Review* 73, 338–59.

Earman, J. (2000) *Hume's Abject Failure: The Argument Against Miracles.* Oxford University Press, New York.

Edwards, J. (1765) *Two Dissertations, I. Concerning the End for which God Created the World. II. The Nature of True Virtue.* S. Kneeland, Boston.

Epicurus (1994) *The Epicurus Reader: Selected Writings and Testimonia,* ed. and trans. B. Inwood and L. P. Gerson. Hackett, Indianapolis.

Faulkner, R. O., Goelet, O., Andrews, C. A. R. et al. (1994) *The Egyptian Book of the Dead.* Chronicle Books, San Francisco.

Feuerbach, L. (1967) *Lectures on the Essence of Religion.* Harper and Row, New York.

Fischer, J. M. (ed.) (1989) *God, Foreknowledge, and Freedom.* Stanford University Press, Stanford.

Fischer, J. M. (ed.) (1993) *The Metaphysics of Death.* Stanford University Press, Stanford.

Flanagan, O. (1991) *Varieties of Moral Personality.* Harvard University Press, Cambridge, Mass.

Flew, A. and Habermas, G. (2004) My pilgrimage from atheism to theism: a discussion between Antony Flew and Gary Habermas. *Philosophia Christi* 6, 197–211.

Flew, A. and MacIntyre, A. C. (1964) *New Essays in Philosophical Theology.* Macmillan, New York.

Flint, T. (1998) *Divine Providence: The Molinist Account.* Cornell University Press, Ithaca, N.Y.

Foley, R. (2001) *Intellectual Trust in Oneself and Others.* Cambridge University Press, New York.

Foster, B. R. (ed. and trans.) (2001) *The Epic of Gilgamesh.* W. W. Norton and Co., New York.

Frankfurt, H. G. (2005) *On Bullshit.* Princeton University Press, Princeton.

Frede, M. (1999) Monotheism and pagan philosophy in later antiquity. In Athanassiadi and Frede (1999), 41–67.

Freud, S. (1961) *The Future of an Illusion,* trans. and ed. J. Strachey, intro. P. Gay. W. W. Norton and Co., New York.

Freud, S. (1962) *Civilization and Its Discontents,* trans. and ed. J. Strachey. W. W. Norton, New York.

Gale, R. M. (1991) *On the Nature and Existence of God.* Cambridge University Press, New York.

Ganssle, G. E. (ed.) (2001) *God and Time: Four Views.* InterVarsity Press, Downers Grove, Ill.

Gavrilyuk, P. L. (2004) *The Suffering of the Impassible God: The Dialectics of Patristic Thought.* Oxford University Press, New York.

Bibliography

Geach, P. (1977) *The Virtues*. Cambridge University Press, Cambridge.

al-Ghazali, A. H. (1994 [1108]) *The Faith and Practice of Al-Ghazálí*, trans. W. M. Watt. Oneworld, Oxford.

al-Ghazali, A. H. (1997 [1095]) *The Incoherence of the Philosophers: A Parallel English–Arabic Text*, trans. M. E. Marmura. Brigham Young University Press, Provo, Utah.

Giussani, L. (1997) *The Religious Sense*, trans. J. Zucchi. McGill-Queens University Press, Montreal.

Goodman, L. E. (1969) A note on Avicenna's theory of the substantiality of the soul. *Philosophical Forum* 1, 547–54.

Guth, A. H. (1997) *The Inflationary Universe: The Quest for a New Theory of Cosmic Origins*. Perseus Books, Cambridge, Mass.

Habermas, G. R. and Moreland, J. P. (1998) *Beyond Death: Exploring the Evidence for Immortality*. Crossway Books, Wheaton, Ill.

Haldane, J. (2003) *An Intelligent Person's Guide to Religion*. Duckworth, London.

Hare, J. E. (1996) *The Moral Gap: Kantian Ethics, Human Limits, and God's Assistance*. Oxford University Press, New York.

Hartshorne, C. (1948) *The Divine Relativity: A Social Conception of God*. Yale University Press, New Haven.

Hasker, W. (1989) *God, Time, and Knowledge*. Cornell University Press, Ithaca, N.Y.

Hawking, S. W. (1988) *A Brief History of Time: From the Big Bang to Black Holes*. Bantam Books, New York.

Hegel, G. W. F. (1984 [1821]) *Lectures on the Philosophy of Religion*, trans. R. F. Brown, P. C. Hodgson, and J. M. Stewart, with the assistance of J. P. Fitzer and H. S. Harris, ed. P. C. Hodgson. University of California Press, Berkeley.

Heschel, A. J. (1951) *Man is Not Alone: A Philosophy of Religion*. Noonday Press, New York.

Hewitt, H., Jr (ed.) (1991) *Problems in the Philosophy of Religion*. Macmillan, London.

Hick, J. (1978) *Evil and the God of Love*, rev. edn. Harper and Row, San Francisco.

Hick, J. (1995) A pluralist view. In Okholm and Phillips (1995), 29–59.

Hick, J. (2000) Religious pluralism and salvation. In Quinn and Meeker (2000), 54–66.

Hick, J. (2001) Soul-making theodicy. In Rowe (2001), 265–81.

Hick, J. (2004) *An Interpretation of Religion*, 2nd edn. Yale University Press, New Haven.

Hick, J. and Hebblethwaite, B. (eds.) (1981) *Christianity and Other Religions*. Fortress Press, Philadelphia.

Howard-Snyder, D. (ed.) (1996) *The Evidential Argument from Evil.* Indiana University Press, Bloomington, Ind.

Howard-Snyder, D., Bergmann, M., and Rowe, W. L. (2001) An exchange on the problem of evil. In Rowe (2001), 124–58.

Hume, D. (1948 [1779]) *Dialogues Concerning Natural Religion*, ed. H. D. Aiken. Hafner Publishing Co., New York.

Hume, D. (1975 [1748]) *Enquiry into the Human Understanding.* In *Enquiries Concerning Human Understanding and Concerning the Principles of Morals*, ed. L. A. Selby-Bigge, rev. P. H. Nidditch. Clarendon Press, Oxford.

Idziak, J. M. (1979) *Divine Command Morality: Historical and Contemporary Readings.* Edwin Mellen Press, New York.

Inwood, B. and Gerson, L. P. (trans.) (1988) *Hellenistic Philosophy: Introductory Readings.* Hackett Publishing Co., Indianapolis.

Irwin, T. (1998) Aristotle. In Craig (1998), vol. 1, 414–43.

Jaki, S. L. (2000) *The Savior of Science.* W. B. Eerdmans, Grand Rapids.

James, W. (1979 [1897]) *The Will to Believe and Other Essays in Popular Philosophy.* Harvard University Press, Cambridge, Mass.

Jaspers, K. (1953 [1949]) *The Origin and Goal of History*, trans. M. Bullock. Yale University Press, New Haven.

Justin, M. (2003) *Dialogue with Trypho*, trans. T. B. Falls, ed. M. Slusser, intro. T. P. Halton. The Catholic University of America Press, Washington.

Kant, I. (1956 [1788]) *Critique of Practical Reason*, trans. L. W. Beck. Liberal Arts Press, New York.

Kant I. (1965 [1781]) *Critique of Pure Reason*, trans. N. Kemp-Smith. St Martin's Press, New York.

Keats, J. (1978) *The Poems of John Keats*, ed. J. Stillinger. Belknap Press, Cambridge, Mass.

Kierkegaard, S. (1983 [1843]) *Fear and Trembling. Repetition*, trans. and ed. H. V. Hong and E. H. Hong. Princeton University Press, Princeton.

Kierkegaard, S. (1985 [1844]) *Philosophical Fragments*, trans. and ed. H. V. Hong and E. H. Hong. Princeton University Press, Princeton.

Kierkegaard, S. (1988 [1845]) *Stages on Life's Way*, trans. and ed. H. V. Hong and E. H. Hong. Princeton University Press, Princeton.

Kierkegaard, S. (1992 [1846]) *Concluding Unscientific Postscript to Philosophical Fragments*, trans. and ed. H. V. Hong and E. H. Hong, 2 vols. Princeton University Press, Princeton.

Kripke, S. (1980) *Naming and Necessity.* Harvard University Press, Cambridge, Mass.

Leaman, O. (1998) Ibn Rushd, Abu'l Walid Muhammad (1126–98). In Craig (1998), vol. 4, 638–46.

Leftow, B. (2005) The ontological argument. In Wainwright (2005), 80–115.

Bibliography

Leibniz, G. W. (1952 [1710]) *Theodicy*, trans. E. M. Huggard, ed. A. Farrer. Yale University Press, New Haven.

Leibniz, G. W. (1989) *Philosophical Essays*, trans. and ed. R. Ariew and D. Garber. Hackett Publishing Co., Indianapolis.

Lemley, B. (2002) Guth's grand guess. *Discover* 23 (4), 32–9.

Lewis, B. (2002) *What Went Wrong?: Western Impact and Middle Eastern Response*. Oxford University Press, New York.

Lewis, C. S. (1956) *The Last Battle*. Macmillan, New York.

Locke, J. (1979 [1689]) *An Essay Concerning Human Understanding*, ed. P. H. Nidditch. Clarendon Press, Oxford.

Locke, J. (1958 [1702]) *A Discourse of Miracles*. Reprinted in I. T. Ramsey (ed.), *The Reasonableness of Christianity, with A Discourse of Miracles, and part of A Third Letter Concerning Toleration*. Stanford University Press, Stanford.

Long, A. A. (1986) *Hellenistic Philosophy: Stoics, Epicureans, Sceptics*, 2nd edn. University of California Press, Berkeley.

Long, A. A. (2004) *Epictetus: A Stoic and Socratic Guide to Life*. Clarendon Press, Oxford.

MacIntyre, A. and Flew, A. (eds.) (1964) *New Essays in Philosophical Theology*. Macmillan, New York.

Mackie, J. L. (1955) Evil and omnipotence. *Mind* 64, 200–12.

Mackie, J. L. (1977) *Ethics: Inventing Right and Wrong*. Penguin, New York.

Manson, N. A. (ed.) (2003) *God and Design: The Teleological Argument and Modern Science*. Routledge, New York.

Marett-Crosby, A. (ed.) (2003) *The Benedictine Handbook*. Liturgical Press, Collegeville, Minn.

Mavrodes, G. I. (1984) Is the past unpreventable? *Faith and Philosophy* 1, 131–46.

Mavrodes, G. I. (2000) Polytheism. In Quinn and Meeker (2000), 139–60.

McDannell, C. and Lang, B. (1988) *Heaven: A History*. Yale University Press, New Haven.

Menssen, S. and Sullivan, T. D. (2002) The existence of God and the existence of Homer: rethinking theism and revelatory claims. *Faith and Philosophy* 19, 331–47.

Menssen, S. and Sullivan, T. D. (2007) *The Agnostic Inquirer: Revelation from a Philosophical Standpoint*. W. B. Eerdmans, Grand Rapids.

Milton, J. R. (1998) Francis Bacon. In Craig (1998), vol. 1, 624–32.

Molina, L. de (2004 [1588]) *On Divine Foreknowledge: Part IV of the "Concordia"*, trans. A. J. Freddoso. Cornell University Press, Ithaca, N.Y.

Montagnon, P. and Eyre, R. (1977) *The Long Search*, vol. 3. Time-Life Video, New York.

Moody, R. A. (1976) *Life After Life*. Stackpole Books, Harrisburg, Pa.

Bibliography

Mulhall, S. (2001) Wittgenstein and the philosophy of religion. In Phillips and Tessin (2001), 95–118.

Nagel, T. (1993) Death. In Fischer (1993), 61–9.

Navia, L. E. (2001) *Antisthenes of Athens: Setting the World Aright*. Greenwood Press, Westport, Conn.

Netland, H. A. (2001) *Encountering Religious Pluralism: The Challenge to Christian Faith and Mission*. InterVarsity Press, Downers Grove, Ill.

Newman, J. H. (1997) *Fifteen Sermons Preached Before the University of Oxford Between AD 1826 and 1843*. University of Notre Dame Press, Notre Dame, Ind.

Nock, A. D. (1998) *Conversion: The Old and the New in Religion from Alexander the Great to Augustine of Hippo*. Johns Hopkins University Press, Baltimore.

O'Connor, T. (2000) *Persons and Causes: The Metaphysics of Free Will*. Oxford University Press, New York.

O'Hara, J. (1953) *Appointment in Samarra*. The Modern Library, New York.

Okholm, D. L. and Phillips, T. R. (eds.) (1995) *Four Views on Salvation in a Pluralistic World*. Zondervan Publishing, Grand Rapids.

Olen, J. (1983) *Persons and their World: An Introduction to Philosophy*. Random House, New York.

Otto, R. (1958) *The Idea of the Holy*, trans. J. W. Harvey. Oxford University Press, New York.

Outka, G. H. and Reeder, J. P. (eds.) (1973) *Religion and Morality: A Collection of Essays*. Anchor Press, Garden City, N.Y.

Paley, W. (1802) *Natural Theology, or Evidences of the Existence and Attributes of the Deity Collected from the Appearances of Nature*. R. Faulder, London.

Pascal, B. (1941 [1670]) *Pensées. The Provincial Letters*, trans. W. F. Trotter and T. M'Crie. The Modern Library, New York.

Passmore, J. (2000) *The Perfectibility of Man*. Liberty Fund, Indianapolis.

Perry, J. (1978) *A Dialogue on Personal Identity and Immortality*. Hackett Publishing Co., Indianapolis.

Phillips, D. Z. and Tessin, T. (eds.) (2001) *Philosophy of Religion in the 21st Century*. Palgrave, Basingstoke.

Pieper, J. (1998) *Happiness and Contemplation*, trans. R. Winston and C. Winston, C. St Augustine Press, South Bend, Ind.

Pinnock, C. (2001) *Most Moved Mover: A Theology of God's Openness*. Baker Academic, Grand Rapids.

Pinnock, C., Rice, R., Sanders, J., Hasker, W. and Basinger, D. (1994) *The Openness of God: A Biblical Challenge to the Traditional Understanding of God*. InterVarsity Press, Downers Grove, Ill.

Plantinga, A. (1967) *God and Other Minds: A Study of the Rational Justification of Belief in God*. Cornell University Press, Ithaca, N.Y.

Plantinga, A. (1974a) *God, Freedom, and Evil*. Harper and Row, New York.

Bibliography

Plantinga, A. (1974b) *The Nature of Necessity*. Clarendon Press, Oxford.

Plantinga, A. (1986) On Ockham's way out. *Faith and Philosophy* 3, 235–69.

Plantinga, A. (1998) God, arguments for the existence of. In Craig (1998), vol. 4, 85–93.

Plantinga, A. (2000a) Pluralism: a defense of religious exclusivism. In Quinn and Meeker (2000), 172–92.

Plantinga, A. (2000b) *Warranted Christian Belief*. Oxford University Press, New York.

Plantinga, A. and Wolterstorff, N. (1983) *Faith and Rationality: Reason and Belief in God*. University of Notre Dame Press, Notre Dame, Ind.

Plato (1961) *The Collected Dialogues of Plato, Including the Letters*, ed. E. Hamilton and H. Cairns. Pantheon Books, New York.

Plato (1997) *Complete Works*, ed. J. M. Cooper. Hackett, Indianapolis.

Pomerleau, W. P. (1998) *Western Philosophies of Religion*. Ardsley House Publishers, New York.

Prior, A. N. (1959) Thank goodness that's over. *Philosophy* 34, 12–17.

Putnam, H. (1975) The meaning of "meaning." In *Mind, Language, and Reality*. Cambridge University Press, New York, 215–71.

Putnam, H. (1997) God and the philosophers. In P. A. French, T. E. Uehling, Jr, and H. K. Wettstein (eds.), *Midwest Studies in Philosophy* 21. University of Notre Dame Press, Notre Dame, Indiana, 175–87.

Quinn, P. L. and Meeker, K. (eds.) (2000) *The Philosophical Challenge of Religious Diversity*. Oxford University Press, New York.

Quinn, P. L. and Taliaferro, C. (eds.) (1997) *A Companion to the Philosophy of Religion*. Blackwell, Cambridge, Mass.

Rahner, K. (1966) Christianity and the non-Christian religions. In *Theological Investigations*, vol. 5. Seabury Press, New York.

Raphals, L. (2003) Fate, fortune, chance and luck in Chinese and Greek: a comparative semantic history. *Philosophy East and West* 53, 537–74.

Ratzsch, D. (2003) Perceiving design. In Manson (2003), 124–44.

Rheinfelder, H. (1928) *Das Wort "Persona"*. N. Niemeyer, Halle, Germany.

Ries, J. (1987) The fall. In M. Eliade et al. (eds.), *The Encyclopedia of Religion*, vol. 5. Macmillan, New York, p. 257.

Rincon, P. (2003) Evidence of earliest human burial. *BBC Science News*, March 26, 2003. Available online at: http://www.news.bbc.co.uk/1/hi/sci/tech/2885663.stm.

Ring, K. (1980a) *Life at Death: A Scientific Investigation of the Near-death Experience*. Coward, McCann and Geoghegan, New York.

Ring, K. (1980b) Commentary on "the reality of death experiences: a personal perspective" by Ernst A. Rodin. *The Journal of Nervous and Mental Disease* 168, 273–4.

Bibliography

Ring, K. and Valarino, E. E. (2000) *Lessons from the Light: What We Can Learn from the Near-death Experience*. Moment Point Press, Portsmouth, N. H.

Rodin, E. A. (1980) The reality of death experiences: a personal perspective. *The Journal of Nervous and Mental Disease* 168, 259–63.

Rowe, W. L. (1979) The problem of evil and some varieties of atheism. *American Philosophical Quarterly* 16, 335–41.

Rowe, W. L. (ed.) (2001) *God and the Problem of Evil*. Blackwell Publishers, Malden, Mass.

Rowe, W. L. (2004) *Can God Be Free?* Oxford University Press, New York.

Rudman, S. (1997) *Concepts of Person and Christian Ethics*. Cambridge University Press, New York.

Russell, B. (1967) *The Autobiography of Bertrand Russell*. Little, Brown, and Company, Boston.

Russell, D. C. (2004) Virtue as likeness to God in Plato and Seneca. *Journal of the History of Philosophy* 42, 241–60.

Sabom, M. B. (1980) Commentary on "the reality of death experiences" by Ernst Rodin. *The Journal of Nervous and Mental Disease* 168, 266–7.

Sabom, M. B. (1982) *Recollections of Death*. Harper and Row, New York.

Sanders, J. (1998) *The God Who Risks: A Theology of Providence*. InterVarsity Press, Downers Grove, Ill.

Schneewind, J. B. (1998) *The Invention of Autonomy: A History of Modern Moral Philosophy*. Cambridge University Press, New York.

Sedley, D. (1998) Stoicism. In Craig (1998), vol. 9, 141–61.

Seneca, L. A. (1932) *Letters to Lucilius*, vol. 2. Clarendon Press, Oxford.

Shoemaker, S. and Swinburne, R. (1984) *Personal Identity*. Blackwell, Oxford.

Simpson, W. K. (ed.) (2003) *The Literature of Ancient Egypt*. Yale University Press, New Haven.

Smythies, J. R. and Beloff, J. (1989) *The Case for Dualism*. University Press of Virginia, Charlottesville.

Sobel, J. H. (1998) *Puzzles for the Will: Fatalism, Newcomb and Samarra, Determinism and Omniscience*. University of Toronto Press, Buffalo.

Sorabji, R. (1983) *Time, Creation, and the Continuum: Theories in Antiquity and the Early Middle Ages*. Cornell University Press, Ithaca, N.Y.

Sterling, M. C. (1993) *Philosophy of Religion: A Universalist Perspective*. University Press of America, Lanham, Md.

Stevenson, I. (1980) Comments on "the reality of death experiences: a personal perspective". *The Journal of Nervous and Mental Disease* 168, 271–2.

Swinburne, R. (1979) *The Existence of God*. Oxford University Press, New York.

Swinburne, R. (1997) *The Evolution of the Soul*, rev. edn. Oxford University Press, New York.

Swinburne, R. (2002) *Is There a God?* Oxford University Press, New York.

Swinburne, R. (2004) *The Existence of God*, 2nd edn. Clarendon Press, Oxford.

Bibliography

Taliaffero, C. (2005) *Evidence and Faith: Philosophy and Religion since the Seventeenth Century*. Cambridge University Press, New York.

Taylor, S. E. and Brown, J. D. (1988) Illusion and well-being: a social psychological perspective on mental health. *Psychological Bulletin* 103, 193–210.

Taylor, S. E. and Brown, J. D. (1994) Positive illusions and well-being revisited: separating fact from fiction. *Psychological Bulletin* 116, 21–7.

Tertullian (1869 [197]) *Apology*. In A. Roberts and J. Donaldson (eds.), *The Writings of Tertullian*, vol. 1, The Ante-Nicene Christian Library, vol. 11. T. and T. Clark, Edinburgh.

Tertullian (1870a [199]) *Prescription Against Heretics*. In A. Roberts and J. Donaldson (eds.), *The Writings of Tertullian*, vol. 2, The Ante-Nicene Christian Library, vol. 15. T. and T. Clark, Edinburgh.

Tertullian (1870b [205]) *De Carne Christi*. In A. Roberts and J. Donaldson (eds.), *The Writings of Tertullian*, vol. 2, The Ante-Nicene Christian Library, vol. 15. T. and T. Clark, Edinburgh.

Tryon, E. P. (1973) Is the universe a vacuum fluctuation? *Nature* 246, 396–7.

van Inwagen, P. (1978) The possibility of resurrection. *International Journal for Philosophy of Religion* 9, 114–21.

van Inwagen, P. (1983) *An Essay on Free Will*. Oxford University Press, New York.

Wainwright, W. J. (1981) *Mysticism: A Study of its Nature, Cognitive Value, and Moral Implications*. University of Wisconsin Press, Madison.

Wainwright, W. J. (1995) *Reason and the Heart: A Prolegomena to a Critique of Passional Reason*. Cornell University Press, Ithaca.

Wainwright, W. J. (ed.) (2005) *The Oxford Handbook of Philosophy of Religion*. Oxford University Press, New York.

Ward, K. (1996) *God, Chance, and Necessity*. Oneworld Press, Oxford.

Ward, K. (2002) *God: A Guide for the Perplexed*. Oneworld Publications, Oxford.

Westphal, M. (1997) The emergence of modern philosophy of religion. In Quinn and Taliaferro (1997), 111–17.

Whitehead, A. N. (1929) *Process and Reality: An Essay in Cosmology*. Free Press, New York.

Williams, B. (1973) *Problems of the Self: Philosophical Papers 1956–1972*. Cambridge University Press, Cambridge.

Winston, D. (1971) The *Book of Wisdom's* theory of cosmogony. *History of Religions* 11, 185–202.

Wittgenstein, L. (1961 [1922]) *Tractatus Logico-Philosophicus*, trans. D. F. Pears and B. F. McGuinness. Humanities Press, New York.

Wittgenstein, L. (1972) *Lectures and Conversations on Aesthetics, Psychology and Religious Belief*, ed. C. Barrett. University of California Press, Berkeley.

Wittgenstein, L. (1980 [1977]) *Culture and Value*, trans. P. Winch, ed. G. H. Von Wright. University of Chicago Press, Chicago.

Bibliography

Wittgenstein, L. (2001 [1953]) *Philosophical Investigations*, trans. G. E. M. Anscombe. Blackwell Publishers, Malden, Mass.

Wojtyła, K. (1979) *The Acting Person*. D. Reidel, Boston.

Wojtyła, K. (1993) Subjectivity and the irreducible in the human being. In *Person and Community: Selected Essays*. Peter Lang, New York, 209–17.

Wolterstorff, N. (1996) *John Locke and the Ethics of Belief*. Cambridge University Press, New York.

Wykstra, S. J. (1996) Rowe's noseeum arguments from evil. In Howard-Snyder (1996), 126–50.

Wynn, M. (2005) *Emotional Experience and Religious Understanding: Integrating Perception, Conception and Feeling*. Cambridge University Press, New York.

Yearley, L. (1993) Conflicts among ideals of human flourishing. In Outka and Reeder (eds.) *Prospects for a Common Morality*. Princeton University Press, Princeton, 231–53.

Zagzebski, L. T. (1991a) *The Dilemma of Freedom and Foreknowledge*. Oxford University Press, New York.

Zagzebski, L. T. (1991b) Critical response. In Hewitt (1991), 125–9.

Zagzebski, L. T. (1996) An agent-based approach to the problem of evil. *International Journal for Philosophy of Religion* 39, 127–39.

Zagzebski, L. T. (2001) The uniqueness of persons. *Journal of Religious Ethics* 29, 401–23.

Zagzebski, L. T. (2002) Omniscience and the arrow of time. *Faith and Philosophy* 19, 503–19.

Zagzebski, L. T. (2003) Emotion and moral judgment. *Philosophy and Phenomenological Research* 66, 104–24.

Zagzebski, L. T. (2004) *Divine Motivation Theory*. Cambridge University Press, New York.

Zagzebski, L. T. (2005) Sleeping Beauty and the afterlife. In Dole and Chignell (2005), 59–76.

Zagzebski, L. T. (2006) Self-trust and the diversity of religions. *Philosophic Exchange* 36.

Zaleski, C. (1987) *Otherworld Journeys: Accounts of Near-death Experience in Medieval and Modern Times*. Oxford University Press, New York.

Index

Index

Index